# Teaching Service and Alternative Teacher Education

NOTRE DAME ADVANCES IN EDUCATION

*Michael Pressley, General Editor*

# Teaching Service and Alternative Teacher Education

## Notre Dame's Alliance for Catholic Education

*Edited by Michael Pressley*

University of Notre Dame Press

Notre Dame, Indiana

Manufactured in the United States of America

Published for the Notre Dame Alliance for Catholic Education by the
University of Notre Dame Press.

The Notre Dame Alliance for Catholic Education thanks the
Lilly Endowment for its generous support in the publication of this book.


*Library of Congress Cataloging-in-Publication Data*
Alternative teacher education : Notre Dame's Alliance for Catholic
Education / Michael Pressley, editor.
    p. cm. — (Notre Dame Alliance for Catholic Education series)
Includes bibliographical references.
  ISBN 0-268-02015-9 (alk. paper)
  1. Alliance for Catholic Education (University of Notre Dame) 2.
Teachers—Training of—United States—Case studies. 3. Community and
college—United States—Case studies. 4. Church and education—United
States—Case studies. I. Pressley, Michael. II. Series.
  LB1715 .A48 2002
  370'.71'1—dc21
                                                            2001005451


∞ This book was printed on acid-free paper.

# CONTENTS

# ACKNOWLEDGMENTS

The teaching service and alternative teacher education program that is described in this book has been generously supported by many people along the way. Many complemented their financial support with their considerable wisdom. The Alliance for Catholic Education has a tremendous debt of gratitude to the following:

Mr. Walter H. Annenberg and the Annenberg Trust
Mr. and Mrs. Robert Biolchini
Dr. and Mrs. Joseph Bitter
Mr. and Mrs. Thomas Brand
Mr. and Mrs. Jim and Trudy Burkholder
Mr. and Mrs. Raymond Chambers
Mr. and Mrs. Lawrence Coss
Mr. Philip Delaney Jr.
Mrs. Donna DeRitis
Mr. Fritz Duda
Mr. Joseph Gallo
Prof. David Gasperetti
Mr. and Mrs. Arnold G. Gough Jr.
Mr. Enrique Hernandez
Mr. and Mrs. Lou Holtz Sr.
Dr. Mary Hughes
Dr. Harry Jenkins
Mr. and Mrs. Richard Kizer
Mr. Charles W. Lamar III
Mr. Samuel J. Lanzafame
Mr. Thomas Larkin
Mr. and Mrs. John Lary
Mr. Edward D. Lewis
Mr. and Mrs. Earl Linehan
Mr. and Mrs. Miller McCarthy

Mr. and Mrs. Kevin D. McGrath
Mr. James McGraw
Mrs. Mary Nash McKenna
Mr. and Mrs. Andrew McKenna Jr.
Ms. Leah Meyer Austin and the Kellogg Foundation
Mr. and Mrs. John J. Micek Jr.
Mr. Thomas Mints Jr.
Mrs. Patricia Morgan
Mr. and Mrs. Richard Muraski Jr.
Mr. Thomas G. Paese
Mr. and Mrs. Jon Rager
Dr. Stephen Ritterbush
Mr. and Mrs. Jim and Colleen Ryan
Mr. and Mrs. Patrick and Shirley Ryan
Mr. Raymond F. Simon and the Helen Brach Foundation
Mr. Joseph Torter
Dr. John A. Walker Jr.
Mr. and Mrs. Michael and Juanita Williamson
Mr. Anthony Brenninkmeyer
The Humanitas Trust
Koch Foundation
GE Fund
UPS Foundation
MCJ Foundation
Mathile Foundation
Our Sunday Visitor Institute
United States Department of Education
DeHaan Family Foundation
Corporation for National Service
Arthur Vining Davis Foundation

Both the University of Notre Dame and the University of Portland
have done a great deal to nurture the fledgling ACE efforts. Notre
Dame has provided summer housing for the program. Both Portland
and Notre Dame have permitted the program to be offered without
charging tuition. Many Notre Dame and Portland faculty and staff
have contributed to the program over the years. We especially have
appreciated the contributions of the presidents of these two universities. Rev. Edward Malloy, CSC, president of Notre Dame, seeded the
idea at the outset and has provided critical support at many important junctures. Rev. David Tyson, CSC, president of the University of

Portland, did much to develop a scheme by which the Portland MAT could serve as the initial licensure experience for the first four cohorts of ACE students.

Throughout this experience, the Congregation of Holy Cross has always been there, with many Holy Cross fathers lending a hand, from Rev. Timothy Scully's founding leadership to the many presiders at the 10 P.M. Masses that are integral to the program. The program would not have so well succeeded without the support of many bishops, principals, and Catholic school faculties and staffs across the United States who have welcomed ACE to their diocesan schools. When ACE has arrived at local sites, often it was the Notre Dame Club that helped out with finding and furnishing a house or apartment or providing a car for the ACE community. Many have been in it together to bring ACE to schools from Charleston to Los Angeles.

# 1

MICHAEL PRESSLEY

## INTRODUCTION

I
t's a Thursday evening in November 1998. The place is an
auditorium at the Hesburgh Library on the campus of the
University of Notre Dame. The building is known to many
for "Touchdown Jesus," a 13-story mosaic reflecting the
Catholic heritage of the school, interpretively nicknamed by its
sports-minded student body and alums. About 150 seniors have
filed into the auditorium, all of them there to learn more about
something they have been aware of since their earliest days at the
university. Specifically, they have come to pick up applications
for the post-graduate experience in teaching operated by the
Alliance for Catholic Education, referred to everywhere on the
campus by its acronym, ACE.

Many of those in attendance at the meeting know former
Notre Dame undergraduates who are now in ACE. They know
that the program provides the opportunity for two years of teaching in a Catholic school in the southern United States. They also
know that ACErs live together in groups of three to seven teachers during their period of service. Most in the auditorium also
recognize that admission to the ACE program is extremely competitive, with some believing rumors that ACE is an almost
impossible admission. Impossible or not, the seniors have come
because they view ACE as an enviable opportunity, offering two
years of meaningful service, a graduate degree from Notre Dame
at no monetary cost, and a lot of fun.

The diversity of the students is striking. There are both males and females, consistent with the 50/50 gender balance in the ACE program. There are majors from all of ND's schools, consistent with the diversity of majors serving the ACE program. Because of the strong general education program at the university, all Notre Dame graduates are prepared to teach in some content area represented in elementary, middle, or high school curricula. Consistent with the university's ethnic and racial mix, there are a few blacks in the audience, more Hispanics, with the majority of the audience being white. The students in attendance are from all over the country, reflecting Notre Dame's national student body. A few are elite athletes, signaled by the sprinkling of ND letter jackets in the crowd.

Most of these students are wondering what is ahead in their lives. Many have come to this meeting because they think that, as part of a meaningful life, they should do some service for those in need. Again, this is consistent with being at Notre Dame, for ND students distinguish themselves by the amount of service they do both during their student years and after they graduate. Others have come because they are convinced specifically that their service should be as teachers, and ACE is one of the most distinctive, service-oriented teacher education programs in the nation.

Fr. Tim Scully is filled with enthusiasm as he addresses the students, making the case that during the past five years, many Notre Dame seniors have been called to ACE. Scully reminds the students of how, in the play *A Man for All Seasons,* St. Thomas More was called to teaching early in his career. He also makes the case, however, that the ACE experience is meaningful in very concrete ways, that ACErs do good as teachers as they live in community with one another, and that they grow spiritually as part of the program. Scully reviews briefly the three pillars of the ACE program—academics, community, and spirituality. He concludes his brief presentation by telling the students, "This program is a blast."

Fr. Scully's presentation is followed by a very professional 18-minute color videotape about teaching in ACE. The film is filled with images of present ACErs in elementary, middle, and high schools, consistent with the kindergarten to grade 12 coverage of the program. These scenes of teaching emphasize the academic development of pupils in Catholic schools. They also represent the academic development of the ACErs, with shots from the first days of teaching as well as images from the ACErs' master's degree graduation in the final frames of the video. The classroom pictures are complemented by images of ACE home life, including visits to several ACE households, or communities. The film highlights that the ACErs eat together, pray with one another, and provide supportive feedback to their housemates about teaching and its challenges. There is little doubt that ACErs in the film like what they do. Moreover, it is clear that what the ACErs are doing is important, with university, church, and school leaders commenting on the tape about the uniqueness of the ACE program and the vitality it injects into Catholic education in the South. The film inspires this audience as it has inspired those already in the ACE program, financial benefactors of ACE, and church, university, and government leaders who support the program.

After the video, the ACE staff explains the application process and that there will be many more applicants than there are places in ACE, but that everyone is encouraged to apply. It is emphasized that ACE is a service program but with value added to its participants through their completion of a master's degree in education as part of the experience. The ACE staff emphasizes that the admission process involves an assessment of past academic successes, the likelihood that the applicant can live constructively in community with other ACErs, and the spiritual commitment of the applicant. Every applicant to the program will be interviewed, typically by a three-person team—a faculty member, an ACE representative (e.g., a staff member or someone who has worked closely with the staff), and a member of the clergy (e.g., one of the rectors from the dorms). Seventy-five will be selected from among the 250 or so who will apply.

Wendy Holthaus stays after the presentation to talk with a student about her days as an ACE teacher. Wendy was a member of the first ACE class, and as such, she watched the invention of the program in summer 1994. Wendy and 39 classmates camped out in the top floors of two of ND's oldest (and, in June and July, hottest) dorms, attending summer school classes that had been put together hastily to prepare the pioneering ACErs for the teaching that they would do the following year. Because in 1994 no one had been to the receiving schools before, Wendy and her classmates knew little about what to expect in the South. As Wendy reflects on her experiences, she confidently assures the potential applicant that things are much more certain now than when she went through the program. Indeed, when she went through the program, Wendy and her classmates concluded that ACE stood for "Always Changing Everything."

Even though ACE is now more stable, it remains a program that continuously reflects on itself and attempts to change for the better when there are opportunities to do so. That continuous reflection and revision is documented in detail in this book.

## THE SCOPE OF ACE

AN OVERARCHING PURPOSE of ACE is to improve Catholic schools, especially in the southern United States, by enabling exceptionally talented young people to teach in them. For some ACE participants, that will mean only the two-year term of service that is directly sponsored by ACE, with them then moving on to another vocation. Some former ACErs are now in medical school, graduate school, and business. Many others will use their master's degree as a vehicle for a career in teaching and education (in recent classes, 80% of ACErs worked in education the year after completing their ACE commitment). Some former ACErs move into public education; more often, they remain in Catholic education, and some even remain in the Catholic schools they served during their ACE participation.

Although this book focuses on ACE participants—the young adults who serve as teachers in Catholic schools—the Alliance for Catholic Education consists of much more. The Alliance for Catholic Education is headquartered at Notre Dame, administratively directed by Dr. John Staud and several associate directors, who are former ACErs. There is a growing staff at Notre Dame supporting this program, with staffers assigned both to ACE proper and to the Master of Education program.

The Master of Education program, which exists only to serve ACE participants, was formalized at Notre Dame in 1997–1998. ACErs entering in summer 1998 were the first class admitted to the ND master's program. Previous to that, ACErs were enrolled in a Master of Arts in Teaching program administered by the Oregon-based University of Portland, whose faculty traveled to the Notre Dame campus during two summers to offer the program. The ND Master of Education program is directed by Dr. Michael Pressley, an educational researcher specializing in teaching, with Dr. Joyce Johnstone serving as its associate academic director as well as the director of ACE outreach. The M.Ed. program now includes four field supervisors, who came to the program with experience in supervision of student teachers. Some of the courses in the M.Ed. program are taught by Notre Dame faculty serving full-time in other programs on the campus. That is, they teach in the M.Ed. program as part of summer school. These faculty have taken on this responsibility because they believe that Notre Dame needs to reverse a quarter of a century absence of education programs from the campus. Many other faculty are recruited from colleges and universities across the country, either to teach at Notre Dame in the summer or to conduct seminars with ACE students over the Internet during the academic year.

From this Notre Dame center, ACE reaches out to other Catholic colleges to recruit ACE participants, including St. Mary's College, University of Portland, Boston College, Holy Cross College, Villanova University, Mount Saint Mary's College of Maryland, St. Joseph's College, Loyola University of Chicago, Loyola College of Baltimore, St. Norbert's College, and College of St. Thomas. Although non-Catholic colleges have provided the occasional ACEr, and each class typically includes one or two students from abroad, most ACErs experienced Catholic education at least at the post-secondary level. In fact, the majority of the ACErs hold undergraduate degrees from Notre Dame. In addition to the higher education participants, each diocese that hosts ACE teachers is considered part of the Alliance. An annual meeting at Notre Dame in April brings together the school superintendents of these ACE dioceses. In short, the Alliance includes institutions of higher education, dioceses in the southern United States, and the ACE teachers themselves. It is a large organization.

During 2001–2002, ACE had 159 participants who taught in 146 schools. The ACErs were about equally distributed between elementary, middle, and high schools. In every case, the ACE participant assumed the responsibilities of a teacher of record, with some mentoring support and some supervision visits from Notre Dame faculty and staff. A total of 25 dioceses were served, from as far east as Charleston, South Carolina, to as far west as Los Angeles, California. There are ACE school sites in 14 states. ACE serves both urban settings and rural locations, with many ACE houses located in smaller cities and towns. Although the full range of socioeconomic statuses is represented among students in ACE schools, ACE particularly focuses on serving schools with large proportions of students in need because of socioeconomic disadvantage. A number of ACE schools are close to 100% Hispanic, and others are close to 100% African American. About 10,000 students are taught annually by ACE participants.

## LIFE IN ACE

THE ACE PROGRAM begins with the summer session, which starts just 10 days after graduation from Notre Dame. For the ACErs who just completed bachelor's degrees at ND, the physical movement is from one dorm to another. For the ACErs coming from other institutions, ACE often is their first encounter with Notre Dame.

For all ACErs, their teacher education experience begins with a retreat at the Moreau Seminary, in a remote corner of the ND campus. Much of the retreat is about orientation to the program, with ACE participants receiving a great deal of information about what is expected of them as members of ACE—as teachers in Catholic schools and as ACE community members. The theme of community is prominent during this weekend, as it will be throughout the two years of ACE involvement.

### COMMUNITY FORMATION

During the summer session, the ACE entering class as a whole is a community. The new ACErs share in the trials and tribulations of a demanding summer school curriculum (i.e., 10 credits), living together in the dorms, eating together in a Notre Dame dining hall, and worshiping together at 10 P.M., Monday through Thursday. Even so, from their admission into the program, ACErs are organized into living communities. Each community of three to seven ACErs is typically distributed across several schools in the diocese being served. During the summer, these living communities do some things together. For example, they eat one dinner a week as a community. Also, one of the four courses taken by first-summer ACErs is a 1-credit seminar in Catholic education, with its most prominent goal being the formation of the individual diocesan-based communities. In the context of this seminar, ACErs engage in a variety of activities with the other individuals who will be in their community house during the next two years.

Each ACE community receives a great deal of assistance in locating appropriate housing in their locales. Sometimes this help is provided by the diocese, sometimes by local Notre Dame club members (i.e., the local branch of Notre Dame's national alumni club), and sometimes by the ACE staff working with former ACErs who know the locale they served previously. The ideal housing for an ACE community is a large house, one permitting each ACEr to have some private space while at the same time providing plenty of community space. Most of the time this ideal is approximated, although in some cases ACErs have ended up in large apartments or in adjacent smaller apartments.

After finding a house, there is the challenge of furnishing it. Although ACErs bring some of their own furnishings, often there is diocesan assistance or help from the local Notre Dame club. Some exceptionally generous gifts have included appliances and, in several cases, cars. This generosity represents in part the appreciation of the receiving communities to the ACErs and Notre Dame for their commitment to improving Catholic education in locales far removed from South Bend.

A key piece of furnishing in an ACE household is the Internet-linked computer. The computer is the community's lifeline to Notre Dame and to their ACE classmates distributed across the southern half of the United States. Since all ACErs are enrolled in distance learning courses through Notre Dame during the school year, the machine takes on an added significance, permitting ACErs to go to school at Notre Dame as they teach in the South.

The house and its furnishings are probably the least important elements in forming the ACE community, however. Most ACE communities decide during the summer how they will structure their lives in order to assure that they function well together. Often, the ACErs make commitments to cook for one another on a rotation schedule, share cleaning and maintenance duties, and resolve how they will share expenses and decision making about how the community expends its resources.

Within a few weeks of arrival in the South, ACE households typically fall into daily and weekly routines. Most ACE communities eat together often, typically the dinner meals during the week. Most ACE communities also decide to have at-home worship sessions, often later in the evening. Many communities decide to join a particular Catholic church for Sunday worship together. Often, only some members of the ACE community own automobiles, which results in the development of school drop-off and pick-up routines, so that all community members have transportation to their schools. Living in an ACE community is a shared and sharing experience.

Very early in the school year, the ACE community is visited by an ND-based ACE staff member. For the most part, by the time of this visit, which usually takes place in September, ACE communities are up and functioning. The visits, however, permit the identification of rough edges of various sorts, providing the ND-based staff an opportunity to appraise how to help communities that are slow in coming together. Sometimes the assistance needed can be provided by the diocese. Other times a local Notre Dame club can be helpful. ND provides some counseling (e.g., when there is an imbalance in responsibilities such that some members of the community are distressed because they are doing a larger proportion of household tasks than other members of the community). For many ACE communities, the members will find it easy to live with one another from the start; for other communities, the search for a harmonious balance of responsibilities and interactions will take a while to achieve.

### Beginning to Teach

There is very little time between the conclusion of the ACE summer session at Notre Dame and the beginning of the teaching duties in the South. For most ACErs, the move begins with a long drive south, either in their own automobiles or with parents.

Once at the school they will serve, ACE teachers are like other first-year teachers for the most part. That means elementary ACE teachers have their own classes, ranging in size from 15 to 25 or so students. For middle school teachers, their assignments usually require multiple preparations; some are responsible for as few as two or three different preps while others have as many as seven a day. High school ACE teachers typically also have multiple preparations, although high school teachers are more likely than middle school teachers to be focused exclusively on classes related to their own college majors.

Like other teachers, ACE teachers answer to a principal. Each ACE teacher also has a mentor at the school site, a teacher who visits the ACE teacher's classroom from time to time and generally attempts to provide some guidance. The ACE teacher is visited several times a year by a Notre Dame–based supervisor from the M.Ed. program (a different person from the ACE staff member who visited the community early in the year). The ND supervisor consults with the principal and the mentor teacher about the ACE teacher's development in the setting. The ND supervisor also observes the ACE teacher's classes and reviews lesson plans as part of the feedback process. During a visit to a community, the ND supervisor typically also spends some time with the ACE community as a whole, perhaps taking them to dinner to explore issues the community might have. By doing so, ND gets a second window on the community formation process fairly early in the year. This is especially critical for those occasions when some remediation is needed (e.g., when a community member is not getting along with housemates).

In short, autumn of the first year in the ACE program focuses on the establishment of the local communities and getting the participants started in their teaching roles. The efforts of many individuals converge to accomplish this goal at 30 or so sites simultaneously—the ACErs themselves, diocesan personnel, Notre Dame club members, ND-based ACE staff, and ND-based M.Ed. faculty.

## MID-YEAR AND SECOND SEMESTER

At the end of the second week of December, a very special event occurs: a reunion retreat of all ACErs, first and second year, in Biloxi, Mississippi. The retreat lasts from Friday evening to early Sunday afternoon, occurring at a conference center on the Gulf of Mexico. Some ACErs drive to the site; more fly. In addition to the ACErs, the ND-based ACE staff come to the retreat, as do a number of faculty serving the M.Ed. program. Other ND community members attend as well, including some rectors from the dorms, all of whom know many of the ACErs.

Much goes on at the retreat. It begins with a dinner and Mass on Friday evening, which is a joyful reunion for the ACErs. The joyfulness is especially apparent when it comes time to share the sign of peace during the Mass, with virtually every ACEr embracing every other ACEr. Saturday is filled with meetings; some are aimed at promoting community, some address the academic program, and some are concerned with spirituality. The meetings continue on Sunday morning, wrapping with a Mass before departure. The December retreat does much to renew the first-year ACErs identification with the larger program and community, following an autumn that was focused on establishing the local community and orienting to a school and teaching as a profession. The retreat also does much to remind the ACErs of their uniqueness. No other teacher education program distributes its participants over so great a geographic region; no other program must hold a national retreat to get the participants together.

The Christmas break is a welcome relief for most ACErs, with many of them returning to their parents' home for the holidays. Very few will be contemplating whether to return to their school for the second semester; with the occasional exception, the typical ACEr looks forward to the second semester. Their home communities are up and functioning, as are their classrooms. The participants know what is ahead much better than they did when arriving in August or September. The second semester goes more smoothly and more quickly than the first semester.

### SECOND SUMMER AND YEAR OF TEACHING

At the conclusion of the second semester, ACErs return to Notre Dame for a second summer session. Although it is not a relaxing summer, with 10 credits of coursework, it is not as demanding as the first summer. For example, there is no teaching practicum for second-summer ACErs. Also, they know the routines and the personalities in the ACE program. Moreover, the second-summer ACErs know much better than they did during the first summer what they will face in the South in the autumn. The second summer is easier largely because there is more certainty about the program and the upcoming second year of teaching.

For many ACErs, the hardest part about the second year is that it ends their ACE experience. The question is what to do next in life. Many decide to stay in teaching. For those who continue teaching in other than their ACE service schools, the most typical move is back to their hometown. Thus, there are now former ACE teachers dispersed across the nation. For those not staying in teaching, often the choice is to attend graduate or professional school, including entry into the seminary. Some ACErs have made plans to marry at the end of their two years of service, occasionally to someone who also had been in the ACE program. In virtually every instance, however, as ACErs complete their second year of teaching, they are grateful for the opportunity to have taught and participated in a program characterized by great camaraderie. Most ACErs feel they had an extraordinary academic experience, a fulfilling community life for two years, and a spiritually inspiring experience.

Given the positiveness of the ACE experience, it is not surprising that ACE graduations are joyous affairs. The ACErs and their families return to Notre Dame in the middle of July for a graduation ceremony complete with a prominent guest speaker, a dinner, and a dance. Although the graduation marks the end of a graduate program and the formal two-year ACE commitment, many ACErs have post-ACE experience with the program. Each summer, a few former ACErs serve as clinical instructors for the graduate program; some, who remain in ACE schools, help mentor future ACErs. ACE is an experience of a lifetime for many participants, with few wanting to leave it behind them entirely.

## WHAT FOLLOWS IN THIS BOOK

ONE OF THE MOST GRATIFYING parts of administering the ACE program is that so many who are interested in education want to know about it. In some instances, they hope to attract ACE to their diocese or community; in other cases, they desire to develop a teacher education program similar to the ACE experience. Some policymakers are attracted to ACE as a model of reform in teacher education. Finally, some young people want to know about ACE because they would like to apply for the program.

Because the ACE effort is complex, explaining it requires a long book. Thus, what follows are chapters detailing the history of the ACE program at Notre Dame, how community and spirituality are fostered within ACE, development and institutionalization of the academic M.Ed. program, fund raising for the program, recruitment of ACE participants, and the differences ACE makes in the lives of its participants. By the end, it will be obvious that a program like ACE is possible only through the coordination of many talents. It will also be obvious that that coordination of talents is worth it, for ACE provides extraordinary service to many students in Catholic elementary, middle, and high schools as it provides a quality service and teacher education experience for the ACErs who participate in the program.

PART I

# HISTORY

*T*he ACE teacher education and service program has a history extending back to school year 1993–1994. The first ACErs were recruited that year, with the resulting ACE I class experiencing their first summer session in June and July 1994. ACE classes I through IV would be educated by the University of Portland faculty. The Notre Dame ACE M.Ed. program began in summer 1998, with ACE V its first class. This history played out in settings as intimate as the founder's office and as public as the information meetings held in the autumn of each year. Although the focus was Notre Dame and South Bend, the history also took place in the ACE communities across the South. The three chapters that follow capture the history of ACE from the perspectives of those who founded the program.

# 2

SEAN D. MCGRAW
TIMOTHY R. SCULLY

# BUILDING ACE

## IMPROVISING ON PROVIDENCE

B uilding the Alliance for Catholic Education (ACE) has been
a journey of faith and substantial improvisation. As we look
back over the past seven years and view the almost miraculous path this organization has followed, the temptation
exists to suggest that we knew from the outset where we were
headed, that we had a game plan, a strategy, from the very beginning. But we most certainly did not. The bald truth is that neither of the authors of this chapter, the founders and initial
catalysts of ACE, had a clue where all this apostolic energy was
leading. Furthermore, neither of us have a formal background in
education, other than our own combined three decades as students in Catholic schools. From the start we were, as the expres-
sion goes, "making it up as we go along." So, as we recount the
lessons we learned in getting ACE off the ground, forgive our
occasional need in the retelling to put some order into what was
an almost entirely incremental and often chaotic process.

How did two political scientists get into the business of supplying teachers to Catholic elementary and secondary schools?
We got involved because Sr. Lourdes Sheehan, RSM, convinced
us that it was a good thing to do. Sr. Lourdes is a soft-spoken,
deeply cultured woman, a native of Savannah, Georgia. She is
passionately committed to Catholic education. When we met Sr.
Lourdes in 1993, Scully had just received tenure at Notre Dame
in the Department of Government and International Studies, and

McGraw had recently returned to Notre Dame from the London School of Economics, where he had completed a post-graduate program in European politics. Both of us were working together on projects related to our common field of interest, comparative politics. But, in retrospect, it is easy to see that both of us were also on the prowl for something more, beyond our strictly academic commitments. In a conversation over dinner in Washington, D.C., Sr. Lourdes, then secretary for education for the National Catholic Conference of Bishops, made a powerful case for Catholic education, challenging Scully and Notre Dame to find ways to get committed young adults into the classrooms of America's neediest Catholic schools.

The challenge sounded like an interesting and important one. The previous year, approximately 70 graduating seniors from Notre Dame had applied for post-graduate volunteer teaching programs. Why not invite such seniors to think about serving, through a Notre Dame sponsored program, as teachers in under-resourced Catholic schools for a few years after graduation? At the very least, why not give it a try for a year as a pilot program? So we decided to give it a shot. We placed a full-page ad in Notre Dame's student newspaper, *The Observer,* which shouted out: "Tired of gettin' homework? THEN GIVE SOME! Be a teacher!" Mind you, we had no clue how many would show up, nor how we would train these prospective teachers, nor where we would place them. But we had to start somewhere, and the place to start, it seemed to us, was with the university students themselves. Was there a promising supply among our graduating seniors of potential classroom teachers?

The response to this question was at once decisive and overwhelming. On the evening of our first recruitment meeting in late fall 1993 (for a program that did not yet exist), the Notre Dame Room in La Fortune Student Center was packed with scores of talented and energetic seniors. The place was electric, and we knew instantly that we had stumbled unwittingly into a deeply felt need among many of our very best graduating seniors. They were hungry for an experience of teaching, and more, of faith and service in community. The hard part was to create a program that might respond effectively to the multiple levels of needs we were uncovering not only among marginalized Catholic school systems, but also among the graduates who sought to join this pioneering effort in teaching.

First, we looked carefully at a few existing initiatives, most notably Teach for America, which provided service to inner-city public schools. We studied Catholic school service programs like Washington's Teaching Service Corps and Chicago's Inner-City Teaching Corps. As we explored the landscape of existing programs, especially in consultation with Sr. Rosemary Collins, SSND, director of the Teaching Service Corps in Washington, we thought long and hard about the distinctive mission that our Alliance for Catholic Education would seek to accomplish. We visited with a number of potential collaborators, most importantly Catholic school superintendents gathered at the National Catholic Education Association meetings in Louisville, Kentucky, and other leaders in the field of Catholic education nationally. Over the course of these conversations, several dimensions of our particular mission in service to Catholic schools began to emerge more clearly.

## FORGING THE MISSION

As we surveyed the challenges faced by other programs seeking to supply teachers to under-resourced schools, it became evident that a key issue faced by all of them had to do with supplying novice teachers with adequate preparation and support. For example, Teach for America had become the target of fierce attacks from educational researchers for its apparent inability to provide professional formation prior to classroom experience ("Who Will Speak for the Children? How 'Teach for America' Hurts Urban Schools and Students," September 1994, *Phi Delta Kappan, 76,* pp. 21–34). Partly as a result of insufficient preparation, and partly as a consequence of inadequate field support, the program was experiencing alarming desertion rates among its teacher-volunteers after only a few weeks of classes. Teachers were often parachuted solo into some of America's most challenging urban environments and asked to perform nearly heroic service. The inevitable frustrations experienced in the classroom by first-year teachers often were reinforced by a lonely living situation, and not infrequently led to a premature exit from teaching.

How could we improve the survival rate of novice teachers? Early on, we settled on three key dimensions, or "pillars," to characterize the distinctive mission of our program: developing *professional educators* who would live in the context of *community* and grow in an eagerness to share and nourish the *spiritual life.* Together, and from the very first conceptualization of our program, these three pillars of teaching, community life, and spirituality would define the mission of the Alliance for Catholic Education. In addition, we determined that our teachers would work in Catholic schools, preferably among the poor, but always in areas where recruiting talented and committed young Christian adults was a permanent challenge. This decision, in turn, meant that we would target small cities and towns where there were few—if any—Catholic colleges or universities supplying qualified Catholic teachers for these under-resourced Catholic schools. This, of course, brought our initial focus in establishing ACE teaching communities to the southern United States.

Our first pillar, developing professional educators, presented a significant obstacle. In the early 1970s, the University of Notre Dame had abolished its Department of Education and more generally gotten out of the business of preparing teachers. The reasons for abolishing the department were many and complex, but in general, the university administration at the time believed that the department was not offering particularly innovative solutions to the challenges posed by schools. In fact, university administrators concluded that perhaps the conventions of the educational establishment were part of the problem. The absence of a Department of Education at Notre Dame presented a mixed blessing for us. On the one hand, and very crucially, we were allowed the freedom to rethink teacher education from the bottom up, from the daily experiences of novice teachers in today's classrooms. We were unencumbered by the normal university and departmental politics and turf wars that can characterize reactions to new initiatives that may present unconventional models. On the other hand, we were faced with a practical problem: how to offer first-class professional training to our teachers so that they could experience success in the classroom. Though the Notre Dame faculty possessed a number of very strong individual researchers spread across various departments who specialized in the field of education, there existed no real infrastructure to support the kind of teacher-training effort that would be required by ACE—especially one geared toward preparing novice teachers in a very brief time to be excellent practitioners in their own classrooms.

At this critical early juncture, we made contact with the president of the University of Portland, Fr. David Tyson, CSC. The University of Portland is a sister institution to the University of Notre Dame, sponsored by the same Catholic religious community, the Congregation of Holy Cross, and enjoys a strong reputation for teacher training in the northwestern United States, especially in the areas of off-site training and distance learning. Tyson understood our need instantly. With characteristic tenacity, he gave the project his blessing and introduced us to the faculty of the School of Education at Portland. After faculty shuttled back and forth between Portland and Notre Dame for several exploratory meetings over the course of a few weeks, providence struck again in the form of the generosity of the University of Portland. The School of Education at Portland agreed to establish an off-site Master of Arts in Teaching (MAT) degree on the campus of the University of Notre Dame for the participants of the ACE program—at cost! This arrangement would allow our ACE teachers to receive the preparation and support they needed during the two years they were in the program, and the certification they would need to stay in teaching beyond the two-year commitment. It was almost too good to be true!

Over the course of the following four years, the faculty of the University of Portland provided exceptional preparation to over 200 teachers in the ACE program and built an accredited teacher-training model that met the needs of the ACE teachers remarkably well. The generosity and genuine care of the faculty of the School of Education, and especially the beloved professor Blaine Ackley, set high standards for future faculty to meet. The sheer amount of hours in curriculum design, supervision, mentoring, and planning represented an almost Herculean effort, but one which the faculty at Portland happily put forward. In particular, an early and recurring challenge had been how to balance the best educational theory with the equally necessary survival tactics from practicing teachers. Portland's School of Education was extremely responsive in trying to address this critical tension within the training dimension of the program. For instance, the program developed a relationship with the South Bend Community School Corporation wherein our ACErs would gain practical experience by working in real summer session classrooms with mentor teachers in the mornings and integrating this experience into their afternoon graduate courses in education. As ACE continued to grow, in numbers as well as in geographic distribution of its teachers, it became increasingly clear that Notre Dame would need to begin to think about taking responsibility for its own teacher preparation for the expanding ACE program.

Designing and implementing the second pillar of the ACE program, serving Catholic schools in the context of community, brought its own set of challenges. To be completely honest, during the initial years of the program, we did not give this dimension the kind of thought and attention it required. It was clear that our young participants wanted to live together a common life of young teacher-disciples. But anyone who has experienced the punishing schedule of a first-year teacher knows that time to devote to relationship-building and community life is strictly limited. Furthermore, when several vigorous and independent young professionals are suddenly tossed together in a house in Lake Charles, Louisiana, and are expected to share meals, prayer, and recreation together, it is sometimes a complete victory if the participants simply avoid killing one another! First-year teaching is an unbelievably demanding job, and novice teachers bring varied needs and expectations home at the end of a long day.

In the months before our first teachers were to leave for the field, we spent weeks on the phone—and on the road—meeting with scores of people from the southern cities where we would be serving, locating housing that would be both affordable and reasonably proximate to the schools where the ACE teachers would teach. It was a scramble, and each diocese presented its own set of challenges. But, in every case, a combination of people emerged among local Catholic school personnel, parents, teachers, and often members of the local Notre Dame alumni club. In one diocese, the local school communities refurbished an old convent by having each school renovate and furnish the room for the teacher who would be serving their school. Almost miraculously, and well before the outset of the school year in fall 1994, we had acquired an "ACE house" in each of the eight locations we would serve that first year.

As we discovered later, establishing and building these local contacts was a significant challenge, considering the distance from Notre Dame. While some ACErs enjoyed relatively sumptuous quarters and had meals prepared for them by local Catholic school enthusiasts, other ACErs struggled with windows painted shut and no air conditioning in the heat of the southern sun. Unhelpful comparisons abounded from one ACE community to another. Ultimately, the ACErs themselves overcame the challenges, always with deep humor and generosity. Equally important was the quality of leadership at the diocesan and superintendent level. In places where this leadership was strong and willing to go out of their way to make things happen, somehow the ACErs more than survived. They flourished.

Partly because of the scramble to put the program together, and partly out of sheer ignorance, we did not impose an overly rigid set of expectations on how each local ACE community would structure common life. Rather (and perhaps naively), we hoped that each local community would develop its own model of Christian living, and that, over time, we could share best practices and success stories. Our hope was that, out of the experience of the ACE communities themselves, an organic model of contemporary Christian lay community might emerge. Though many examples of clerical religious communities were available, we wanted a model to come forth that would respond uniquely to young men and women who, though intensely religious, generally felt called to live and serve as committed Catholic lay people. We turned for help to a band of four young teachers from Washington's Teaching Service Corps (three were Notre Dame graduates; the fourth, a Georgetown graduate, has since begun a doctorate in theology at Notre Dame). We invited them to provide advice and counsel from their experience as novice teachers who had lived together in a Christian community. These zealous young teachers, two men and two women, generously agreed to spend the summer at Notre Dame that first year to mentor our pioneering class and share their own best practices in teaching, community life, and prayer. They were an invaluable resource to us, especially since neither of us had had any firsthand experience living the life for which we were preparing our youthful pioneers.

The most deliberate effort we made to prepare our initial participants to live a healthy and engaging Christian community life consisted of an eight-week seminar called Personal and Professional Growth and Development, a required course designed in collaboration with the faculty at the University of Portland. This seminar, which met every Tuesday and Thursday evening during the course of the summer, focused attention on themes relating principally to the task of integrating teaching, Christian community life, and spirituality. Relying primarily on the members of Notre Dame's Campus Ministry staff and the four Teaching Service Corps teachers, we tried to help the ACErs find ways to balance the demands of teaching as a ministry while also living generously a common life. For instance, we provided personality indicators and taught effective communication skills in an effort to enhance mutual understanding and tolerance among the ACErs. We also offered a multitude of techniques and suggestions for individual and communal prayers. Whether it was reading Flannery O'Connor's *Mystery and Manners* to communicate a deep sense of the Incarnation in the uniqueness of southern culture, or learning *Lectio Divina* as a personal or communal exercise, the ACErs were continually invited to see their entire experience through a lens of faith.

The summer schedule was punishing, and our greatest challenge was simply to overcome the fatigue and lack of energy among the ACErs. We had already taken an orientation weekend in April, two days in the middle of their Senior Week prior to graduation, and only given them 10 days of vacation before beginning the summer session. Now we had them in the classrooms of the South Bend public schools for three to four hours in the morning and in their own graduate courses in education for another three to six hours in the afternoon and evening, leaving them with a few hours for preparation time and—with luck—a few hours of sleep in an overheated fourth-floor dorm room with no air conditioning. Often, the last thing the ACErs wanted to do was to have another class dealing with issues that were not yet a reality in their lives. Add to this packed summer experience daily schedule changes, classroom changes, dining hall mix-ups, etc., and one could see how the ACErs were not always pleased with our "making it up as you go along" strategy. In fact, after several meetings where we listened to the ACErs' frustrations, complaints, and suggestions, ACE became not so affectionately known as Always Changing Everything, instead of the Alliance for Catholic Education.

Learning to adapt and be flexible in the context of a pioneering program characterized much of the early experience in ACE. After our first year of experience, both during the summer and in the field, we were able to adjust our professional program to address the specific community and spiritual life challenges facing the ACErs. For instance, intra-community issues often centered on the varied teaching, coaching, and extracurricular commitments that prevented some of the ACErs from being present at house activities. Inter-community issues that developed often focused on comparing the unequal salaries or accommodations between the different communities. For example, some ACErs were unable to live in the same house because of concern among local Church leaders that coed housing might cause scandal among the faithful. Living in single-sex adjacent apartments, instead of a common house, sometimes led some ACErs to conclude they were being cheated out of a rich experience of common life that other ACErs obviously enjoyed and talked up. With each new issue, we struggled to catch up to the unfolding needs and promise of these young teachers, hoping to provide a rich experience of service and faith in the context of community.

Ultimately, we want to provide an experience during the two years of involvement in ACE whereby ACErs learn to become agents of community-building in their schools, local parishes, and broader communities. To accomplish this, we need to be much more deliberate and systematic in drawing the lessons from the best practices that our hundreds of ACErs themselves have experienced, and we must discover incentives for our current ACE communities to adapt these practices to their own local circumstances. Hopefully, while we can point toward some successful models, we will always provide a significant degree of freedom for our participants to discover what combination of practices will best draw out the gifts and talents of every member of each local ACE community.

The third pillar of the ACE program involves an invitation to the participants to develop their own personal and ecclesial faith and spirituality. Much like the community life pillar, this dimension of the ACE program has only gradually evolved as we have accumulated valuable experience over the past seven years. From the outset, ACE spirituality focused on the person of Christ Teacher, and has employed Gospel stories of Jesus' constant invitation to his followers to a deeper and more wholehearted discipleship as the central organizing theme of our common life and service. Christ Teacher has increasingly provided a rich common language and culture with which our participants can identify to interpret the daily struggles and triumphs of first-year teaching. Indeed, Christ Teacher is the central image that we have self-consciously attempted to infuse throughout the academic and community life dimensions of the ACE experience. The Gospel and the language of discipleship provide the commonly agreed-upon context and meaning for the ACE experience. Though admittedly the most delicate dimension of the program to elaborate, ultimately this invitation to deepen and nourish the life of discipleship in Christ will provide the most lasting impact on the lives of our program participants and the children and school communities they serve.

As we initiated the program, we certainly had no preconceived set of spiritual exercises for our young teachers to undertake. Rather, we planned each day as it unfolded. Prayer was an integral part of everything we did, both as an administrative team and as a program. We were conscious of the fact that the whole endeavor was, above all, a work of the Holy Spirit. At the heart of our prayer, always, has been the Eucharist. If ACE has a spirituality at all, it is one that places the Eucharist at the center of our lives, every day. It is difficult to remember a single activity that we undertook as a staff, or faculty, or admissions committee, or gathering with our young participants that did not begin and end with prayer, often at the Eucharist. The Eucharist is the perfect prayer of the Church, and the Lord nourished and sustained us as a young program around that life-sustaining table. Every evening during the summer program, many of the participants and staff gathered in a campus residence hall chapel for Mass as a way to close, or at least punctuate, the day and place the rush of activities in the hands of the Lord. In fact, ACE celebrations of the Sunday Eucharist have become so popular on campus during the summer that the Campus Ministry has formalized the event and invited the broader university summer school community to participate. Though we had very little idea how to shape a spirituality that would be inviting and relevant to young teachers, we clung to the Eucharist in intimate and relatively informal settings as the central act of worship and thanksgiving of the ACE program. It still is.

As was the case with community life, our delivery vehicle for the spiritual life component of the program consisted of our evening course two days a week, Personal and Professional Growth and Development. Here we outlined, and tried to model, the basic structure of possible prayer modalities. We encouraged the ACErs to explore a variety of options and find a road to the interior life that appealed to each participant. We cautioned the ACErs that the spiritual life was often the first dimension of life that was dropped once things became too busy. By introducing the ACErs to people of faith whose life of prayer had infused and supported their service to the Church, we hoped to inspire the ACErs to develop this same longing for God in their own lives.

With each passing week, as we tried to listen to the spiritual needs and aspirations of the ACErs, we attempted to respond with liturgical expressions that might resonate in some way. Very much in the spirit of improvisation, we developed certain liturgical expressions that have since become part of a growing set of ACE rituals. For example, when we gathered our pioneer class of participants in the initial April retreat, an occasion when all the new ACE participants and diocesan school superintendents gather for a "get to know you" orientation weekend, we developed a set of liturgies to frame the event. In the same way, the initial retreats of the summer, the mid-summer retreats, the Missioning Mass and celebrations at the end of the summer, and the Advent retreat in Biloxi, Mississippi at mid-year, all presented occasions for us to bring rich liturgical language to express the movement of our participants toward discipleship with Christ Teacher. With the passage of several years, each of these liturgies, though with adaptations along the way, became familiar benchmarks in a participant's journey until the program's completion with graduation. Over time, though completely unintentionally, we developed a "twelve-step journey" of spiritual life and development in ACE spirituality, a journey that we are continually adapting to the needs of the ACErs themselves (see Chapter 9, this volume). It is our hope that a more

encompassing and coherent spirituality will imbue the ACE experience with an organic relationship to the one Teacher.

The ACErs want that. In particular, many ACErs have suggested
that they need help redefining where they find God, especially in the
midst of loneliness and deep personal changes. In a recent post-ACE
survey, the three most significant challenges to the ACErs' faith once
they have graduated from ACE were identified as (1) the inability to
become part of an active faith community, (2) a sense of loneliness
and one's relationships being disconnected to one's life of faith, and
(3) a lack of integration of one's work and one's faith life. The need
to frame the entire experience more explicitly in spiritual language,
symbols, and liturgies focused on Christ Teacher has become increasingly apparent.


## RECRUITING TALENT AND PROMISE

WHAT MAKES ACE interesting and exciting, in the end, is the
character of the ACE participants themselves. So how in the world did
this cohort of talented seniors, who could be doing just about anything
after graduation, come to decide that working for below-minimum
wage in Catholic schools was what they wanted to be doing? The only
answer to this question, in our experience, rests in the deep faith commitments that motivate and energize the wonderful young applicants
who seek to join ACE. We recounted earlier how surprised we were to
find the initial recruitment meeting jam-packed with dozens and dozens
of faith-filled world-beaters. Our first year, nearly 5% of the senior
class applied to the program. In the second year, 7%. In the third year,
nearly 10%! In terms of quality, again, simply amazing! Many of the
leaders of Notre Dame's graduating class have expressed a desire to
give something back to the schools that provided them with the values
and skills to become young leaders in the faith, and they see teaching
as a good way to do it.

We have learned some valuable lessons in trying to build a pool of
talented and motivated young teachers for our program, both at Notre
Dame and beyond. First, it does not hurt to have high standards for
admission into the program. We made it clear from the start that,
although strictly academic measurements were relevant, we would not
determine admission to ACE exclusively, or even primarily, in terms
of academic distinction, but rather more broadly on leadership potential and perceived (though often inchoate) teaching skills. In fact, after

we designed the application form (borrowing liberally from similar teacher-service programs), we formed a common set of admission criteria together with veteran Catholic schoolteachers and administrators prominently present among the residence hall staff at Notre Dame. From the very start, we enjoyed the luxury of having far more qualified applicants than we could accommodate in the program, and so entry into the program gained the reputation of being quite competitive. The reputation was to our advantage. Of the 100 applicants in our first year, a majority graduated from college with honors, studied a broad variety of different academic disciplines, and was involved in a vast array of extracurricular activities. We accepted and placed as teachers 40 of these original 100 applicants in our first year. As a result of the increasing interest in our program and our decision to grow slowly, we have gone from accepting 40% of our applicants to where we can only accept 25%—even though nearly 75% of all applicants have obtained an undergraduate G.P.A. of 3.5 or higher and were among the strongest undergraduate student leaders in service programs and other extracurricular activities.

ACE has decided at the programmatic level to work hard to attract under-represented groups to join the ranks of our teacher corps. First, ACE chose from the very beginning to achieve gender parity among its classes of teachers. Not only did our schools request male teachers, but we also realized that community life would be strengthened if there were equal numbers of men and women. We also worked hard to recruit minority applicants to our program. As the program has expanded, we have moved to schools serving Hispanic and African American populations that are in great need of teachers who can provide sound role models.

Each year, interviewing the applicants to the program is a deeply moving experience for the members of the admissions committee. The stories of generosity, courage, and faith that the young applicants share in carefully structured, one-hour interviews are testimonies to the fact that something terribly right is happening over the course of these young Catholics' lives of faith and service. If concerns about Generation X or Generation Y are plaguing social commentators, it would be enough to tame the most cynical among them to sit through an afternoon of these interviews. Whether it has been a teacher who challenged and loved them, a service experience as a tutor or youth counselor that has captured an inner call to live the Gospel through service to others, or the presence of deep friendships that have enkindled their faith, in each and every case the applicants have a hunger for a deeper experience of God, and they seek to gain this in ACE. (See Chapter 12 for more about recruiting.)

Almost from the beginning, the temptation for us has been to grow too quickly, and to accept the many invitations from multiple dioceses across the country that have requested ACE teachers. For a number of reasons, we decided to grow more slowly and maintain the highest possible quality among the participants, as well as to continue to be able to interact intensely and personally with each participant. Just as strong personal relationships initially brought the ACErs to the program, further leadership formation depended on deeply personal interactions within the program to call forth fully the leadership gifts of our participants. Therefore, the key to our contribution has been and will be quality, not quantity. If we are to help meet the future staffing needs of the more than 8,500 Catholic elementary and secondary schools across the nation, it will be partly by replicating the ACE model at other Catholic and Christian colleges and universities.

### PARTNERSHIPS ARE KEY

Launching an ambitious service-teaching program from an institutional base such as that offered by the University of Notre Dame provided a ready infrastructure and set of networks that allowed us to mobilize the resources to implement our vision. From the very start, Fr. Edward Malloy, CSC, president of the university, supported the idea and gave us the green light to move forward; he even provided us with our first seed grant of $5,000 to get started. Within the broader Notre Dame community, a number of important institutional allies came forward to offer support. Particularly encouraging were early meetings with members of the Notre Dame faculty from various academic departments who maintain an abiding interest in education. Leaders among the faculty such as Maureen Hallinan in sociology, John Borkowski in psychology, Clark Power in liberal studies, and others offered to help build a local educational initiative to support the training of the ACE teachers. These same faculty colleagues would continue to play a critically important role as we began to look to house a more ambitious institutional effort for education on the campus at Notre Dame. The well-known lesson here, of course, is that senior faculty allies are a *sine qua non* in building a lasting institutional presence within a university community.

The steady encouragement and contributions made by the university's Office of Campus Ministry, especially its director, Fr. Richard Warner, CSC, have been absolutely essential to the success of ACE. Campus Ministry provided an unending supply of expertise and talent in helping to shape the retreats and the community and spiritual life pillars of the incipient program. Other members of the administration got behind the idea as well. The university agreed to provide free housing during the summer to the ACErs, and to provide classroom space and office support for the program's needs. The help of University Relations was also enlisted early on to assist in the task of identifying potential friends and benefactors to provide seed money to cover the costs of implementing the early stages of the program. Other units of the university, ranging from the university counsel, to development and internal auditing, to graphics and design, to catering, all provided an exceptionally receptive institutional infrastructure that made ACE possible within our impossibly tight time horizon. (See Chapter 4 for more about the role of campus-level support in development of the program.)

Though partnerships within the Notre Dame community were crucial in providing a necessary institutional setting for launching the ACE program, other institutional partners outside the university played key roles in the development of the program. We wrote earlier about the essential contributions made by the University of Portland's School of Education, especially in designing and implementing a training model for the ACE teachers during the first four years of the program. The National Catholic Education Association, especially the office of chief administrators, became a focal point for identifying superintendents of Catholic education who would be likely collaborators for this effort in their local dioceses. Identifying the right superintendents as collaborators in the field turned out to be an important factor accounting for the success of our program's efforts. Annually, the chief administrators' meetings have provided an opportunity for a growing fellowship of ACE superintendents to network with one another, and for the ACE staff to exchange mid-semester check-ups with these our most valued partners. Indeed, the mutuality of this partnership would be recognized by the National Catholic Education Association just one year after we began, when ACE was awarded the C. Albert Koob Award for the most significant contribution to Catholic education in 1994.

The Department of Education of the National Catholic Conference of Bishops also played an important partnership role with ACE in building this Alliance for Catholic Education. First of all, the presence of Sr. Lourdes Sheehan, RSM, as secretary for education enabled us to gain a national perspective readily, providing sage and seasoned counsel as our young program expanded into unknown territory. Sr. Lourdes's ability to assess the sometimes complicated local political realities embedded within the southern diocesan school systems where we served provided an invaluable resource. Moreover, her association with our program afforded us an unimpeachable calling card with local ecclesiastical authorities. Sr. Lourdes's commitment to ACE made it possible for us, as newcomers to the field, to gain instant credibility among key superintendents, and her reputation, together with Notre Dame's, made an unbeatable combination.

Locally, we became very engaged in collaboration with both the South Bend Community School Corporation (SBCSC) and the Diocese of Fort Wayne–South Bend in developing ways to improve and initiate summer programs in our local schools. Initially, the SBCSC offered our new teachers an opportunity to teach and gain practical experience that complemented their graduate courses in education. Yet our work with the SBCSC allowed their summer programs to increase their enrollment while increasing teacher-student ratios. Furthermore, our third summer ACE was able to help the local Catholic schools begin their own summer school session, taking advantage of both ACE graduates who had returned for the summer and the new ACE teachers who were in training. Both of these local institutions have helped ACE enhance its own educational program while at the same time allowing ACE to serve the needs of our local school children.

As we continued to think about the different dimensions of our program, it became clear to us that we would need a steady flow of financial resources to accomplish our goals, over and above the fees paid by participating schools. Though the long-term prospects for endowing this annual shortfall appeared achievable, like any new program in the short-term, we needed to scramble for money. A number of individuals and private foundations and corporations were exceptionally generous with support for our incipient program, well before we had placed our first teacher. In addition, and quite fortunately, our plans for beginning ACE coincided almost identically with President Bill Clinton's notion for encouraging national service in the form of the Corporation for National Service. We set to work to prepare an application for the corporation, and with the help of Fr. Ted Hesburgh, CSC, our local congressman Tim Roemer, and others, we were invited to join this federal effort as a National Demonstration Grant program, one of 11 pioneer programs selected nationally from among institutions of higher education. As an Americorps program, the ACE program received a limited amount of administrative support annually, but more importantly, each of our participants automatically became eligible for a grant of $4,725 annually to be applied either to further graduate education or to offset federal loans outstanding from undergraduate study. When we announced this news to our first-year program participants on the sweatiest night of the summer, after a long day's work in the South Bend summer schools, there was instant jubilation! Our partnership with Americorps has been a very significant one, allowing Notre Dame's ACE program to network among service-teaching programs nationally.

Other grants and private donations have been secured over the years, beginning with friends and family, to larger, multi-year grants from foundations and corporations. Establishing these important financial relationships has taken considerable time and energy, but these relationships both allowed us needed flexibility and challenged us to continually articulate our vision to a critical audience. We have learned that resources always support good ideas. Given the abiding presence of the Holy Spirit, the enthusiasm of those in the program has quickly spread to those who have heard about what we are doing and want to become involved. As we look to the future, especially with the prospects of replicating the parts of our experience that might be of use to other institutions, that network of partnerships and alliances on behalf of the future of Catholic schools must continue to grow.

## THE PRESENCE OF THE CONGREGATION OF HOLY CROSS

ACE IS INFUSED with the missionary spirit of the Congregation of Holy Cross, a community whose members define themselves essentially as "educators in the faith." Indeed, the French founder of the congregation, Fr. Basil Moreau, formed the band of religious priests and laymen to respond to the critical need for Catholic schools in the wake of the destruction left behind by the French revolution. Today, this community follows the founder's exhortation to teach so that God, as he put it, "may be known, loved, and served." The congregation has sponsored dozens of elementary and secondary schools throughout the United States, as well as several colleges and universities. The University of Notre Dame is both the first apostolate founded in the Americas by the congregation, as well as the most widely recognized.

Holy Cross manifests a "can do" and "whatever it takes" spirit, a spirit that characterized the original missionaries from this French community in the mid-19th Century. The founder of the University of Notre Dame, Fr. Edward Sorin, CSC, epitomized this kind of ambition and vision in the field of education, boldly christening L'Université de Notre Dame du Lac in the forests of northern Indiana, dedicating the work to the mother of Jesus. More than perhaps anything else, the faith, drive, and ambition of the Congregation of Holy Cross at Notre Dame has fueled the exciting trajectory of this newest alliance for Catholic education.

Given the founding apostolic vision of the Congregation of Holy Cross, it is natural for members of this religious community to find ways to respond to the contemporary challenges faced by Catholic schools in America. Like Holy Cross, ACE has been an intensely and purposefully collaborative initiative, one where lay men and women collaborate with priests to prepare a new generation of teachers for America's Catholic schools. Clearly, the future leadership of our vast network of Catholic schools in America, the most important institutional legacy we possess as a Church for the evangelization of culture, will undoubtedly be held by lay men and women. They must be well prepared to carry out this mission. Naturally, members of the Congregation of Holy Cross have found a special urgency in Notre Dame's reinvolvement in service to K–12 education across the United States.

The way in which community life in ACE is structured to support the apostolate of teaching, and not the other way around, also borrows from the Constitutions of the Congregation. In some ways, the life of an ACE teacher mirrors, for two years, the life of a religious living in the context of Christian community to serve the educational needs of the local Catholic Church. This is precisely why the congregation was founded in France in the first place! The relatively unencumbered spirituality of the program, with Christ Teacher as the only true model, and the Gospel as our only rule, draws directly from the spirituality of the Congregation of Holy Cross. With the Eucharist at the heart of our daily prayer, and a deep devotion to Mary, Notre Dame, the first teacher of Jesus, ACE at Notre Dame is a natural outgrowth of the charism of the founding religious community.

One of the most rewarding aspects of ACE for the two authors of this chapter is the response of several participants of the program each year to an invitation by the Holy Spirit to enter the Congregation of

Holy Cross, presumably to continue the work of Catholic education. That the talented leadership cadre of ACE, such as Lou DelFra, CSC, and others, have chosen to join forever this band of "educators in the faith" can only enrich, deepen, and renew the contemporary vocation of the congregation to serve Catholic education, especially among schools in service to the poor. Thus, ACE has not only returned Notre Dame to a dimension of its apostolic vision that is essential to the role of Holy Cross in evangelizing culture through preparing committed Catholic school teachers, but the program has also brought to Holy Cross a renewed strength and vitality in its own future work in education.

## IDENTITY MATTERS

Young people yearn for identity. One lesson we learned is that the identity of a teacher is a powerful and attractive one, which allowed us, as a program competing for the strongest applicants with other volunteer programs, a certain advantage. Another advantage, frankly, is that the life of a first-year teacher is unbelievably busy. Being stretched and consumed by a work that really matters provides deep satisfaction and builds character. In fact, the tremendous responsibility placed on these ACE teachers to become leaders in their schools, parishes, communities, and world of Catholic education has been one of the most influential reasons the ACErs experience so much personal, professional, and spiritual growth. We want ACErs to know the value of hard work, balanced by the nourishment and support provided by prayer and community life.

Building a new program requires that some attention be given not only to the identity of the individual program participants, but to the identity of the ACE community as well. During our first summer, when we asked our ACErs to help us think about a logo for the program, one of our number, a talented artist, drew up a colorful circle of children with "Alliance for Catholic Education" surrounding them all. It was an instant hit and has become widely recognized on campus to represent ACE and service to Catholic education. Rituals are also an important component of forming identity; the yearly ritual of unleashing a new ACE T-shirt emblazoned with the ACE logo and distributing it to the first-year teachers at the end of the summer has become a great community builder. The tradition includes not telling the ACErs what color the T-shirt will be in any given year, which inevitably leads to wide rumor-mongering and speculation. (See Chapter 8 for more about community-building in the program.)

Over the past several years, we have been able to build a relatively strong institutional culture within ACE by developing symbols, traditions, and rituals that mark rites of passage over the course of the two years in the program. For example, at the completion of the summer training effort, we celebrate the sending forth of our ACE teachers to their various diocesan schools across the country in a rousing Missioning liturgy. Through our local bishop, John D'Arcy, who has encouraged the development of ACE in countless ways since its inception, we always invite a senior leader of the Catholic Church to be principal celebrant for this liturgy, people such as Cardinals Laghi, Keeler, O'Connor, Law, Mahoney, and McCormick. The presence of these senior Church leaders provides an opportunity for ACE to identify with the larger teaching mission of the American Catholic Church. At this liturgy, we give each second-year ACE teacher a bronze medal of Christ Teacher, a medal that proclaims our mission "to make God known, loved, and served." At the Eucharist that marks graduation, we give each graduate a striking image of Our Lady, Notre Dame, in a reposeful and quiet posture. After all, she was the first and most excellent teacher of Jesus himself. Paying attention to regular ritualized acts, liturgy, and special places, like the Grotto at Notre Dame where we celebrate in prayer at graduation, is crucial in establishing the larger framework of meaning within which the ACE participant appropriates his or her own new identity as teacher in the footsteps of the Master.

## ALWAYS CHANGING EVERYTHING

FROM THE VERY OUTSET of this program, we listened carefully to our various constituencies and responded as effectively as we could to changing circumstances and needs, often having to trade off competing goods. We changed the schedule, the course contents, the teaching assignments, the housing arrangements, the mass schedules, always trying to keep up with the competing demands with which we were confronted nearly every day. As pioneers, we had no routines and were not exactly sure where we were going. So that first summer—no, first year—was a bit chaotic, to say the least.

Prof. John Borkowski, a senior member of the Psychology Department at Notre Dame and one of the program's great supporters, said after the first year, "If I didn't believe in the presence of the Holy Spir-it before ACE, I certainly do now!" His remark is entirely under-standable, since building ACE required a continual response to the improvisations of the Spirit. It still does. If we glance backward in time over the initial building of the American Catholic School system in the nineteenth and early twentieth centuries, what is striking is the improvisation and risk upon which it was built. Our program has grown surprisingly over the past several years, and it has deepened and strengthened its institutional linkages both within Notre Dame and with the broader work of Catholic education across America. Whatever else might be said about what the future holds for this edu-cational initiative, Notre Dame will continue to try to contribute in meaningful ways to the exigencies and challenges faced by Catholic schools as they move into the 21st Century. Whether this leads us to replicate ACE in cooperating higher educational institutions across the land, or to offer training and certification to promising leaders and administrators of Catholic education, or to serve more deliber-ately the needs of Catholic education in and around South Bend, or all of the above and more, will depend on where the Spirit, in Her great providence, wishes to take us. We pray that we might have the courage and faith to respond.

# 3

MICHAEL PRESSLEY

# DEVELOPMENT OF THE ACE
# M.ED. PROGRAM

I pick up the story of the Alliance for Catholic Education in 1997, with the current Notre Dame program developed between summer 1997 and school year 1999—2000. Like many programs, this one was invented as it happened.

### SUMMER 1997

I CAME TO NOTRE DAME the first week of June 1997 to head a master's program in education, one that would enroll students in the ACE program. Earlier in the year, the decision had been reached by Notre Dame and University of Portland officials to transfer responsibility for the master's degree academic experience from the University of Portland to Notre Dame. For the class entering in summer 1998, Notre Dame would have to offer the first half of a teacher education program, and in summer 1999, the entire Notre Dame M.Ed. program would have to be up and running.

I lived with the program in summer 1997, residing in the same dorm where the male ACErs lived and eating in the same cafeteria that served the ACErs. These close contacts permitted me to understand the program from the perspective of the students. I also wanted to understand the program from the faculty's perspective, believing that the Portland faculty's experience with ACE had to be filled with insights about how the program could be delivered given the constraints involved in offering a master's level graduate program with only 15 weeks of face-to-face contact on the campus (i.e., 8 weeks the first summer and 7 weeks the second summer).

## INTERACTIONS WITH THE PORTLAND FACULTY

The Portland program as it operated at Notre Dame required students to enroll in four 3-credit courses in each of two summers. The students were enrolled in two courses for the first half of the summer and two courses for the second half. The coursework was heavily oriented toward classroom teaching methods, although there were also courses in topics such as foundations of education and exceptionality. In addition to the coursework, students participated in other activities. For example, even before the summer began, students entering in summer 1997 had been required to do observations of students in South Bend schools, with reports on these observations due early in summer 1997 and graded as part of one of the courses. Also, there were weekly meetings of all the ACErs with the ACE staff, typically on Sunday evening. The get-togethers focused on community-building.

In order to understand the Portland program, I visited not only some of the classes but also the various social settings where the Portland faculty met. Many of the Portland faculty came to the 10 P.M. Masses, and I was able to join some of their informal discussions before and after the service. A number of the Portland faculty had their meals in one restaurant on the campus, so I began taking some of my meals there, joining in the lunch or dinner table conversations. There were days I ate several lunches so that I could interact with the students in North Dining Hall and with the Portland faculty in the campus restaurant. My conversations with the Portland faculty were very informative, especially about the needs of the students in the program.

## INTERACTIONS WITH THE STUDENTS

The most salient characteristic about breakfast was that the first-year ACE students had to eat rapidly in order to get to their summer placement in the South Bend schools. Students very much looked forward to their morning of work in the schools. Often students would talk about what they had planned for the class they were teaching or special challenges that were occurring in the setting they served. All of the new ACErs saw the summer service in the schools as helpful to them in their formation as teachers.

Breakfast also was revealing, however, about the stresses that students in the ACE program felt, especially around the end of courses (i.e., 4 and 8 weeks into the program) when students spent much of the night working on projects and papers that were due. As a veteran of university life, I knew that end-of-term periods often are stressful, with loss of sleep common, but the end-of-term stresses witnessed in summer 1997 seemed especially extreme.

Mealtime conversations revealed a variety of ACEr perceptions about the weaknesses and strengths of the program. A recurring theme was distress about many assignments that seemed inauthentic because they did not relate directly to the teaching that would be undertaken in the fall. For example, there were many complaints about planning lessons that would never take place, assignments intended only as practice in planning lessons. The ACErs believed they should be planning actual lessons for their autumn classes. Another common complaint was that the ACE participants felt disconnected from the Portland faculty; this disconnection was striking compared to the strong sense of community and connection they felt with the ACE staff. One memorable analogy was that the faculty-ACEr relationship was like an "I-thou" relationship, which many ACErs considered inappropriate, since community is a huge emphasis in ACE. More positively, the ACErs remained enthused about the program, with virtually everyone very much looking forward to teaching in the fall.

Despite the strong sense of community among the ACErs, first-summer ACErs seemed to mix little with second-summer ACErs. The ACE community in summer 1997 was divided along class lines! The two cohorts took no classes in common. Their schedules did not put them in the cafeteria at the same time for breakfast and lunch. The Sunday evening activity designed explicitly to build community and which included both ACE classes was a bust for the most part. Those Sunday evenings just did not click.

I often thought about this when I attended the 10 P.M. Mass. On the positive side, the Mass was sometimes inspirational, with the celebrants obviously doing some hard thinking about what they could say to the ACE participants that would relate to the ACE experience. Sometimes, there was simple but inviting music provided by ACE participants. The services were held in one of the more beautiful and modern chapels on the campus, and the quietness of 10 o'clock in the evening often contributed to the appeal of the services. Finally, the 10 P.M. Mass was the only activity, besides class, that was shared by ACE participants and at least some faculty. On the negative side, not many ACE participants attended the 10 P.M. services, and during the final week of summer 1997, the attendance was downright small, reflecting that many participants could not cope with the academic load and their spiritual development simultaneously. Also, too many of the homilies were not connected to the themes and experiences of the ACE program. Finally, there was little mixing of the ACE participants and the faculty at the services.

### JOURNEYS TO INDIANAPOLIS

In summer 1997, ACE participants had many questions about the accreditation of the new master's program that Notre Dame would offer and when this program would be able to recommend its graduates to the state of Indiana for licensure as teachers. Gaining state accreditation occurs over a number of years rather than months, and I knew that I had to confront this issue directly and immediately for the program to be approved by summer 2000, when the first participants would graduate from the Notre Dame program.

Early in the summer, John Staud (acting director of ACE), Tim Scully (founder of ACE), and I went to Indianapolis to meet with state officials for an informal discussion about accreditation. The state people were especially intrigued because it seemed Notre Dame might be perfect for a pilot testing of the new state standards, which were then emerging. These standards were based on ones approved by the National Council for Accreditation of Teacher Education (NCATE), with the expectation that teachers would be accredited on the basis of performance more than by the simple accumulation of academic credits. Particularly central to the new state standards were the principles developed by the Interstate New Teacher Assessment and Support Consortium (INTASC) (see Table 3.1), and the idea that the summative evaluation of a candidate for teacher licensure be based on a portfolio of professional accomplishments. By the end of this meeting, I knew that the Notre Dame program would have to be very different from the Portland program that had served ACE for its first four years. The INTASC principles prescribed coverage that was somewhat different from the Portland program, and the summative portfolio requirement was very different from anything in the Portland approach.

**TABLE 3.1**

*INTASC Principles*

1.  The teacher understands the central concepts, tools of inquiry, and structures of the disciplines he or she teaches and can create learning experiences that make these aspects of subject matter meaningful for students.

2.  The teacher understands how children learn and develop, and can provide learning opportunities that support their intellectual, social, and personal development.

3.  The teacher understands how students differ in their approaches to learning and creates instructional opportunities that are adapted to diverse learners.

4.  The teacher understands and uses a variety of instructional strategies to encourage students' development of critical thinking, problem solving, and performance skills.

5.  The teacher uses an understanding of individual and group motivation and behavior to create a learning environment that encourages positive social interaction, active engagement in learning, and self-motivation.

6.  The teacher uses knowledge of effective verbal, nonverbal, and media communication techniques to foster active inquiry, collaboration, and supportive interaction in the classroom.

7.  The teacher plans instruction based upon knowledge of subject matter, students, the community, and curriculum goals.

8.  The teacher understands and uses formal and informal assessment strategies to evaluate and ensure the continuous intellectual, social, and physical development of the learner.

9.  The teacher is a reflective practitioner who continually evaluates the effects of his or her choices and actions on others (students, parents, and other professionals in the learning community) and who actively seeks out opportunities to grow professionally.

10. The teacher fosters relationships with school colleagues, parents, and agencies in the larger community to support students' learning and well-being.

The state officials indicated that they thought Notre Dame was in an ideal position to implement the new requirements, and they were excited about working with Notre Dame in their implementation. The state officials also indicated, however, that Notre Dame should seek professional help in the development of its program from someone well informed about teacher education in Indiana. In fact, the head of the Indiana Professional Standards Board all but told the ND visitors that they should hire a consultant, someone already directing an Indiana-based teacher education program.

In July 1997, I made a second trip to Indianapolis to participate in a training workshop sponsored by the state for potential examiners in the state's reaccreditation process. The workshop largely was to acquaint examiners with the NCATE standards and the INTASC

principles as well as with the emerging portfolio approach to summative evaluation of teacher licensure candidates. There was a lot of
anxiety at the meeting, since most of the potential examiners were
teacher educators from programs in Indiana colleges and universities,
programs that were designed in light of and aligned with the old
teacher accreditation standards in the state. In fact, there was a great
deal of doubt among the attendees that their institutions could come
into compliance with the emerging standards. As the new kid on the
block, I listened to the reactions and said little.

The Indianapolis workshop was my first encounter with Joyce
Johnstone, who then headed the teacher education program at a small
Catholic college in Indianapolis, Marian College. I sensed from the
start that she might be the right person to serve as our consultant.
Joyce was an obvious Indiana insider, and she had extensive background in Catholic education. She could provide Notre Dame with
the state perspective translated in ways that would make sense and be
acceptable in a Catholic higher education context.

Also at the Indianapolis workshop was a faculty member from the
St. Mary's College teacher education program, the program serving
undergraduates at Notre Dame who wanted certification in teaching.
(St. Mary's is Notre Dame's sister institution and is also located in Notre
Dame, Indiana.) She told me about some perceptions—actually, mis-
perceptions—within the St. Mary's community about Notre Dame's
launch into teacher education. I recognized at that point that there was
a need to do some educating at home about the intent and scope of the
new Notre Dame program.

## CONCLUDING MOMENTS OF SUMMER 1997

Late in the summer session, the ACE II participants graduated from
the program conducted by Portland. What I could not miss when
speaking with graduating ACErs was their conviction that they had
done something worthwhile during their two years of ACE. They were
very satisfied with their experiences in the program. Moreover, so were
their families, despite a few parents' trepidations about a son or daugh-
ter using a $100,000 undergraduate education as a springboard for a
master's degree in education and a possible teaching career. At the
graduation reception there were many stories of academic growth, fulfillment in community, and spiritual development. No one could have
left that graduation and not believed that ACE was a good thing. As

is true for every graduation night, however, when it ends, there is a return to the real world, which for me in summer 1997 was the final week of the academic session being experienced by members of ACE III and IV.

The final week of the summer 1997 session was very revealing about many issues. Every meal in the dining hall provided illustration of the stresses of the intensive summer school experience. The participants also made clear that they felt the summer had not been a good balance of the three pillars of the ACE program: professional education, community, and spiritual life. Many were particularly distressed that they had learned little during the summer about how to stimulate the spiritual growth of their students, despite the fact that the Portland faculty included a number of the religious. Also, many ACErs were very tired; some were acutely aware that there would be no break for them between the end of the summer session and the beginning of their teaching in a K–12 classroom in the South.

These problems weighed heavily on my mind as I contemplated the program that I would propose for ACE. The program had to be designed so that the load was lighter in the summers and more meaningful. It had to be staffed with people who would be committed to working with the participants as community members and organized so that participants and faculty would communicate more. There had to be more time and opportunity for spiritual development.

On the very last Wednesday evening of the summer 1997 session, however, the mood changed. All the work had been handed in. What remained were some recreational and symbolic activities. Thursday was devoted largely to a trip to the Michigan dunes, with most of the ACE participants and the ACE staff joining in this day at the beach. In the evening, there was a ceremony at the Grotto, which is Notre Dame's replica of the shrine at Lourdes, a place of prayer and for devotion. Each group that would form a community household received a candle at the ceremony, which they would use as part of their at-home worship during the school year. A party at the campus club, featuring an Irish band and food, followed the Grotto ceremony, with succeeding celebrations in local watering holes.

At this end-of-summer party, for the first time, I was introduced to one of the benefactors of the program, who had been invited by Fr. Scully for the explicit purpose of increasing the benefactor's connection to ACE. What became clearer than ever to me in this meeting was that one of the reasons ACE was so successful was that it made sense to Notre Dame benefactors. I recognized that for the Notre Dame

M.Ed. effort to thrive, it would have to make sense to Notre Dame benefactors, something Fr. Scully knew already.

The second first for me at the party was my introduction to a cardinal of the Church, who would preside at the concluding religious service for the program, the Missioning Mass. The cardinal seemed determined to bring ACE to his home diocese. This was my initial encounter with expansion pressures on ACE. I recognized that the temptation to expand would have to be balanced with other elements of the Notre Dame M.Ed. program.

The final Friday began with the Missioning Mass, presided over by the cardinal archbishop who had lobbied me the night before, and who continued his campaigning during the homily, also directing his expansion message at the program benefactor who attended the Mass. As part of the service, each ACE III participant received a Christ Teacher medal to commemorate the completion of one year of service to Catholic education. Most importantly, all participants were blessed by the cardinal as they set off for their new assignments. This Mass was simply exuberant. The music was provided by instrumentalists and choralists from the ACE community, with the singing continuing in gospel fashion for a full 10 minutes after the cardinal departed. Even though there was a huge picnic waiting in a tent outside the chapel, the ACErs were so into the service that no one wanted to leave.

The final two days of the 1997 summer session gave me much to think about. What was most striking was just how enthused the ACErs were as they participated in the ceremony at the Grotto and in the Missioning Mass. The very same people who had appeared exhausted or discouraged on Monday and Tuesday seemed rejuvenated by the events on the final Thursday and Friday. Everyone seemed charged about getting to the schools they would be serving and getting to the business of teaching. I wondered if the energizing effects of the final few days might be injected into the program for the entire summer. Could the ACE M.Ed. experience be structured to incorporate the spiritual elements and activities that seemed so energizing to the ACErs during those final few days of summer 1997?

### SUMMARIZING SUMMER 1997

As I reflected on the challenges of launching an M.Ed. program at Notre Dame and what the formal credit demands should be, I recalled the emphatic feedback that there was just too much coursework in the summer sessions. Yet the meetings in Indianapolis left no doubt that the new state requirements focusing on performance would require a great deal of formal coursework and would add new pressures by requiring students to develop professional portfolios. I knew after the summer that the relevancy of every assignment in the program needed to be apparent. A recurrent ACEr concern was being asked to do many tasks that were, at best, approximations to teaching rather than connected to the actual teaching they would be doing in the fall. The ACErs seemed especially to yearn for experiences that would inform them more about how academic, community, and spiritual developments interlink.

I developed many good personal relationships with the ACErs while living, eating, and worshiping with them. The ACE staff knew the ACErs well. In contrast, the ACErs did not have much in the way of personal and community relations with the faculty serving their program. It seemed strange to me that this program, which emphasized community development, so separated students and faculty. Moreover, it also seemed strange that it so separated the ACE IIIs and IVs. I had a lot to think about as I prepared to put together a program that would make sense for the ACErs and pass muster with university and state stakeholders.

## SCHOOL YEAR 1997–1998

SEVERAL TASKS absolutely had to be accomplished in autumn 1997 if the M.Ed. program was to begin operation in summer 1998, and none were small. First and foremost, it was essential that the degree program be approved by the university, which required that the Graduate Council and Academic Council take action. For that to happen at a university as careful as Notre Dame about its academic programs, the proposed program had to promise to be excellent. Moreover, the program had to be proposed at the level of detail specified in the university's graduate catalogue—individual courses in sequence. Thus, one major task for autumn 1997 was to invent the curriculum.

A successful proposal would also include information about the faculty who would serve the program, which was a major challenge, since in August 1997, the program could boast of only one faculty member—me. Some Notre Dame faculty had indicated to me that they wanted to be involved with the M.Ed. program, but all of these individuals already had full-time responsibilities on the campus. Some had volunteered the names of others on campus who also might be interested in participating in the program. Also, I had a promise from the administration that I could fill in gaps with guest faculty appointments from outside the University of Notre Dame, although in August 1997, I had yet to talk with a single individual about the possibility of coming to Notre Dame in summer 1998 and beyond to serve the M.Ed. program. Thus, a second major task for autumn 1997 was to invent the faculty.

Then, there was the need to begin the accreditation process. As of August 1997, the entire guidance from the state of Indiana about how to do an accreditation using the emerging system was to follow the guidelines in *Standards, Procedures, and Policies for the Accreditation of Professional Education Units,* which was published by the National Council for the Accreditation of Teacher Education (NCATE). Like many such manuals, this one was exceptionally vague about what needed to be done to satisfy the requirements it specified. Thus, a third major challenge for autumn 1997 was to figure out how to deal with the state.

## September 1997

Letters were distributed during the summer to all faculty and professional staff on the campus, soliciting self-nominations of faculty members for the to-be-created M.Ed. program. Faculty who indicated an interest were invited to information meetings in the fall. By the time of the first meeting, I had roughly sketched out the curriculum for the M.Ed. program (see Table 3.2). The first summer would include a teaching practicum in South Bend schools as well as coursework in teaching, educational psychology, and Catholic education. In addition to these three 3-credit courses, there would be a 1-credit seminar relating ideas about Catholic education to the academic and community experiences of the ACErs. The second summer would include three 3-credit courses, one in human development appropriate to the ACEr's teaching level (i.e., elementary, middle, or high school), a course in exceptionality also appropriate to the teaching level, and a seminar in teaching methods appropriate to each ACEr's content specialization. The 1-credit seminar in Catholic education would also be required in the second summer, so that once again, each ACEr would have a 10-credit load. The total of 10 credits was arrived at because of two factors. One, the graduate school permitted a maximum of 10 credits to

**TABLE 3.2**

*Courses in the Notre Dame M.Ed. Program as Conceived in 1997–1998*

Introduction to Teaching (3 credits) (first summer)

Introduction to Reading and Writing *or* Introduction to Middle School Teaching *or* Introduction to High School Teaching (3 credits) (first summer)

Educational Psychology (3 credits) (first summer)

Exceptionality in Elementary School *or* Exceptionality in Middle School *or* Exceptionality in High School (3 credits) (second summer)

Child Development *or* Early Adolescence *or* Middle Adolescence (3 credits) (second summer)

Seminar in Content Area Instruction (e.g., Math Education, Language Arts Education) (3 credits) (second summer)

Directed Readings in Content Area (e.g., Math Education, Language Arts Education) (3 credits) (Internet seminars)

History of Education *or* Social Foundations of Education *or* Moral and Ethical Education *or* Philosophy of Education (3 credits) (Internet seminars)

Seminar in Catholic Education (2 credits) (1 credit each summer)

Student Teaching (12 credits)

Portfolio Compilation Course (3 credits) (second school year)

---

be earned in a single summer; two, I remembered how the ACErs struggled with the heavier credit load in summer 1997.

The meetings with potential faculty, which were well attended, concentrated on the nature of the curriculum after providing a general overview of the purpose and philosophy of the program. A recurrent theme emanating from the faculty was that the new M.Ed. program must function well, because so many ND students were so looking forward to participating in it. A subsidiary theme was that faculty in attendance wanted reassurance that their own students would be able to participate in the ACE M.Ed. I left each of the faculty sessions with between three and five names of individuals interested in serving the ACE M.Ed. as faculty.

I also left these sessions with a better idea about some of the campus anxieties surrounding the program. Faculty wanted to know whether this program signaled the return of a School of Education at Notre Dame, which seemed to be a fear for some. For others, there was some resentment of the new M.Ed. program, for they had friends who had been in the education program that was ended by the university in the 1970s. A few were concerned that Portland was being cut out of the ACE effort unfairly, unaware that Portland's departure was due to the pressure on their resources created by the growth of the ACE program over its first four years. The most frequent concern, however, was with respect to Notre Dame undergraduates pursuing education credits through St. Mary's College. Specifically, there were fears that Notre Dame's M.Ed. program would discourage students from enrolling in the St. Mary's courses, and thus do harm to St. Mary's education program, which already was suffering from under-enrollment pressures.

As I listened and learned at the sessions for faculty, I also began trying to discern what needed to be done in autumn 1997 to meet the state accreditation expectations. The most important step was to file a "preconditions" document in accordance with the preconditions process specified in the *Standards, Procedures, and Policies* book provided by NCATE. The state demanded this documentation 18 months before an accreditation visit. Since the accreditation visit needed to occur in summer 1999 for ND to be accredited in time for the first graduating class in summer 2000, there was no time to spare.

The preconditions document required descriptions of the unit offering the education degree, information about the personnel serving the program, documentation of the program's policies and procedures, evidence of continuous internal evaluation, information about admissions procedures and policies, detailing of assessments of students in the program, information about Notre Dame's institutional accreditation, and specification of the university's nondiscrimination policies. Although some of this was institutional boilerplate, much of it required invention in consultation with faculty who were likely to participate in the program. Much of that invention would happen in the month of October, although we made a good start on generating this paperwork in September 1997.

Beyond the state accreditation, a motivation for generating the paperwork was that it could do double duty, serving to inform the governing councils at Notre Dame about the program. To get that process started, Fr. Scully scheduled a luncheon meeting in mid-September between the ACE and M.Ed. people and the deans of the graduate school. The agenda was to discuss what had to occur for the Graduate Council to approve the M.Ed. program, with that approval necessary before the program could be taken before the Academic Council. The deans indicated they would do everything possible to facilitate the process so that the program could begin to operate in summer 1998. That meant the program would have to be reviewed by the Graduate Council at its mid-November meeting, with the paperwork describing the program in the hands of each member of the Graduate Council at least two weeks before the meeting. Much of the preconditions and curriculum had to be invented by the end of October 1997!

## OCTOBER 1997

October 1997 was busy with additional development of the curriculum and identifying faculty. Once the individuals most likely to serve the program were identified, meetings were scheduled to review the preconditions document, with about 10 to 15 faculty and ACE staff members attending each session.

What became apparent during the work on the preconditions document was that the biggest part of the task would be meeting precondition 8, which required detailed specification of the programs that ACE M.Ed. participants would follow—that is, the program that math teachers would take, the one for English teachers, etc. The state now wanted something very different from what historically had counted as precondition 8. They wanted programs described with respect to how they met the new state standards, including how the programs assured that participants met the INTASC standards. When I called the state for information about how to do this, the reply I received was, "We'll get back to you." I persisted until receiving a commitment from state officials to have the Professional Standards Board generate a response at a meeting near the end of October, a response that would be binding. Even though the meeting took place in October, however, it would be well into November before I knew what would be required to meet precondition 8.

In October, the St. Mary's issue came to a head, with many questions being posed across the campus about the ACE and St. Mary's education relationship. Early in the month, I met with ND vice president Carol Mooney, whose job it was to interact with St. Mary's on Notre Dame's behalf, and we agreed that a meeting with the appropriate St. Mary's officials was needed as soon as possible. A few weeks later, traveling to St. Mary's on a rainy autumn morning, Vice President Mooney and I explained to a St. Mary's vice president and to the head of teacher education that there was no conflict between ACE and the St. Mary's teacher education effort. ACE was so selective that a student who wanted to become a teacher had no guarantee of an ACE

M.Ed. admission. Most of these students would go the traditional route and seek education courses and licensure through St. Mary's.

Moreover, with respect to participation in ACE, St. Mary's applicants were treated as equal to Notre Dame applicants, with the $60,000 educational advantage conferred by ACE as much a plum for St. Mary's students as for Notre Dame students. In fact, much of the meeting was spent reflecting on the educational opportunity afforded by ACE to St. Mary's graduates. We also pointed out that the ACE M.Ed. was consistent with an agreement made with St. Mary's in the early 1970s, establishing that undergraduate teacher education would be the purview of St. Mary's, while the right to offer graduate work in education would be in Notre Dame's portfolio. This existing agreement came as something of a surprise to the St. Mary's representatives, and I was grateful that Notre Dame so carefully archived every administrative decision.

By the end of the meeting, the St. Mary's vice president seemed more positive than at the outset, although it was clear the head of teacher education still had serious reservations. The follow-up letter from the St. Mary's vice president that arrived a few weeks later, however, confirmed that St. Mary's could live with the ACE M.Ed. program. An important tension surrounding the ACE M.Ed. effort had evaporated. At least at the top levels of St. Mary's and Notre Dame, there was a clear understanding that the ACE M.Ed. was not threatening the survival of the teacher education program at the sister institution.

As this was going on, there were concerns among the ACE staff about the upcoming summer session, because two programs would be operating simultaneously: ACE IV students would be completing their second-summer coursework with Portland; ACE V students would be doing their first-summer coursework in the Notre Dame program. There was also budgetary uncertainty, but my tactic was to avoid a confrontation at this point with respect to the budget. I was determined to bring in a summer 1998 budget that would be well under $100,000.

To do so, I made the decision that two of the three 3-credit courses would be offered as large sections. Thus, Introduction to Teaching would enroll all of the ACE IV students during the first half of the summer session, and Educational Psychology would enroll all of the ACE IV students during the second half of the summer. Each ACEr would also take a methods seminar consistent with the developmental level of the students they would be teaching; each of these sections would have no more than 25 participants. There was a need to identify five faculty members for the 1998 summer session as well as faculty members and school-based teachers who could supervise the practica. By the end of October, we had tentatively identified all of the faculty members and two of the three practica supervisors. The M.Ed. program was beginning to be a concrete reality rather than merely a paper-based concept.

## NOVEMBER 1997

The ACE and M.Ed. staffs succeeded in delivering a program document to the Graduate Council early in November. Fr. Scully had talked to a number of members of the Graduate Council about the merits of the proposal in advance of the document delivery, and I felt confident that the program would be well received at the mid-November meeting. Indeed, every late October and early November encounter with a member of the Graduate Council increased the confidence of those identifying with the ACE M.Ed. effort. For example, on a flight from Chicago to South Bend, I sat next to a council member who praised the merits of ACE and made clear she was in favor of Notre Dame providing an M.Ed. degree to ACErs. In her eyes, the program not only made academic sense but was consistent with Notre Dame's missions of serving other Catholic institutions and supporting the poor.

The discussion portion of the Graduate Council meeting centered on familiar issues. There were questions about the wisdom of reentering a program area that the university had decided to forego a quarter of a century earlier. There were questions about whether the former education faculty, a few of whom remained on the campus, should be included in the new program. The relationship between the proposed program and the existing St. Mary's program was probed. In the several months since these questions had first been posed at the faculty information sessions in September, the ACE M.Ed. administrators and staff had opportunity to think hard about all of them and formulate answers that were consistent and compelling. The discussion in the Graduate Council went well. The vote did, too, with the final tally being 22 in favor of approving the program and 3 opposed.

Throughout the autumn, there had been on-and-off consultation with Joyce Johnstone, the Marian College professor I had met in Indianapolis in the summer. She read and reacted to the paperwork being generated by the Notre Dame group and, as a paid advisor to the program, began to mediate the discussion with state officials. The program was headed in the right direction from her perspective, and she was having success convincing the state officials that this program made sense. Joyce made frequent trips to Notre Dame, and the entire Notre Dame leadership flew to Marian on one occasion in the fall. Fr. Scully began to believe that Joyce should be a full-time staffer in the ACE M.Ed. program.

November would also bring some confirmation that the proposed ACE M.Ed. program was consistent with the best thinking about the reform of teacher education. The long-awaited final report of the National Commission on Teaching and America's Future, *What Matters Most: Teaching for America's Future,* was released. The M.Ed. program was consistent with many of the recommendations in the report. The commission endorsed streamlined alternative programs, ones focusing on learning theory, development, teaching methods, and intensively supervised, long internships. The ACE M.Ed. was shaping up to be such a program. The report called for aspiring teachers to have many more experiences with minority and disadvantaged students. The two-year period of ACE service in the South was definitely consistent with this direction. The commission called for mentoring to be a centerpiece of teacher education, and mentoring was prominent in the planned ACE M.Ed. program. The commission was concerned that teacher education be redesigned to increase the likelihood of well-qualified teachers choosing to serve under-resourced schools, and of course, ACE's focus on the disadvantaged was consistent with the commission's conclusion that intellectual capital needs to be directed to schools serving the poor and disadvantaged. The commission also urged that efforts be made to educate teachers in the use of technology, and the ACErs were well matched to this recommendation: ND's campus is completely wired, so that all its graduates emerge with years of immersion in technology; ACE participants from other universities would have similar immersion experiences with technology. Like NCATE, the commission called for performance-based assessment of new teachers, which was consistent with the performance and portfolio approaches being incorporated into the ACE M.Ed. program in response to the emerging Indiana standards. The commission also explicitly favored the INTASC principles that drive the Indiana standards and Notre Dame's program. In short, the emerging ACE M.Ed. program looked terrific in light of the commission's report.

The final piece of big news in November 1997 was that the state provided information about what Notre Dame needed to do to fulfill precondition 8. Basically, it boiled down to preparing hundreds of pages documenting exactly which courses students would take depending on their specialization, specifying in detail how the coursework would result in fulfillment of the INTASC standards. Moreover, on November 15, a firm deadline for submitting all of the preconditions to the state was set: January 15, 1998, just two months after we received the notification about how to fulfill precondition 8.

## DECEMBER 1997

Notre Dame's Catholic tradition stimulates a festive Advent season. The campus is tastefully decorated, there are choral concerts, and seasonal celebrations abound. For the ACE M.Ed. staff, there was a great deal of Christmas partying in early December, and then it was back to the office for the ACE M.Ed. leadership to crank out pages fulfilling the specifications of the state's precondition 8. When I opened Christmas packages with my family on Christmas Day, the documents the state had demanded for delivery in January 1998 were ready for the printer. With the help of a commercial printing and mailing service, the mission for the state was accomplished the Saturday after Christmas.

That Saturday evening, I reflected on the accomplishments of the autumn. I felt that God surely must be blessing this program, for formidable task after formidable task was accomplished in four short months. The only major task with respect to the M.Ed. program that had to be accomplished during winter semester was to meet with the Academic Council for their approval of the program. The paperwork that had just been shipped to the state would provide more than enough documentation for the Academic Council to judge the M.Ed., so that no new writing was anticipated in the winter semester, a welcome relief given the flurry of writing that had occurred in late November and December to fulfill precondition 8.

On Monday, following several prescheduled medical tests, I was diagnosed with advanced esophageal cancer. There was a 90% probability that the disease eventually would prove fatal. In the evening, I informed my family and those with a need to know of the terrible news. One with a need to know was Tim Scully. In the days that followed, I got my affairs in order and began to make inquiries about treatment. On Tuesday evening, I went to the Grotto for a prayerful reflection. Part of that meditation was the insight that perhaps it was God's will that I get the ACE M.Ed. effort only as far as I did, that I was the appropriate instrument for laying the groundwork, but there was someone better for overseeing the operation of the program. I also reflected that if it was God's will that I continue in this work with the ACE M.Ed. or any other task, I was prepared for that, but if my work on earth was nearing completion, I could accept that as well. After all, a central tenet of my life has been "Thy will be done."

I had survived another form of cancer in my youth and always believed there was as much miracle as medicine in that survival. As I reflected on the new illness, I honestly believed that there might be another mix of miracle and medicine this time. That mixing not only occurred in the winter semester of 1998, but it occurred in a way that permitted the ACE M.Ed. effort to proceed exactly on schedule and without compromise.

The miracle began as a series of phone calls in the hours after the Grotto reflection. One of the calls was from Fr. Scully, who, while at a dinner in Panama, happened to be seated with a leading medical authority who was well informed about esophageal cancer. The doctor told Fr. Scully about a cutting-edge treatment that seemed to be increasing greatly the odds of surviving advanced esophageal cancer. The doctor also provided a list of names of physicians in the United States well qualified to administer the treatment. When Scully called with the information, I was more than prepared to hear it, for I had just gotten off the phone with a physician friend who had indicated there was a fairly new treatment for esophageal cancer, but he was not certain where the treatment could be obtained. Additional inquiries would send me to the University of Wisconsin–Madison to receive the treatment. When I reconstructed the timeline of the events, I realized that Tim Scully had probably been at dinner with that Panamanian doctor shortly after my prayerful reflection at the Grotto.

## Winter Semester 1998

While I was in treatment in Madison, Tim Scully, John Staud, and their associates made progress. Early in winter 1998, Notre Dame offered Joyce Johnstone the associate directorship of the M.Ed. program, beginning with summer 1998. She accepted, and her participation in the ND program immediately accelerated.

The big event of the semester for the M.Ed. program was the Academic Council meeting. Scully, Staud, and Johnstone edited the documents submitted to the state to craft a description of the program for the council members. I was in no shape to participate in preparing it. I continued to hope that I might be able to make the Academic Council meeting, but that hope seemed dashed when the meeting was scheduled for March 19, the same week I was scheduled for surgery following the aggressive regimen of chemotherapy and radiation administered in January and February. I knew that Scully, Staud, and Johnstone would do a good job presenting the program, but I had great regret that the program I had so carefully devised would be taken to the Academic Council by others.

As March approached, Scully accelerated his politicking on behalf of the program. His position then as associate provost and vice president permitted many opportunities to interact with the members of the university faculty who served on the Academic Council. Although the many conversations increased his confidence that the program would pass, Scully was accustomed to over-preparing for such votes rather than taking success for granted. He would advocate on behalf of the proposal to the Academic Council right up until the hour of the council meeting.

There was one surprising turn of events for me. In late February, my surgeon advised me that he would not be able to perform the operation until the first week of April. That meant I could go home for most of March, needing to be at the hospital only one day each week. As a consequence, on March 19, I performed the only task I would perform on the Notre Dame campus in winter semester 1998. With Johnstone and Staud on each side of me, I made the presentation to the Academic Council and fielded questions. That I could do so seemed a bit miraculous to me, for March 19 was the first day in several months that I felt like a healthy human being, and in fact, when I looked in the mirror, I appeared to be my old self. Some on the council did not realize that I was very ill, until Notre Dame's president, Fr. Malloy, mentioned the illness when he thanked me at the conclusion of the meeting.

To the delight of everyone involved with the ACE M.Ed. effort, there had been no serious challenges to the program from the council members. Indeed, many of the questions were prefaced with laudatory comments about the ACE effort. Those comments presaged the vote, which was 44–0 in favor of approving the ACE M.Ed. program. The program was on the books.

When I visited the Grotto following the meeting, I thanked God for that afternoon. That evening I had another bout of nausea, the result of the chemotherapy and radiation. The three weeks between the Academic Council meeting and surgery were uncomfortable ones, and after March 19, I would not have another two-hour period when

I was completely free of symptoms. Somehow, miraculously, I had been in good shape for the one afternoon that mattered most to the ACE M.Ed. effort.

What remained after that in the spring semester was attending to the nitty-gritty involved in running the summer school program. John Staud scheduled the classrooms and made the arrangements for housing and board for faculty and students. He was accustomed to such work, having cooperated closely with Portland during its four years at Notre Dame. Staud and the ACE staff did a magnificent job, with everything ready to go in summer 1998, which permitted the initial evaluation of at least the first half of the M.Ed. program.

### SUMMARIZING SCHOOL YEAR 1997–1998

During school year 1997–1998, the ACE M.Ed. was formulated, approved, and staffed. The only way that the many tasks of the year could have been accomplished was through great cooperation among the ACE staff, the university's administration, and the emerging M.Ed. administration and faculty. The year's tasks were also accomplished through great persistence, for example, in communicating with the state for needed clarifications and in dealing with political turf issues on the Notre Dame and St. Mary's campuses.

### SUMMER 1998

THE PLAN FOR SUMMER 1998 with respect to the newly admitted ACE V participants was for each of them to take 10 credits. During the first four weeks, they enrolled in Introduction to Teaching, which I taught. During the second four weeks, members of ACE V enrolled in Educational Psychology. For all eight weeks, the students also took a methods course in teaching at the developmental level they would serve in the fall (elementary, middle, or high school), did practice teaching in a South Bend school, and experienced the 1-credit integrative seminar in Catholic education. I was not physically ready to teach during the first week of June—recovery from surgery was anything but smooth in May. Joyce Johnstone filled in for me until I was equal to the task at the beginning of the second week, although there were days when I was pretty shaky, having to nap on a couch in the lounge of the lecture building following the class.

In general, however, the summer courses went very smoothly. Especially gratifying was that the 1-credit integrative seminar in Catholic education was very successful, with the faculty in charge of it assembling a variety of presentations and experiences that seemed meaningful to the students. In addition, the students and faculty felt connected to one another. One innovation that I devised based on my experiences in the previous summer was to provide lunch for the faculty in the same dining hall where the students ate. This arrangement worked out wonderfully, with faculty meeting students at every noon meal. Moreover, all of the faculty attended some of the Masses, and some of the faculty attended most of the Masses. There was a real sense of community between the ACE Vs and their teachers.

Both the Intro to Teaching and the Educational Psychology courses were large sections, with all ACE Vs enrolled in these courses. On the plus side, meeting together every day fostered a sense of community and, in particular, provided a forum through which the various members of the ACE community could communicate with the group as a whole. Yes, there was one professor in charge of the section, but frequently other faculty members sat in, as did ACE staffers. When the ACE staff just absolutely, positively had to get a message to the ACE V students, they simply showed up at the Teaching or Ed Psych class to make an announcement.

A disadvantage was that the large sections made it hard to keep track of attendance, and sadly, about a half dozen individuals seemed to miss a great deal of class. Also, the grading burden on the faculty leader was very heavy, accentuated because each of the large courses only met for four weeks. The faculty members in charge of these courses felt that they were always grading during their four weeks of teaching. These problems motivated rethinking of ACE M.Ed. class sizes for summer 1998 and beyond, but also motivated some hard thinking about how ACE M.Ed. courses could be structured so as to contribute to the building of community.

The conclusion of summer 1998 for the ACE Vs did not seem quite as intense and crazy as the conclusion of summer 1997 had been. Even so, there was a great deal of assessment pressure at the end of the term. Also, there were a few miscommunications in which ACE staffers provided one direction and faculty members another (e.g., about when summer practicum experiences concluded).

As was the case in summer 1997, the symbolic events concluding the summer were a highlight for everyone. The candlelight service at the Grotto lasted longer than it had in summer 1997, with many more candles lit. The Missioning Mass featured Cardinal O'Connor of New York, whose personal reflections on his own teaching of special education students connected well with the ACErs. The chapel overflowed with ACErs, their families, faculty, and friends of the students and the program. In summary, Summer 1998 was a very successful launch of the ACE M.Ed. program.

### AUTUMN 1998

ALL CONNECTED with the ACE M.Ed. program felt a need to do some final shaping of it, to decide once and for all how big courses would be, the sequencing of courses, and the relationship of courses offered concurrently. Thus, in August and September 1998, Johnstone, Scully, Staud, and I carried out a series of meetings intended to design the program as it would occur in 1999 and 2000, including specification of its budget. These were the constraints:

- There would be 10 hours of coursework per student in summer 1 and summer 2, consistent with the graduate school limit of 10 hours of coursework in any summer session.
- There could be 9 to 12 hours of work in school year 1 and in school year 2, with 6 hours for full-time supervised student teaching at a Catholic school in the southern United States and the remaining hours in distance learning experiences. This would provide the extensive supervision called for in the report of the National Commission on Teaching and America's Future. The distance learning experience would provide another experience with technology, consistent with the call for extensive experience in technology in many of the teacher education reform initiatives.
- The coursework would include the courses specified in Table 3.2. Such coursework is consistent with the INTASC principles, the report of the National Commission on Teaching and America's Future, and with teacher education programs at a number of colleges and universities in Indiana.
- Completion of the program would require acceptance of a portfolio of teaching accomplishments before summer 3, with this portfolio written up as an autobiography about the participant's development as a teacher. Each class in the ACE curriculum was expected to generate activities that could be starting points for port-

folio entries. Thus, when ACErs were asked to prepare lessons in a course, the lessons were to be for the upcoming year, with the ACErs responsible for evaluating the lessons and integrating the evaluation in the portfolio of professional accomplishments. The portfolio requirement was intended to stimulate a focus on authentic teaching tasks in the coursework.

- Graduation would be in summer 3.

Besides the constraints, there were also some desires. One was to avoid the large sections used in summer 1998. It seemed that the community-building advantages provided by the large sections might be accomplished in other ways (e.g., by having the same groups of students take several courses together, such as all the elementary teachers enrolling in the same two classes, all the middle school teachers doing so, and all the high school teachers doing so as well; by having students in the two ACE classes in residence during the summer take at least some of their courses together). A second desire was to keep the costs of the program under control, and certainly not to exceed the funds that were available to pay for the program.

In the end, Johnstone, Scully, Staud, and I agreed on the following scheme for summers 1999 and 2000:

- In both summers 1999 and 2000, first-year students would take Intro to Teaching (in three sections of 25 students) and a methods course appropriate to their level of teaching (i.e., elementary, middle, or high school methods). The three sections of Intro to Teaching and the three methods courses would be linked such that all elementary students would be in one section of Intro to Teaching and the same students would be in elementary methods, all middle school students would be in one section of Intro to Teaching and the same students would in the middle school methods, and all high school students would be in one section of Intro to Teaching and the same students would in the high school methods. The professors in the linked courses would be encouraged to coordinate their coverage and work with the 25 students enrolled in the two courses as a community of learners, encouraging cooperative learning among students and integration across the courses.

- In both summers 1999 and 2000, second-year participants would take courses in human development and exceptionality, with three groups of 25 students in linked development and exceptionality courses (e.g., elementary teachers would take child development and exceptionality at the elementary level, middle school teachers would take early adolescence and exceptionality in middle school, and high school teachers would take middle adolescence and exceptionality in high school). The instructors in the linked courses would be encouraged to build communities of learners, encouraging cooperative learning among participants and across the course contents.

- In both summers 1999 and 2000, all students would take the 1-credit seminar in Catholic education, with the instructors encouraged to make the experiences both inspirational and informative. By having the students in both resident ACE classes participate in this seminar, the hope was to increase feelings of community across the two ACE classes, breaking down the class consciousness sensed in summer 1997.

- In summer 1999, all students would take a content-area seminar (e.g., math education, science education, language arts education). These courses would enroll across the two ACE classes, with the goal of increasing the sense of community by breaking down the segregation by class.

- In summer 2000, all students would take educational psychology in sections no larger than 25 students. Once again, each section would include members from both ACE classes in residence as part of the breakdown of class distinctions within ACE.

- During school years 1999–2000 and 2000–2001, all students would take 6 units of student teaching. Seminars over the Internet would be offered during the school year, with these covering methods in the content areas as well as foundational issues in education (i.e., history, philosophy, social foundations).

- During school years 1999–2000 and 2000–2001, more ACE houses would include members from both ACE classes currently in the program, again as part of the breaking down of class distinctions.

There were also reflections on activities auxiliary to the M.Ed. courses, with decisions to continue the retreats in the summer and to determine how the retreat during the middle of the school year could be more cost effective. All previous mid-year retreats brought together all ACErs and staff to a common meeting center somewhere in the South (e.g., in Biloxi, Mississippi, in December 1997 and December 1998). The travel expenses associated with such a trip were enormous, and thus, the possibility was being considered to attempt several more regionalized retreats, ones that ACErs could reach by driving. An additional motivation for considering this option was that smaller retreats promised greater personal communication between ACErs and staff.

Another activity reviewed was the 10 P.M. Mass. Specifically, there was agreement among the staff that some efforts needed to be made to link the Mass more directly to the ACE focus on education. Admittedly, it was not clear how this would play out, but Scully promised to communicate to the priests celebrating the 10 P.M. Masses that every effort should be made to craft homilies that would connect with education as a topic or with the specific experiences of the ACErs.

As Autumn 1998 concluded, I was putting the finishing touches on a faculty who could deliver the program planned for summer 1999. Ten of the faculty working in the program were Notre Dame based, in addition to one school administrator whose degrees and college teaching experience were Notre Dame. The remaining half dozen members of the faculty were distinguished members of schools of education across the country, including the University of Michigan, University of Georgia, Texas Christian University, UCLA, Indiana State University, and Case Western Reserve University. Many of the faculty brought national reputations to the program; many brought extensive school-based experiences. In addition to the regular faculty, each content-area seminar and several other classes would be staffed with clinical faculty—distinguished teachers in the South Bend area who would co-teach courses, providing many insights about day-to-day life in classrooms.

Other administrative activity gained momentum. Joyce Johnstone worked throughout autumn 1998 to assemble information for accreditation documents. By November, she had no doubt that the ACE M.Ed. program would meet the March 1999 deadline for filing accreditation paperwork with the state, well in advance of a July 1999 site visit by an accreditation team. The planning for the ACE M.Ed. operation in 1999 and 2000 was under control. During the Advent season, everyone associated with the ACE M.Ed. effort was able to answer all queries about the program confidently. Things had gone well in summer 1998 and during the autumn semester.

As the year concluded, however, the ACE and M.Ed. administration could never get off their minds the constant pressures to expand. Requests were received frequently, but expansion had to be balanced with the need to keep the program small enough to be excellent. Moreover, it was impossible to escape the realization that much more money needed to be raised if there was to be a permanent Notre Dame–based faculty large enough to support the program in the years ahead.

1999

FROM JANUARY TO MAY of 1999 was very busy. A new class, ACE VI, was admitted in spring 1999, following a procedure that was by then paradigmatic. Students applied by late January, with the application including personal statements from the applicant as well as three letters of recommendation—one from a faculty member, one from a person who had seen the ACE applicant function in a living situation (e.g., dormitory head resident), and one from a personal friend. Then, every individual was interviewed by a three-person team: an ACE staff member, a faculty member, and someone associated with campus ministry. Many such teams were needed to accomplish all the interviews that took place in spring 1999, each lasting an hour.

The newly admitted 1999 class was the largest to date, with 75 reporting for the start of the summer session at the end of May. As always, the class was gender balanced. Academically, ACE VI was the strongest class ever. Much was learned in the summer of 1998 and during the 1998–1999 school year about the academic demands of the new program. There was a slightly greater attrition for the class that had entered in 1998 (ACE V), with some attrition reflecting the challenges of the program for participants entering with undergraduate grade point averages below B. Hence, John Staud and his colleagues were more concerned about grades during the admissions process in spring 1999 than they had been previously, although grades alone did not guarantee a place in the class. It had to be apparent in the essays, letters, and interviews that the individual was committed to and would benefit from the community and spirituality aspects of the program. Of course, first and foremost, there had to be a sense that the individual would be a good teacher.

ACE VI and V came together in summer 1999, the first summer session when the ACE academic program was offered entirely by Notre Dame. Yes, Portland would conduct the graduation in July for the ACE IV class, but all ACE instruction in summer 1999 was the responsibility of Notre Dame.

During spring 1999, Joyce Johnstone worked hard with everyone involved in the ACE M.Ed. experience to assemble a paper trail of support for the program's accreditation review. She also worked out visits for members of the accreditation team so they could get to know Notre Dame in advance of the actual accreditation visit. This included attendance by team members at the April retreat on the campus, which is held annually for superintendents of dioceses hosting ACE teachers and newly admitted ACErs. The accreditation team visitors were extremely impressed by the degree of commitment to the program from the superintendents, who uniformly spoke enthusiastically about the program. They were also impressed with the energy and intelligence of the students entering the program. The April retreat was a strong start on the accreditation visit process.

As the spring semester proceeded, some faculty involved with ACE were wrapping up their first year of Internet seminars with students, since methods courses were offered online during 1998–1999. There were also two sections of an online course on moral and ethical education. Basically, these courses were offered via listserve. There had been a number of start-up hassles, from getting students to sign on at all, to developing Internet skills in students, to having assignments sent to Notre Dame and graded in a timely fashion. In the spring, faculty were getting to the finish line for the courses, but it had been a long journey. Sadly, a few students had not participated at all in Internet courses and had to do substantial make-up work in the summer.

More positively, there were some great exchanges on the Internet seminar listserves. For example, in the course on elementary methods, as the school year ended, the elementary-level ACE teachers debated how to handle possible retentions. There was much discussion about the research-based conclusion that retention is ineffective as well as about local policies, sometimes favoring retention and sometimes not. For several ACE participants, the Internet discussion assisted them tremendously with what were difficult decisions about children in their classrooms. Thus, despite the hassles with the Internet seminars in 1998–1999, there was an emerging understanding that the Internet seminars could serve as powerful forums for teaching and learning, permitting the connection of theory, research, and teaching in actual classrooms.

Much was different in summer school 1999 compared to the Notre Dame offerings in summer 1998. First, there were many more sections of courses than in previous ACE summer schools, with classes much smaller than in the large lectures of summer 1998. Second, for the first time, there were classes taken by members of both ACE classes. In summer 1999, these were content-area methods seminars. They varied in size from small (about 10) to large (about 30), but they permitted a mixing of ideas between ACErs who had a year of experience and ACErs who had yet to be in the field. Third, courses that had operated in the previous summer generally seemed to flow better in summer 1999 (e.g., the 1-credit course focusing on community retained what had worked in 1998 and improved on what had not).

As good as the summer school experience was for the ACE V and VI students in summer 1999, there were some concerns. In particular, many of the first-summer students seemed very stressed by the academic demands, especially just past the midpoint of the summer. The faculty and I noted the need for some very hard study of the schedule to distribute due dates and exams across the summer rather than permit many evaluation events to occur close in time.

Most courses offered in summer 1999 were very well received by the ACErs. Also, even though there were many more faculty serving the program, and many more faculty who were visitors to Notre Dame, there was a real sense of community and camaraderie among the faculty as well as between faculty and students. A number of social events were for both faculty and students. Also, a generous proportion of the faculty made it to the evening Mass, especially the visitors who were living in the graduate student housing complex. They walked over to Mass together, stayed and talked with students afterward, and then walked home together. As had been the case in summer 1998, faculty ate with students in the dining hall. In short, there was a very strong sense of community in summer 1999, with many factors contributing to it, from classes shared by the two ACE cohorts, to social events, to greater participation in worship opportunities.

Despite the stresses produced by a demanding and condensed schedule, everyone felt pretty good about summer 1999 as it was occurring and after it concluded. In addition, by being so close to the students, the faculty really did appreciate the pressures the students were under, with this providing great motivation for the faculty to work with the ACE administration to create a better ACE summer schedule in future years.

One reason to feel very good was that the accreditation visit, which occurred in the middle of July, went very well. The visiting team not only found the paperwork in order but also were much admiring of the classes and ACE experiences that they sampled. Everyone in the program was enthused about ACE and let the team know it. At the end of the visit, the head of the accreditation team met with the ACE leadership to inform them that accreditation was virtually certain. Yes, there were a few matters that needed attention in the years ahead, including the development of a much larger permanent faculty, a clarification of the governance structure, and some small modifications to the curriculum, but there was nothing required that would be impossible to accomplish. The accreditation team definitely felt good about witnessing the first standards-consistent, performance-assessed program in the state of Indiana.

Another challenge for the program was with respect to spirituality. Although weekday evening Mass attendance was up slightly, a good night would include only 25% of the ACE participants. More positively, the Sunday evening Mass was becoming an event. This was due largely to the efforts of Steve Warner, whose Summer Folk Choir really enlivened the services. The really great news for ACE was that the summer 1999 choir was largely composed of ACErs, reflecting that singing in the Summer Folk Choir was included as part of an ACE course experience in contemporary liturgical music. Sunday Mass was packed with ACErs and many others on campus, providing a very favorable window on the program to many students attending summer school and many groups visiting the campus for special institutes and events during the summer session.

The enthusiasm on Sunday night made clear the potential for spirited spirituality in the ACE program; the lack of attendance at Mass Monday through Thursday also made clear that the spirituality being offered during the week was not connecting. A bright spot was that on one weekday night, a few students and Steve Warner experimented with a Taize prayer session. Although only a few showed up, those who were there left enthused, with that group determined such alternatives would become part of ACE spirituality the next summer.

A significant event during summer 1999 was the ACE IV graduation, the last time the ACE experience would include Portland. At the ACE IV graduation ceremonies, the University of Portland received a number of accolades for their contributions to the ACE program. The Portland group headed home feeling honored by the experience, and the Notre Dame group headed home realizing that now the entire ACE responsibility really was on their shoulders.

The week after the graduation was the traditional closing of the ACE program. Classes ended on Wednesday. Thursday morning was for meetings with students in anticipation of student teaching during the upcoming year, including sessions about field supervision and Internet seminars. Thursday afternoon was spent at Warren Dunes. On Thursday evening, there was a candlelight prayer service at the Grotto, presided over by Cardinal Law of the Diocese of Boston. Friday morning was the Missioning Mass, presided over by Cardinal Law. This Missioning Mass was more electric than the ones in past years, reflecting, in part, the very large choir of ACErs who provided the folk music. Steve Warner's class had really increased ACErs' commitment to the music of the Folk Choir, and Stanford-Keenan Chapel on the ND campus was fully alive with that music during missioning and for an encore, continuing 10 minutes after the mass concluded.

On Friday afternoon, the ACErs packed cars and headed out, some straight to their schools in the South but most going home for a few weeks off before the school year began. For the ACE administration and staff, the afternoon was spent in a meeting of the Alliance for Catholic Education national advisory board, which came to campus twice a year. Although many of the participants at the advisory board meeting were exhausted, both from the events of the past 24 hours and the events of a very full summer, it was a meeting filled with promise. There were discussions about how ACE could expand westward in the next year, probably to Los Angeles and possibly to Phoenix. There was the possibility of the U.S. Congress providing some support so that Notre Dame could work with other colleges and universities wishing to replicate the ACE effort. There was discussion of a number of foundations with interests in ACE. On the horizon was a meeting with an important donor interested in the area of exceptionality. Plans were being laid for a mini-conference involving this donor, ACE faculty and staff, Notre Dame administrators and trustees, and a few nationally prominent professors in the area of exceptionality. The meeting was to discuss possibilities for the study of exceptionality at Notre Dame, with the expectation that ACE would play a prominent role in it.

Saturday morning, on a plane to Pittsburgh, I sat beside one of the very best teachers in ACE V and had a wide-ranging discussion about the summer. She was very satisfied and looking forward to the upcoming school year. She was ebullient about how much better the 1999 summer session had been compared to the 1998 session, pointing out that everyone in ACE V recognized the enormous effort that must have occurred during the school year to develop the 1999 summer experience. I revealed to her that I was heading to my 30th high school reunion, grateful to be able to do so given the health challenges of the past year and a half. She confided in me that just one year earlier, she and all of ACE V had prayed together that I would be with them in summer 1999. Both this young woman and I understood at that moment just how closely knit the ACE participants, faculty, and staff were becoming as a community.

In the early autumn, Staud, Johnstone, Scully, and I would confront an issue raised by the accreditation team—the murky governance of ACE and the teacher education program. There was no doubt the accreditation team was right to cite the program for a deficiency in this area. There were four individuals prominently involved in the governance of the program—Staud, Johnstone, Scully, and me. None were quite certain just where our responsibilities began and ended, with the result that there was student uncertainty about authority. It was a relief to all of the participants to confront the problem squarely in this meeting, and the boundaries were drawn rather easily, with Staud ultimately responsible for financial and pastoral affairs, Johnstone in charge of outreach functions, and me overseeing academics. The division matched the directors' expertise to three huge responsibilities in the program, although Staud, Johnstone, and I also agreed to meet regularly to keep emerging issues in the lines of sight of all three, and to consult with one another about all decisions of consequence. With respect to difficult items falling between the cracks of responsibility, we agreed to accept a majority-rule model.

In making this agreement, Staud, Johnstone, Scully, and I were aware of what had been the most painful experience of the past year. A total of 10 students had departed from the ACE V class. Each had a different reason for leaving, from wanting to marry, to dissatisfaction with their specific teaching assignment. There were also close calls, with some students almost quitting the program. Some of these might not have been so close had the leadership team been articulating better, working together to come up with solutions to problems rather than sometimes unknowingly working at cross-purposes (e.g., one director discussing one option with a troubled ACEr and another director discussing an alternative option). A top priority for the leadership team was to reduce attrition in ACE VI and subsequent ACE classes. We were convinced we could do so by working together more closely.

As the autumn leaves turned, the meeting on exceptionality with the potential donor took place. Prospects were very good that resources would be forthcoming for a research and teaching center dedicated to improving the learning of students, especially students who struggle when given only conventional instruction. The possibility of congressional support for replications of the program at other colleges and universities became more real, with such support written into the budget being considered by the Congress. An outstanding group of faculty was committed to teach in ACE in summer 2000. Meanwhile, the courses on the Internet were going better than those offered the year before, with most Internet professors using the WebCT capacity that Notre Dame recently had purchased. The November recruiting meeting for ACE was well attended, as was a dance sponsored by ACE, which was held in the student union at the end of fall semester.

One of the most notable events of the late autumn, however, was the early December retreat in Biloxi. As in previous years, there was a kick-off Mass, many sessions dedicated to spirituality and community, and a concluding Mass. This year, the spirit was especially high. The faculty, staff, and ACErs felt a real closeness during the experience. By the end of the weekend, the ACE faculty and staff were certain that the Biloxi retreat was a must event for ACE to continue, that this retreat promoted a strong identification with the program about halfway through the year, providing a booster shot of commitment to ACE. A number of the ACE faculty and staff were on the same plane home, with delays turning it into a 13-hour trip, providing plenty of opportunity to reflect on just how fantastic the Biloxi weekend had been. There would be no more talk of cutting out Biloxi in favor of smaller mid-year, regional retreats.

## 2000

AT THE END OF JANUARY 2000, when the ACE application deadline came, more than 250 applicants competed for 80 spots in the new class. As in past years, every applicant was interviewed. As the interviewing proceeded, there was a strong sense in the admissions committee that an outstanding class was being formed.

The congressional money came through early in 2000, setting in motion the adventure of replicating the program at other colleges and universities. Plans for summer 2000 continued to be formulated. In particular, a new approach to the first week for the new ACE students was developed. The week would focus on classroom management, philosophical and empirical foundations of Catholic education, and use of technology in schools. It would be an intense week, conducted entirely by the Notre Dame–based faculty and staff. One goal was to make certain that from the very first week in ACE, the permanent faculty and staff would be close to the ACErs.

March 1 was an especially important date in the spring. This was the due date for ACE V participants to file their portfolios with the M.Ed. program. Everyone made it, except that an accommodation was necessary for one student whose school burned down about a month before the portfolio was due. Most of his portfolio was in the school building at the time of the fire. That student put together a videotaped portfolio, documenting how he had met the standards required by the program and the licensure process.

As the faculty and staff reviewed the portfolios that came in, it was clear that they were outstanding as a group. Yes, some were much better than others, but only a very few required that the ACEr do any additional work (several ACErs were asked to provide revisions to their portfolios in order to strengthen the evidence that they had met the program standards). All 60 of the ACE V students who had stayed with the program for the full two years completed their portfolios successfully and qualified for the July 2000 graduation.

When the summer session arrived, the first week with the new ACErs was intense and very successful. Videotapes about classroom management were followed by discussions; the lectures about the special nature of Catholic education became lively lecture hall discussions, with lots of spirited commentary; students received an introduction to their computer lab and the technology contained in it. As intense as the first-week experience was, no one complained.

This first week for the ACE VII participants was capped off with a party at my home. It was a beautiful summer evening, permitting both outdoor and indoor activities. Boom boxes supplied the music as ACE VII mixed with faculty and staff over dinner, followed by dancing, games, and lots of conversation. The party started at 5 and lasted until almost 11. The members of ACE VII, the faculty, and the staff clearly enjoyed each other's company. There was no doubt at the party that every student in ACE VII felt the program was terrific. One young woman, who had given some thought to dropping out of ACE just before the summer began, was emphatic that, after a week of ACE, she knew the program really was for her, that she had learned an enormous amount during the first week and felt immersed in a learning and loving community of educators.

Members of ACE VI arrived at the beginning of the second week of the summer term to begin their second summer program. Many of them remarked how much they were looking forward to the second summer. They would be reunited with friends, but they also were looking forward to being in classes; this year, they would have something to share based on their classroom experiences.

Given the positive first week for ACE VII and the enthusiastic return of ACE VI, it was not surprising that courses went very well for the rest of the summer, with the adjustments in the schedule seeming to reduce some of the pressures noted in past summers. During summer 2000, the course integrating across the two ACE cohorts was "Cognition, Instruction, and Assessment." Each of the nine sections was dedicated to a particular content area. For example, the 20 ACE VI and VII math teachers had their section with an expert in math education; the 10 ACE VI and VII foreign language teachers spent their summer thinking about how ideas in cognition, instruction, and assessment applied to second language acquisition. As in the previous summer, these courses tended to form mini-communities within the larger ACE community.

In summer 2000, the spiritual commitments of the ACErs were very apparent. A daily indication was the increased attendance at Mass. It was not unusual for 50 or more ACErs to appear at 10 P.M. in Dillon Chapel. The ACE office also offered alternative prayer sessions, for example, saying the rosary or participating in a Taize-style prayer experience. In summer 1999, music was all too infrequent in the daily ACE Mass. In summer 2000, there was folk music every Wednesday; several Masses featured a group of students who offered more traditional church music. On Sunday, Stanford-Keenan Chapel was overflowing with ACErs and many others from around campus; every Mass there was a real celebration, with the liturgy enriched by the Summer Folk Choir, most of whom were ACE students studying contemporary liturgical music.

The spirituality was apparent in more subtle ways as well. More faculty began their classes with prayers. The Intro to Teaching course offered during the first week covered a number of topics in Catholic education, which triggered many spirited discussions about the difference spirituality made in Catholic compared to public school settings. Also, it was difficult to visit the Grotto during summer 2000 without encountering an ACEr. In short, there was serenity amidst the hubbub of ACE activity as ACErs, faculty, and staff immersed themselves in an experience that was as spiritual as it was academic.

Also noteworthy were student-organized evenings where ACE VI teachers shared with their ACE VII counterparts their best teaching tips. Elementary, math, science, foreign language, language arts, social studies, and religion teachers all had such get-togethers, with the typical session lasting about two hours. These meetings reflected a real giving by ACE VI participants and a real commitment to learn as much as possible by the ACE VII participants.

During summer 2000, for the first time, the ACE program had its own computer lab, located in the architecture building, which was right behind the men's and women's dorms that served ACE. The lab was often packed to capacity, with ACErs working alone and working together. The place permitted many personal connections between ACErs as it provided great opportunities for them to work with state-of-the-art computing experiences.

At the end of the second week in July, Notre Dame graduated ACE V, the first Notre Dame Master of Education class. Even though graduations are always high spirited, this one seemed especially so. Genelle Adelman let all know that she would be the very first person to receive the new M.Ed. degree. And so she was when I placed the hood over her at about 2:15 on Saturday, July 16, 2000, for Genelle led the class in alphabetical order across the stage. The speakers from the podium were very upbeat. Governor Mark Racicot of Montana provided the keynote address, noting with pride the disproportionate number of Montanans in ACE (i.e., six), given the tiny population of his state. He made clear to the ACErs the concern of public officials across the country about education and emphasized how critical it was for more programs like ACE to emerge. As a member of the advisory board of the Corporation for National Service (Americorps), he also acknowledged the exemplary record of accomplishment of ACErs within the Americorps program, with their more than 90% completion rate. The governor gave the ACErs plenty of reason to feel good.

So did Tim Green, the spokesperson for the class. Rather than have the individual with the highest G.P.A. speak, the ACE faculty and students decided to elect a class spokesperson. Tim was the runaway winner, perhaps predictable given his infectious humor. Tim more than rose to the occasion for this graduation speech, providing hilarious reminders of ACE V's pioneering experiences with distance learning on the Internet and the larger lecture approach attempted in summer 1998. Tim also offered profuse thanks to the many who had contributed to the success of ACE, acknowledging with gratitude the efforts of Notre Dame administrators and faculty as well as the support of diocesan officials. Tim's speech was received with enthusiastic laughter and applause.

Fr. Malloy, president of the University of Notre Dame, concluded the presentations, first by noting just how daunting it was to follow Tim Green, and that it had been easier to follow President Clinton as a speaker, which he had done just a few days before. Fr. Malloy then went on to praise the ACE V class and the ACE program in general, and to make clear the commitment of the university to this alternative approach to teacher education and to America's Catholic schools.

The graduation ceremony was followed by a graduation Mass that filled Stanford-Keenan Chapel. As had become the tradition at ACE folk choir Masses, the chapel absolutely rocked. No one could miss that Frs. Malloy and Scully, who presided over the event, were beaming with pride, that this occasion made obvious that the Catholic church has a great future. The enthusiasm of the Mass carried over into a dinner followed by a dance. There could be no greater evidence of community than occurred at the dance, with ACErs, parents, ACEr brothers and sisters, faculty, ACE staff, and the children of faculty and staff mixing it up to Latin rhythms late into the evening. Most striking, the dance floor included large numbers of individuals from ACE V, VI, and VII, joined by some staff members from ACE IV, and guests from ACE I, II, and III. The ACE community concept clearly was cutting across years and cohorts in summer 2000.

Following the ACE V graduation, there was only one more week of summer session for ACE VI and VII. The end-of-term pressures were not as pronounced as in past years. The one source of new pressure was some new courses aimed at enriching the curricular knowledge of students (e.g., in computers, art, and coaching as character education). These were designed so that 1 credit of lecture would be provided at the end of the summer term, with the courses continuing on the Internet during the school year. Bunching the lectures for these courses at the end of the term was probably not a good idea; it made for a lot of new reading and writing just as students were trying to wrap up other things and get ready to head out. The administration of ACE noted the need for an adjustment with respect to the scheduling of these courses to avoid the end-of-term crunch.

The events of the final two days (candlelight service at the Grotto on Thursday night, the last-night party, Missioning Mass on Friday morning, and final ACE lunch) were now paradigmatic. They were a bit sad, however, as members of both ACE VI and VII reflected back on what had been a meaningful and joyous summer, hating to see it come to an end.

One striking difference between the summer 2000 concluding moments and the final days of previous ACE summers was the huge California presence at the concluding events, coinciding with the send-off from Notre Dame of eight ACErs who would serve in Los Angeles. Cardinal Roger Mahoney of Los Angeles, now the ranking U.S. cardinal, presided at the Grotto prayer service and at the Missioning Mass. He brought with him several Los Angeles–based members of the Notre Dame Board of Trustees. The entire Los Angeles contingent, including the eight ACErs heading to Los Angeles, had a private meeting with Cardinal Mahoney and the ACE administration on

Thursday afternoon. The Los Angeles contingent made clear that they would do whatever was required to make ACE a success in L.A. Before the meeting was ended, a plan to get the ACErs another car was being hatched, and one of the board members gave all of the ACErs tickets to the Notre Dame–Southern Cal game in November. Mahoney made certain that the ACE house had a personal spiritual counselor, the monsignor serving the Cathedral of Los Angeles.

Such commitment was typical, for all of the dioceses receiving ACE teachers do much to support the program. None of the ACE officials take such commitments for granted. All connected with ACE recognize that the Alliance for Catholic Education depends greatly on the benefaction of many. After interacting with the eight very bright young people heading for Los Angeles, we had every reason to believe that at least several of these young people would become career Catholic educators. The ACE leadership is confident that the benefaction supporting the program will pay long-term dividends for Catholic schools and the country.

THIS CHAPTER is being written shortly after the conclusion of the summer 2000 ACE experience. Although the summer was a success on every count, there was one especially positive accomplishment: no one had dropped out during this summer session. In part, it was due to improved courses, with the best professors from previous summers being retained and the newly recruited professors proving to be exceptionally good teachers who were dedicated to all aspects of the program. Their dedication to community translated into a faculty that was ever constructively present in the students' community. Student community was enriched by the first week of immersion in Intro to Teaching that was provided to ACE VII. Community also was affected very positively by the many small classes that permitted great interaction between ACErs, as well as by the student-organized sessions on teaching. The ACE community ate together every day, and a large proportion prayed together often. The ACErs also partied together, including at a number of receptions organized by the program but also at more informal gatherings (e.g., nights at the local minor league ballpark, evenings that often included ACErs from several cohorts as well as faculty and staff). One parent who attended the Missioning Mass remarked that she had never seen a church so filled to the brim with people so completely committed to one another. By summer 2000, the ACE M.Ed. program at Notre Dame was accomplishing its goals of being an alternative teacher education experience, a community-building approach, and a spiritual community.

## A WEEK IN THE LIFE OF AN ACER

ONE WAY TO REFLECT on the history of the ACE M.Ed. program is to consider a week in the life of a typical ACEr during the summer school. In doing so, it will be clear that the decisions made during program development continue to impact every member of the program every day in June and July.

For the typical week in the summer, we select the last week in June, beginning with Sunday afternoon. Our typical ACEr is in the computer lab, a room filled with ACErs, all of whom are working away on assignments. Both ACE classes have courses that will conclude either this week or next, and thus, final assignments loom large. The assignment our typical ACEr is working away at involves designing a set of lesson plans that will be tried out next year. This is consistent with most of the major assignments this typical ACEr will have in the program, since the program is completely oriented to development of authentic teaching skills. The best way to do that is to have students reflect on their teaching, design new teaching and curriculum, and then, during the school year, test out their ideas. Eventually, the ACErs will reflect on their implementation of their ideas and fold a summary of their reflections into their professional portfolios.

This Sunday afternoon, the typical ACEr works away at a computer station, occasionally interacting socially with the other ACErs in the room. She has an extended conversation with one of the other ACErs, who is working on the same class assignment. Both reflect on various options they are considering with respect to the teaching they are planning. The typical ACEr spends about 10 hours a week in the computer room. She knows she can get peer assistance when it is needed. This is an ACE community workspace.

By the end of the afternoon, great progress has been made on the assignment. The ACEr then heads to dinner, eating at a table filled with members of both ACE VI and VII. The talk is about assignments that are due but also about how one of the communities finally knows where it will be living; the diocese has located a big house that will be affordable for ACE students.

After dinner, the ACEr walks to Stanford-Keenan Chapel. She is taking the Liturgical Music and Education course offered by Steve Warner and Karen Schneider-Kirner. The course includes an hour and a half of instruction on Sunday night, followed by Summer Folk Choir rehearsal, and then participation in the Summer Folk Choir at the 10 P.M. Mass that all of ACE and much of the rest of the campus attends.

As always, Steve and Karen are a wealth of information, with the presentations in this class always interesting. This ACEr is especially struck by Steve's remark that the music at Mass must always add to the liturgy, and Steve offers many insights about how this can occur. Once the formal presentation is over, choir practice begins. During the first week or two of this class, this ACEr was lost during choir practice, never really certain when she was supposed to be singing. Now, the music is becoming familiar and choir practice is a lot of fun, as is singing in the choir during the actual Mass.

Following Mass, the ACEr strikes up a conversation with the professor in the course that had occupied her attention that afternoon. She decides to let the prof know some of her frustrations while wrestling with the final project. The ACEr and prof end up taking a walk on this gorgeous summer evening, talking as they do so, managing a stop at the Grotto during the 45-minute discussion. This is just one of several times when this ACEr has had post-Mass walks with ACE faculty, staff, and participants. The 11 o'clock to midnight slot is a time when many ACErs trade reflections with others connected to the program. Shortly after midnight, however, the ACEr tucks in, for she must be up at 6:30 to make it to breakfast at 7 and then head off to a local Catholic school for the 7:45 start of the practicum day.

At Monday morning breakfast, the ACEr meets with two other ACErs who are also doing their teaching practicum at the same school. They leave the dining hall together and car pool to the school site. On the way, they discuss their lesson plans for the day, lessons that had been worked out over the weekend. This ACEr is very excited because she is going to try to teach some first grade students about predicting before reading. Last week in Professor Cathy Block's course, the ACEr learned this was one of the first comprehension strategies that should be taught, one that even Grade 1 children can learn to use habitually. Similarly, the other two ACErs in the car each have new ideas they are going to try. The ideas reflect what they are learning in class as well as in interaction with other ACE participants. The ACEr recognizes on the ride out to the school that a beginning ACE teacher is never going it alone.

This ACEr's mentor teacher at the school was a member of ACE V hired by the program to serve as a lead teacher this summer in this school as well as to mentor a new ACEr. Because this is only the new ACEr's second week in the school, she does some teaching this morning but also a lot of observing. The experienced teacher provides lots of explanations to her as asides. The morning passes quickly, with the 13 students in this summer school class working hard all morning. During the last half hour, the ACEr works individually with a student who is really struggling with writing. The ACEr helps the student sound out words, providing tips about how to remember which direction Bs face when Bs are printed. By the end of the morning, the ACEr will have had some experience teaching a whole group, some one-on-one tutoring experience, an opportunity to interact with a parent who wanted to observe her son in class, and some feedback from the mentor teacher about the morning's progress. The ACEr feels good, for it all went well. The ACEr departs the school determined to work hard on lesson planning in the evening, for her field supervisor will visit the classroom tomorrow.

Lunch in South Dining Hall is not quite as rushed as breakfast. The ACEr eats with three other ACErs with whom she'll be living in the coming school year. The two women and two men discuss what they have recently learned about the schools they will be serving in the autumn. The diversity of the ACE teaching experience is evident as these four ACErs talk. Two are elementary teachers, one a middle school teacher, and one a high school teacher. All are looking forward to teaching. Many of their discussions with second-summer ACErs have been about life in southern Catholic schools. They are beginning to believe that their lives down south will not be as foreign as they thought. Their superintendent is in South Bend this week for an ACE-sponsored superintendents' institute. She impressed all four ACErs when they met her in April at the kick-off retreat. On this visit, she will be able to provide specifics about their assignments. All are looking forward to that information, for there remain many gaps in their understanding about the communities and schools they will be serving.

After lunch, the ACEr goes to her 1 P.M. class, Cognition, Instruction, and Assessment for Elementary Teachers. The professor is a distinguished Australian educational psychologist, Valentina McInerney. Today's topic is cooperative learning, which the ACEr read about in a chapter in the assigned text, one co-authored by the professor. Professor McInerney breaks the class into small cooperative-learning groups so that students are immersed in cooperation as part of the lesson on cooperative approaches to teaching and learning. The time flies for the members of the class.

Then comes Elementary Reading and Writing, taught by Cathy Block. Professor Block hands back a written assignment, publicly announcing a strength of each paper as she returns it to its author. Then comes a discussion about how to select children's literature to be consistent with social studies and science topics that are part of the Grade 1 curriculum. There are lots of questions, which the professor uses as stimuli for discussion. Over the course of the two hours, a lot of information about using children's literature is presented and mulled over by the professor and students thinking together. Nancy Masters, our ACEr's field supervisor, is auditing the class. The ACEr and Nancy later talk briefly about the observation that will occur the next day. "Just relax and be yourself," Nancy tells the ACEr. "You'll do great." The ACEr recognizes once again that ACE is a supportive community.

The afternoon ends; our ACEr heads to the computer lab to get a start on course assignments and tomorrow's lesson plan. She'll stay at the lab until 6:40, then head for dinner. Quite a few ACErs take dinner late, so she eats at a table occupied completely by ACErs. They talk about the pace of this week. The ACEr talks about the enormity of the assignment in Dr. Block's class, which requires pulling together lesson plans by integrating suggestions made throughout the course. All the comments at the table reflect students who are learning much about contemporary educational practices.

Following dinner, the ACEr heads back to the dorm room, sensing that the lesson planning she needs to do could be done best there rather than at the computer lab. She does not want to occupy a computer station when there are ACE classmates with greater need of those machines tonight. ACErs often think about their classmates; the cooperative and community goals of the program definitely are reflected in the ACEr's behavior after four weeks in the program. At about 9:50, the lesson plan is ready and the ACEr heads to Mass.

When the ACEr gets to the chapel, there are about 50 ACErs and faculty quietly reflecting. Both Professors McInerney and Block are present; so are two of the directors of the program. The celebrant is Tim Scully, who founded the ACE program and continues as an administrator. Scully's homily takes the day's readings and offers insights about their value for someone with a teaching vocation. As is true at every Mass during the summer session, the ACE congregation is appropriately reflective during the homily. When it comes time to begin the eucharistic prayer, Fr. Scully invites everyone in the chapel to gather around the altar. This proves to be an intimate experience given the smallness of Dillon Chapel. During the Lord's Prayer, the participants hold hands. As at every ACE Mass, the sign of peace is prolonged; most individuals make contact with every other person in the chapel or almost every person. That exchange often is a hug—sometimes an intense embrace—rather than a handshake. Everyone takes communion, with several ACErs serving as eucharistic ministers.

After Mass, our ACEr mingles with members of both ACE classes, speaks briefly with Professor Block, and then heads back to the dorm to spend just a few more minutes reviewing tomorrow's lesson plan that will be watched by Nancy Masters. Then, she goes to bed.

Every day during this week is as busy as Monday was. The observation on Tuesday is a bit disappointing for the ACEr because several students choose to misbehave during the visit, although Nancy Masters is impressed at how well the ACEr handles these students. Wednesday is especially long, as Wednesdays have been all summer. In addition to the day classes, there is the 1-credit integrative seminar from 8:30 to 10 P.M. The main activity in the seminar this week is a discussion between the ACEr and future housemates about how to divide responsibilities in the house. She finds integrative seminar activities very interesting and important, but she feels very tired at that time of the evening. Perhaps the fatigue is especially noticeable because Wednesday is the night for music at the Dillon Chapel Mass, which means she has to put in a half hour of practice from 8 to 8:30 before the integrative seminar, and then must be really active during the Mass. Wednesday is the hump in the week.

Thursday features a set of special speakers in the afternoon in lieu of the regular classes. Our ACEr leaves halfway through because there are assignments due on Friday, and she needs every bit of time to get the work done. This ACEr has noted that many of her classmates decide to work in the computer lab or in their dorm room rather than attend every class when assignments are coming due. What helps is that the professors recognize the pressures and seem to understand such absences.

By Friday evening, this ACEr feels very satisfied, for every assignment has been completed for the week, and she feels very good about the work that she submitted. There was some sadness, however. With Cathy Block's class completed, Professor Block is heading home to Texas Christian University. The intense contact in ACE with wonderful professors is great, but the downside is that the contact ends too soon.

Late Friday afternoon, the ACEr leaves campus for a relaxing weekend at another ACEr's parents' cottage. The ACEr is back on campus on Tuesday afternoon and at the Pressleys' home by 6 P.M. for the ACE Fourth of July party. The ACEr and about 30 other members of ACE VI and VII stay late enough to watch the fireworks. It feels like a real Fourth of July, celebrated with lots of new friends made in the first month of the ACE program. There are also several out-of-town guests, two of whom were authors of one of the textbooks that some ACErs were reading in a class. Lots of accomplished educational researchers, teacher educators, and distinguished contributors to the American educational scene visit the program during the summer, and when they do, they always visit as much with the students as with the faculty.

Summer 2000 is an immersion in a beginning teaching experience for this ACEr, but it is much more—an immersion in the culture of American education, including learning from leading research contributors, working with cutting-edge educational software, and mixing with administrators and teachers working across the nation. The ACEr knows that few teacher education experiences can equal this one in exposing its participants to a range of resources.

## WHAT WE LEARNED ON THE JOURNEY

SINCE 1997, everyone involved in designing and administering the ACE program learned a great deal about all that has to be accomplished to begin a teaching service or teacher education program at a university. Those lessons include the following:

- Such a venture requires a core of faculty and administrators with diverse expertise, including those who are good at academic programming, accreditation, fund raising, and campus politicking. The core faculty and leaders must interact fluidly with one another to accomplish the many tasks that need to be coordinated to put a program on the books.

- It helps to have some version of the program running before attempting to get the program on the books. A program that is up and running serves as proof that the program is viable and permits informed reflection on what is right with the program and what needs to be improved. The Notre Dame team learned a great deal from the Portland experience with ACE, and the Portland experience demonstrated that teacher education was viable at Notre Dame.

- It helps to have a conceptual framework that is shared by the stakeholders in the program. The three ACE pillars of professional education, community, and spiritual life again and again reminded the development team of what the program needed to be and how it had to be unique compared to other teacher education efforts.

- There will always be those who disagree with aspects of the program. Such criticisms need to be taken seriously and, if valid, responded to by reconstruction of the program when it is possible to do so (e.g., student complaints led to a decreased credit load in the summer sessions). Sometimes complaints simply represent a lack of information. The ACE program developers spent a lot of time informing the Notre Dame community about the program, including dealing with a number of rumors that were not true. The overwhelming approval votes for the program probably would have been much less overwhelming if the various rumors about the ACE M.Ed. had not been dealt with constructively.

- When a program succeeds, there is pressure to expand. It is important to know the limits of expansion, for delivery of an excellent program depends on keeping the program a manageable size. As this book is being written, the ACE program is capped at 80 new participants a year in order to preserve the quality of experience that is possible with the present numbers.

- If there is magic in the ACE program, it is produced by feelings of community within it and the moments when the spirituality is inspirational. For such a community to thrive, great care must be taken with respect to recruitment of faculty and students. The ACE M.Ed. program demands faculty who are excellent as scholars and teachers but also excellent in connecting with students, including with respect to their spiritual development. The ACE M.Ed. demands students who are as committed to the concepts of community and spiritual development as to academic development. Good programs are good because of the people in them. Thus, a special obligation in developing an innovative program such as the ACE M.Ed. was the identification of faculty and student community members who would be comfortable with the program as they developed academically, as community members, and spiritually.

As I reflect on all that was accomplished in a very short time, I also recognize that the task of developing the ACE M.Ed. program is anything but over. Good programs continually reinvent themselves, with perpetual reflection on what is going well and what could go better. Based on program successes and failures, there are appropriate reconstructions of the coursework and professional development experiences that constitute the program.

**TABLE 3.3**

*Changes in the Notre Dame M.Ed. Program since Its Conception*

---

Introduction to Teaching (first summer) *(now divided into a 1-credit introduction to teaching offered during the first week to first-summer students, with 2 credits now given for the first-summer practicum)*

Introduction to Reading and Writing *or* Introduction to Middle School Teaching *or* Introduction to High School Teaching (3 credits) (first summer)

Educational Psychology (3 credits) *(now "Cognition, Instruction, and Assessment," with 9 separate sections representing each teaching area and one section for students with extensive background in psychology; now offered every other year, enrolling both first- and second-summer students, and thus, connecting across the ACE cohorts in the program)*

Exceptionality in Elementary School *or* Exceptionality in Middle School *or* Exceptionality in High School (3 credits) (second Summer)

Child Development *or* Early Adolescence *or* Middle Adolescence (3 credits) (second summer) *(an advanced section of development now offered for students with substantial background in development)*

Seminar in Content Area Instruction (e.g., Math Education, Language Arts Education) (3 credits) *(now offered every other year, enrolling both first- and second-summer students, and thus, connecting across the ACE cohorts in the program)*

Directed Readings in Content Area (e.g., Math Education, Language Arts Education) (3 credits) *(offered as summer + Internet courses beginning in 2002–2003)*

History of Education *or* Social Foundations of Education *or* Moral and Ethical Education *or* Philosophy of Education (3 credits) *(social, historical, empirical, and philosophical foundations now integrated into courses on music, art, and educational technology in the curriculum; moral and ethical education continues to be offered, but complemented by courses exploring moral education and coaching as well as service learning; all of these courses offered as summer + Internet courses beginning in 2001–2002)*

Seminar in Catholic Education (2 credits) (1 credit each summer)

Student Teaching (12 credits)

Portfolio Compilation Course (3 credits) *(offered as summer + Internet course beginning in 2001–2002)*

---

Thus, although at the time of this writing, I am confident that the ACE M.Ed. is a good program, I am equally confident that it will become a better program as more is learned about teacher education from doing it. For example, as this is being written, the program is reflecting on our first venture into the visual arts this past summer. We are also reflecting on the first version of a course about coaching as character education, with plans developing to expand this offering and complement it with at least one other course on coaching. Rather than continuing to offer Internet seminars, I experimented this past summer with starting courses in the summer and continuing them during the school year over the Internet. It now seems likely that the "summer + Internet" approach will replace the purely Internet approach. (The changes in the program since its beginning are summarized in Table 3.3).

During the very first summer of ACE, the students quipped that ACE stood for "Always Changing Everything," since their program that first summer really was invented as it was carried out. After seven years of ACE, the pace of change is a bit slower but the commitment to changing for the better remains.

# 4

JOYCE V. JOHNSTONE

# INSTITUTIONALIZATION OF CHANGE

Change in higher education does not occur easily, even with internal moral imperatives and with external monies. The ACE program at the University of Notre Dame was a radical change: Notre Dame had been out of the education business for 25 years and lacked an experienced teacher education faculty to help shape the direction of the program; there were no historic ties between Notre Dame and the targeted dioceses; few of the students who would be recruited for this service program had the cultural readiness to work in under-resourced schools in the South, as few came from the geographic region or the socioeconomic status of the children they would serve. However, Notre Dame entered this developmental process with many advantages, which would enable institutionalization of this visionary Catholic service program.

## INTERNAL FACTORS

In studies of institutionalization, several internal and external factors have been identified that influence the process of change, sometimes as enablers and sometimes as inhibitors. The internal factors that enhanced Notre Dame's ability to establish ACE included: (1) relevance to the mission of the university; (2) administrative support; (3) the skills, consistency, and power of and respect for the change agent; (4) faculty support; (5) compatibility with university requirements; and (6) the university climate for change.

### RELEVANCE TO THE MISSION OF THE UNIVERSITY

The mission and values of an institution must guide and direct any change project (Chickering, Halliburton, Bergquist, & Lindquist, 1977; Levin, 1980; Baldridge, 1980; Seymour, 1988; Curry, 1992; Townsend, Newell, & Wiese, 1992). Compatibility with the norms, values, and goals of an institution must be maintained for any change project to reach institutionalization, and these values guide and direct the curriculum, selection of faculty and students, policies and procedures, and culture. Moreover, the leaders of the institution must be committed to these values. The history of teacher education at Notre Dame reflects a long-standing commitment to Catholic education, beginning in 1904, and to the guidance and preparation of this country's Catholic youth. Furthermore, Notre Dame has a deep culture of service, with a higher proportion of undergraduates participating in service activities than any other university in the nation.

In 1977, Notre Dame closed its education department. In 1993, when the ACE vision of providing teachers in service to under-resourced Catholic schools emerged, however, the university embraced the ACE program with vigor. Faculty, administrators, and alumni alike saw ACE as a program central to the mission of the university, a program involving teaching and research that benefited not only its participants but also Catholic schools across the South. ACE exemplified the commitment to service and faith imbedded in the mission of Notre Dame. As Fr. Tim Scully, vice president and senior associate provost of the university, wrote in a May 21, 1999, article for the *Wall Street Journal*:

> These days there is a lot of talk about values, much of it vague. We
> believe that Catholic schools owe their charges teachers who view
> their jobs as vocations and who understand the importance of
> example. This understanding is at the heart and soul of the pro-
> gram, not some "extra." Accordingly, we have developed a spiritu-
> ality based on Christ the Teacher, a spirituality that is real, that
> does not pretend to be easy but always promises to be reward-
> ing. . . . If Catholic institutions do not take the lead in ensuring a
> generation of teachers every bit as dedicated and committed as the
> ones who taught us, who will?

## ADMINISTRATIVE SUPPORT

Successful change projects begin with firm administrative support (Levin, 1980; Baldridge, 1980; Townsend et al., 1992), reflected by a willingness to encourage change, embrace new ideas, and support program development (Curry, 1992; Levin, 1998). It is born of a trust in the leadership and faculty expertise. Without such support, initiatives coming from departments, faculty, or individuals struggle.

Fr. Edward Malloy, president of the university, had that willingness. In the 1998 address to the faculty, he stated, "We have complained upon occasion about the quality of grade and high school instruction in this country. We have a chance through ACE to make a huge difference, to influence the way people think about educational training because of the experimental nature of what is going on."

The power of the administrative leadership with regard to program change also stems from its ability to encourage and fund desired academic programs and to kill or discourage or financially starve undesired programs (Levin, 1980). Fr. Malloy demonstrated this power by offering financial support to ACE during the planning stages. The officers of the university almost to a person were stakeholders in ACE. Two of the university officers—the counselor to the president, and the vice president and senior associate provost—sat on the executive committee of the ACE Advisory Board, as did the wife of the provost. Additionally, the vice president for finance and chief investment officer was also on the ACE Advisory Board.

The ACE admissions committee was composed of 33 administrators, faculty, and rectors who divided into groups of three to interview each of the hundreds of ACE applicants, a commitment of approximately 20 hours each winter. An associate dean of the Graduate School not only sat on the admissions committee but also taught in the program. The counselor to the president and director of Campus Ministry were actively involved in this process. Other administrators on the admissions committee included the two assistants to the president, the executive assistant to the provost, the director of the Office for Students with Disabilities, and the coordinator of the Office of Multicultural Student Affairs.

Support of the administration also was demonstrated by the flexibility and problem-solving approach of the Graduate School, the Registrar's Office, the University Libraries, and the Office of Instructional Technology as the program administrators worked to refine and improve this unique program. The Graduate School made accommodations for

deadlines and paperwork pertaining to both admissions and graduation. The University Libraries system worked hard with the program
administrators to provide relevant resources to the ACE teachers for
research in coursework and classroom teaching. The Registrar's Office
kept in constant communication, addressing the complexities of the education program, including the distance learning component. The registrar said, "I try to give a lot of leeway to new programs, knowing there
will be bugs to work out." When administrators develop that climate
for change, as they did with ACE, they in effect begin the process of
change (Curry, 1992).

### The Change Agent

The genesis of the ACE program was the creative vision of Fr. Tim
Scully. Reviewers of educational change (Rogers & Shoemaker, 1971;
Zaltman & Duncan, 1977; Levin, 1980, 1998; Seymour, 1988; Curry,
1992; Johnstone, 1994) stress that the role of the change initiator cannot be overemphasized. Zaltman and Duncan (1977), in an extensive
review of the literature on change agents, found the following basic
qualities essential in a change leader in order for lasting change to
occur: technical skill, administrative ability, good interpersonal relations, passion and commitment for the project, acceptance of constraints, and leadership qualities including poise, backbone, political
finesse, and emotional maturity.

Motivated by the desire to leverage Notre Dame's resources to
ensure that Catholic schools maintain quality teachers in their classrooms, Fr. Scully worked tirelessly to develop, maintain, and expand
the mission of ACE. As vice president and senior associate provost,
he was in a position of power to lay the idea on the table. Then he
spent close to a year visiting potential client dioceses and schools, not
only to understand their needs, but to develop a program that would
take Notre Dame's most valuable resources—the passion, quality, and
commitment of its students—and match them to the needs of the
diocesan schools. Fr. Scully was also in a position to secure the needed resources, both monetary and support services, to launch ACE. He
began by securing a planning fund from the president of the university and then tapped donors and foundations for initial operating
funds. Then he built an endowment so that ACE would not be funded through university operating funds. He obtained a commitment

from the university that summer room for the ACE teachers would be absorbed, and finally, that all tuition for the graduate degree would be waived. Finally, he used his political skills to have ACE named an Americorps demonstration program, providing both programmatic money and student vouchers for the funding stream.

Johnstone (1994) found that in the most successful academic change projects, the change agent remained at the university and remained a passionate advocate until the change project was institutionalized, often in 8–10 years. Fr. Scully continues to lead the ACE effort, as chairman of the ACE Advisory Board and as director of the Institute for Educational Initiatives, which houses ACE. His duties and position at the university have changed over the past seven years, and he is now the executive vice president of the university. However, his commitment to ACE has not wavered. He has the respect of the Catholic leadership in the country, the able faculty and staff he has assembled, and the students who choose to give two years of their lives to fulfill his vision. His strong and continued leadership for the ACE program is critical to its success.

## Faculty Support

It is remarkable that ACE began in a university without a school or department of education. However, Notre Dame did benefit from faculty and administrators who were themselves products of Catholic schools, supported Catholic education by placing their own children in Catholic schools, and did research on children and schools within the frameworks of the disciplines of psychology and sociology. Many Notre Dame faculty, including Fr. Scully, had taught in elementary and secondary Catholic schools.

A group of arts and letters faculty played powerful behind-the-scenes roles in the ACE development. Clark Power, chair of the Program in Liberal Studies, John Borkowski, the Andrew J. McKenna Chair in Psychology, and Maureen Hallinan, the William P. and Hazel B. White Chair in Sociology, led the initial efforts. From the very beginning, these faculty were included as stakeholders, as members of the advisory board and admissions committee, and by 1997, as a core group to help recruit a director for the envisioned graduate program and to assist him in the development of the curriculum. All continue to serve as fellows in the Institute for Educational Initiatives, which houses ACE.

For any change project to remain on the academic landscape, it must have sustained faculty support (Levin, 1980). For the first few years of ACE, the University of Portland delivered the graduate program at Notre Dame. Notre Dame watched the concept of ACE grow during the Portland years, before they had to make a decision about reinstitutionalizing graduate education at Notre Dame. Importantly, when Michael Pressley was hired to design a graduate program, its development did not depend on competing for faculty positions or other resources. ACE was designed with its own endowment so that it would not require money from the general revenues or from the operating budget of the university. The initial support for ACE, therefore, faced no serious faculty challenge other than a mandate that any graduate education degree be as rigorous as other degrees offered by the Graduate School.

The arts and letters faculty lent their talents to ensure the success of the ACE program. Currently, six tenured arts and letters professors teach ACE courses (Pressley, Howard, Turner, Power, Narvaez, Werge) as do eight nontenured faculty and administrators (Brandenberger, Poorman, Barry, Bredemeier, Shields, Matthias, Schneider-Kirner, Warner). All of these Notre Dame ACE faculty were open to learning about the latest advances in teacher education and contributing to the development and refinement of the curriculum.

In addition to Pressley, the ACE program added four teacher-educators since the graduate program began in 1998 (Johnstone, Daunt, Moreno, Watzke). By recruiting arts and letters faculty who are passionate about the ACE mission and having them work alongside the education faculty who have been brought to ND as experts in pedagogy, ACE built a strong foundation of quality and support for the graduate program.

One problem that often besets new change projects is overworked faculty. Many colleges and universities share the problem of overcrowded curricula and faculty stretched to the breaking point with teaching and research loads and many committee assignments (Wimpelberg, King, & Nystrom, 1985). By contrast, the majority of the ACE courses are taught in the summer when faculty members have the most flexibility. Although faculty may be working on research, no faculty member is teaching more than one course for ACE during this time, and university committees do not meet.

The ACE faculty model was designed to capitalize on the talents and availability of nationally renowned scholars who can commit for a summer class on the Notre Dame campus or an Internet class from their home campus. More than 15 of these "national faculty" have swelled the faculty ranks, from diverse universities such as the University of Maryland, Texas Christian University, University of Nebraska, University of Michigan, Ball State University, University of Georgia, University of Virginia, and Brock University. Several of the national faculty have a strong commitment to the program, returning to teach in it year after year. Projects are people (Baldridge, 1980; Townsend et al., 1992), and the graduate faculty of ACE complements the commitment of the ACE students.

### ACADEMIC REQUIREMENTS

Excessive and restrictive general education requirements are generally considered inhibitors to change (Johnstone, 1994). Because ACE is a graduate program, few general education requirements apply. The ACE participants must take the GRE, but they can postpone the test until after they know that they have been admitted to ACE (March), as long as it is taken before the first summer courses begin (June).

Because of the enormous interest in ACE, the program accepts outstanding students from its large pool of applicants—the average undergraduate G.P.A. from the 2000 cohort was 3.4—if ACE wishes to admit a student with less than a 3.0 G.P.A. based on other criteria, the Graduate School admits the student on probationary status pending a 3.0 during the first summer.

Additional flexibility is provided by the distance-education component of the program. Approximately 50% of the curriculum is taught on campus during the summers, 28% is taught through Web-based delivery, and 22% is site-based in the participating schools. This flexibility allows for an immersion graduate program in teacher preparation leading to an initial license.

### CLIMATE FOR CHANGE

Change requires leadership, risk-taking, solid planning, and the cultivation of a change-accepting environment (Seymour, 1988). A sense of organizational momentum helps (Townsend et al., 1992). Lasting change occurs in organizations that have cultivated a change-accepting environment (Levin, 1980).

At Notre Dame, the momentum for change accompanied by academic excellence is electric. During the last decade, Notre Dame concentrated its energies on addressing the joys, challenges, and rewards of teaching. This commitment is reflected in programmatic enhancements, such as the creation of the Kaneb Center for Teaching and Learning and the development of its Educational Leadership Program, as well as in establishment of the Institute for Educational Initiatives. State-of-the-art facilities have also taken center stage, most visibly in the new College of Business Administration complex and in Debartolo Hall, both of which are high concept and Internet based. By 1997, Notre Dame's computer technology infrastructure was in the top 1% of all colleges and universities in the nation. A new performing arts center and new science teaching facilities are underway. Notre Dame continues to improve its status as one of the premier Catholic universities in the world.

Financial problems can certainly pose a barrier to change. Program expansion is unlikely to occur when teacher education administrators are justifying the cost effectiveness of existing programs (Bergquist, 1978). Because the ACE program is self-sufficient, its development and expansion have been applauded. This is especially true because most of the resources that came to ACE would not have been given to the university for any program other than one concentrating on preparing strong graduate students for teaching in under-resourced schools.

For some institutions, it may not be the proper time to initiate change; competing initiatives may defeat a proposed program. Although Notre Dame had other programs in the developmental and neophyte stages, university stakeholders did not see ACE as a threat to their programmatic ideas, and thus, intramural competition for resources did not affect ACE.

All program initiatives should play to the institution's strengths. If a proposed program requires competencies, skills, or relationships not present at the university, the program either should not be attempted or should be undertaken in collaboration with other resources. The strength of ACE was the congruence with the mission of Notre Dame; the administrative, alumni, and faculty support; the talent and vision of Fr. Tim Scully; the timing of the initiative both for the university and the schools that are served; the relative ease of mounting a graduate education program at Notre Dame, especially when it can generate its own resources.

## EXTERNAL FACTORS

No matter how favorable the factors may be to initiate change on a campus, institutionalization of that change, the weaving of the program into the fabric of the institution, requires that the college or university consider external factors, which can derail the initiative. The ACE program, a teacher-service program leading to initial licensure, had several external factors to consider: (1) national and state accreditation issues, (2) the relationship to the schools and dioceses, and (3) consortia linkages and replication.

### National and State Accreditation Issues

Accreditation is often seen as a factor in maintaining program quality and as a protection against program erosion (Daly, 1983). The possibility of losing accreditation if changes are not made becomes a powerful motivator (O'Neil, 1997). In Indiana, all teacher education programs are required to meet the standards of the National Council for Accreditation of Teacher Education (NCATE). As Notre Dame embarked on the development of a graduate-level teacher education program, the NCATE standards were certainly monitored as programmatic decisions were made, but the program administrators did not feel enslaved or even encumbered by them.

More important than the national standards for accreditation was the State of Indiana redesign for teacher education. Notre Dame entered the teacher education landscape just as Indiana was in the midst of a radical change in its license system. The Indiana Professional Standards Board had adopted the principles of the Interstate New Teacher Assessment and Support Consortium (INTASC) as the cornerstone of its new system, a system in which all licenses would be standards based and performance assessed. While many teacher education institutions in the state were challenged to mesh their current course and credit-based programs with this reality, this approach allowed Notre Dame the freedom to design a graduate-level initial license program that could capitalize on the competence of its candidates, and on the two full years of classroom experience during which the ACE teachers could demonstrate their knowledge and performance on the standards. Additionally, Notre Dame had no entrenched courses or faculty members demanding to teach favored content in a

particular way. The ACE program designers, using the Indiana standards as a framework, were able to conceptualize and deliver a curriculum that capitalized on the creative direction in which the state
was heading. The new state licensing approach enhanced the university's ability to develop this alternative yet experiential approach to
teacher licensing.

## RELATIONSHIP TO THE SCHOOLS AND DIOCESES

Teacher education programs depend a great deal on quality field
experiences to provide students with relevant connections for course
content. The ability to place students in classroom settings that model
appropriate practice is something faculty cherish. The ACE program
had two placement challenges: (1) provide school-based experiences
for the ACE teachers in the summer prior to their first year of service
as a classroom teacher, and (2) prepare ACE teachers for the cultural
context of the schools and children they would serve. Strong relationships with both local schools for summer placements and with the
receiving dioceses and schools in the South, therefore, were essential.

Because the ACE program recruited primarily liberal arts, science,
and engineering majors who had little or no school-based experience
with children, the summer practicum where they could observe good
teaching and practice their skills was of paramount importance. It also
presented one of the greatest challenges in the program design. In
South Bend, few public schools had summer programs, and the
Catholic schools had none. The summer placements that could be
found were often remedial, based on a summer calendar that did not
mesh well with the ACE eight-week calendar, and staffed by teachers
who had seniority but did not always represent best practice.

The ACE staff responded to these circumstances by approaching
the Ft. Wayne–South Bend Diocese and offering to establish and subsidize summer programs and classes in the Catholic schools. In cases
where current Catholic schoolteachers were not available to staff these
classes, the program hired ACE graduates to teach as summer mentors for the beginning ACE students. Each summer, approximately 10
ACE graduates came back to campus to teach in the diocesan summer school program, providing classroom placements in which the
newly accepted ACErs practice teaching.

Each year, ACE worked with the diocese to plan the summer program. Although there was a fee to the children for these classes, ACE

assumed responsibility for the costs not covered. The ACE staff also worked with three public school districts in the South Bend area and continued to increase and refine the relationships, a process that requires a sustained commitment.

The most critical component of the Alliance for Catholic Education is the relationship between the university and the southern dioceses where the ACE teachers are placed. Initially, the client dioceses were chosen because of the relationships and ties of individuals in those dioceses with Sr. Lourdes Sheehan, the first director of ACE. More recently, individual dioceses have contacted ACE seeking ACE teachers, and selection as an ACE site has been determined by a number of factors, including level of need, quality of the diocesan leadership, and the desire and capacity to fulfill the ACE vision.

Once dioceses joined the ACE alliance, all participants attended to their shared commitments. The diocese was responsible for locating and furnishing a residence for the ACE community, identifying teaching needs in a timely manner, appointing mentor teachers for each ACE teacher, and completing all required evaluations for the M.Ed. program. The ACE staff matched prospective ACE teachers to the designated openings, sent the applications to the dioceses for their approval, and completed any paperwork required to ensure that the ACE teachers can be teachers of record during their two years of service. ACE also tried to replace a graduating ACE teacher with a new recruit.

Problems arose when there was lack of a common vision, ineffective communication, and infrequent opportunities for face-to-face interaction. ACE staff met with diocesan superintendents at least three times each year: twice in their dioceses while visiting the ACE teachers at their sites, and once at an April retreat at the university.

Because ACE superintendents expressed a need to connect with each other, ACE sponsors a summer sabbatical for the participating superintendents. In the summers of 2000 and 2001, ACE superintendents met on campus for a five-day experience. This summer program had five purposes: (1) provide opportunities and resources for spiritual renewal; (2) discuss the latest research on education, especially Catholic education and the forces affecting education today; (3) share successful programs and strategies in the area of development, leadership, and curriculum; (4) explore the challenges of maintaining and expanding Catholic education; (5) participate in a shared liturgical life. By providing such opportunities to strengthen the diocesan voice within the alliance, Notre Dame continues the healthy development of its diocesan partnerships.

## Consortia Linkages and Replication

At the inception of ACE, no other Catholic teacher-service programs also provided initial licensing through an alternative graduate education program. One of the most revealing signs of the continued success of ACE is that despite its fairly rapid growth, the demand for ACE teachers from the dioceses across the country outpaced the capacity to supply all requests. The ACE leadership decided not to expand beyond 160 ACE members in order to maintain programmatic intimacy and continuity. Therefore, alternative methods of expansion were explored, including replication of ACE by partnering with other institutions interested in developing their own alternative teacher-service programs.

First, ACE developed the Office of Educational Outreach, headed by Joyce Johnstone. Then, early in 1999, Notre Dame began to work with its advocates in Washington, D.C., to secure federal funding for the partnering initiative. In the fall of 1999, Notre Dame received $500,000 in federal appropriations to partner with four institutions in developing alternative teacher-service programs that contained the tenets of the ACE program. Upon learning of the federal appropriation that Notre Dame received, a private foundation approached ACE, seeking to capitalize on the federal initiative and support three additional institutions in their efforts to develop ACE-like programs. Simultaneously, ACE received a grant from an additional private foundation, part of which was directed toward assisting Seton Hall University in developing an ACE program. Each of the partnering programs agreed to remain true to the ACE mission of providing teachers for under-resourced parochial schools while maintaining professional teacher development, spiritual development, and community living (i.e., four to seven teachers living together for mutual support).

Notre Dame sent letters to more than 60 faith-based colleges and universities that had strong commitments to service, inviting them to apply as partnering institutions. Eight institutions were chosen: Providence College, Valparaiso University, Seton Hall University, University of Dayton, University of Portland, Loyola Marymount University, Christian Brothers University, and a consortium of Baltimore colleges including the College of Notre Dame, Loyola College, and Mount St. Mary's. A ninth institution, Creighton University, began replication efforts in the summer of 2001. Each program will build on its own institutional strength and character as it partners with Notre Dame over the next five years, providing variations on the theme of ACE.

Some may recruit older students; some may define community differently; some may have a greater or more diverse spiritual component. All parties will learn from the successes and challenges that each institution encounters.

Teacher shortages in Catholic schools are a national problem. Given the quantity of Catholic teachers needed, no one institution alone can make a significant impact. However, institutions focusing on specific regions of the country can make significant progress in alleviating the shortage of Catholic educators in their region, and if all of the regions of the United States are eventually covered, then all the Catholic institutions working together can make a national impact on teacher shortages. ACE places its teachers in 13 states in the South and Southwest; initially, each partnering institution will work with from one to four dioceses located in their vicinity. These efforts will provide teachers in 12 additional states.

ACE views the work with the partnering institutions as one the most vital movements in Catholic education. The momentum generated over the past eight years must be sustained and enlarged. The national need for faith-filled Catholic educators is so acute that only together, in partnership with like-minded institutions, can a solution be effected. Hence, Notre Dame is seeking to expand its network of partnering colleges and universities, hoping to add new institutions every year.

Participation in consortia can help institutions deepen the strength and scope of their teacher education programs (Sharp, 1982). For example, in reaching out to share the ACE vision, Notre Dame deepened its own commitment to institutionalizing ACE. Thus, this consortia linkage, like the other external forces of accreditation, state regulations, and relationships with schools, has had a positive effect on the ability of Notre Dame to institutionalize the ACE program.

## RELEVANCE OF THE FACTORS

FOR CHANGE TO OCCUR, administrative support must be firm, as demonstrated by a willingness to encourage change and support program development. Faculty leadership must be strong and active for the change project to be approved and accepted by the larger college community, for in the democratic academic power structure and openness of the academy, faculty have the power to scuttle any initiative. Both of these factors were evident in the development of

ACE. Additionally, the change agent must be able to understand the full scope of the project and to empathize with the change targets, whether they be faculty, students, parochial schools, or all of these. The change agent must also be able to empower others so that they will assume ownership for the project. At Notre Dame, Fr. Tim Scully had a vision for Notre Dame's influence on Catholic schools and had the charisma and skill to attract others—students, diocesan leaders, faculty, administrators, and donors—to that vision.

For the change project to become institutionalized, change factors must remain intact. If, for example, administrative support for the project wanes, essential funding could be cut. At Notre Dame, the entire university community continues to applaud ACE. Likewise, if the change agent leaves before institutionalization occurs, new priorities assume importance without a champion who truly believes in the project, and the necessity of the change dims. Fr. Scully continues to be the standard-bearer for ACE; ACE continues to draw national attention and support because of his leadership.

Other factors that influence the maintenance of the change project are the relevance of the project to the mission of the institution, the relationship to accreditation and state regulations, and the relationship to the target schools. The mission and values of the institution must guide and direct any change project; without congruence between the mission and the goals of the change project, the initiative will die. If the project falls outside the boundaries of the mission and goals of the institution, regardless of its intrinsic merit, it will have little worth to the institution. Notre Dame not only attended to congruence to mission in its inception of ACE but also looked carefully at mission relatedness when selecting partnering institutions. Administrators believe that those institutions that have a strong culture of service as a function of their mission will have a greater likelihood of success in this teacher-service program.

The relationship of the change project to state regulations is important because the state requirements may reinforce the importance of the project. The move to standards-based performance assessment by the Indiana Professional Standards Board allowed for the birth of the innovative ACE program. On the other hand, state regulations that ignore the curricular implications of the project or that cause undue hardship in maintaining the project may sound the death toll.

Having quality field placements is a necessity for teacher education students. ACE has had the ability to choose dioceses and schools with strong leadership and a desire to help the neophyte ACE teachers. These placements reflect the philosophy of ACE, an important enabler for the health of the program. Communication between Notre Dame and the ACE schools is respectful, consistent, and productive. The university and the schools are able jointly to provide optimum reflective practice for the program, thereby enhancing the work of institutionalizing the program.

The ACE program at Notre Dame has been a labor of love. Those involved, the administrators, faculty, students, and donors, are passionate about its mission of providing faith-filled, talented teachers for some of the country's most impoverished schools. It will continue to shine as a model of teacher service in the image of Christ Teacher.

## REFERENCES

Baldridge, J. V. (1980). Managerial innovation. *Journal of Higher Education, 51*(2), 117–134.

Bergquist, W. H. (1978). Relationship of collegiate professional development and teacher education. *Journal of Teacher Education, 2*(2), 39–41.

Chickering, A. W., Halliburton, D., Bergquist, W. H., & Lindquist, J. (1977). *Developing the college curriculum: A handbook for faculty and administrators.* Washington, DC: Council for the Advancement of Small Colleges.

Curry, B. K. (1992). *Instituting enduring innovations: Achieving continuity of change in higher education.* ASHE-ERIC Higher Education Report No. 7. Washington, DC: George Washington University, School of Education and Human Development.

Daly, N. (1983). Coping with limited resources. In American Association of Colleges for Teacher Education, *Teacher preparation in small colleges: Regular educators and the education of handicapped children* (pp. 1–22). Washington, DC: Author.

Johnstone, J. (1994) *Curriculum change in small colleges.* Unpublished doctoral dissertation, Indiana University, Bloomington.

Levin, A. (1980). *Why innovation fails.* Albany: State University of New York Press.

Levin, A. (1998). Succeeding as a leader; failing as a president. *Change, 30*(1), 42–46.

O'Neil, E. (1997, June). Using accreditation for your purposes. *AAHE Bulletin.* Washington, DC: American Association of Higher Education.

Rogers, E. M., & Shoemaker, E. F. (1971). *Communication of innovations: A cross-cultural approach.* New York: Free Press.

Seymour, D. T. (1988). *Developing academic programs: The climate for innovation.* ASHE-ERIC Higher Education Report No. 3. Washington, DC: Association of the Study of Higher Education.

Sharp, B. (Ed.). (1982). *Dean's grants projects: Challenges and change in teacher education.* Minneapolis: University of Minnesota.

Townsend, B. K., Newell, L. J., & Wiese, M. D. (1992). *Creating distinctiveness: Lessons from uncommon colleges and universities.* ASHE-ERIC Higher Education Report No. 6. Washington, DC: George Washington University, School of Education and Human Development.

Wimpelberg, R. K., King, J. A., & Nystrom, N. J. (1985). Private teacher education: Profiles and prospects. In A. Tom (Ed.), *Teacher education in liberal arts settings.* Washington, DC: American Association of Colleges for Teacher Education.

Zaltman, G., & Duncan, R. (1977). *Strategies for planned change.* New York: Wiley.

PART II

# THE THREE PILLARS: PROFESSIONAL EDUCATION, COMMUNITY, AND SPIRITUALITY

*T*he goal in developing the ACE program was to intermingle academic development of teachers, their development in community, and their spiritual development. The metaphor of three parallel pillars never seemed quite right, although the "three pillars" phrase lives on, perhaps only because of semantic inertia. Perhaps a better metaphor would be a cable with three intertwined strands, with each strand a different metal. The cable as a totality is much stronger than each of the component strands, capable of standing upright and supporting weight, even though no one strand could stand upright or support weight.

To understand the cable, however, it is necessary to understand the individual strands. Analogously, to understand ACE, it is necessary to understand the conceptual and pragmatic foundations of the academic, community, and spiritual strands of the program. Still, readers should not expect a pure separation of academic, community, and spiritual dimensions in these chapters, for none of the components is ever completely separated from the others as ACErs participate in the total experience that is ACE teacher service and education.

**5**

MICHAEL PRESSLEY
JOYCE V. JOHNSTONE

# ACADEMIC DEVELOPMENT

## INTELLECTUAL FOUNDATIONS OF THE ACE MODEL

We are writing this chapter in late August 2000, following the two-month summer session offered at Notre Dame for ACErs. All 150 of them will be teachers of record in Catholic school classrooms this academic year, despite the fact that very few of them have a teaching license. Most are Americorps volunteers, teaching in schools that serve needy children. They are working for a small stipend and some student loan forgiveness.

The purpose of the summer session was to provide basic teacher education for these 150 young people. Now that they are at the site, there are other tasks. Thus, earlier today, we packed some boxes of grammar workbooks for shipment to one of our teachers who serves in a school with very few textbooks. We took a phone call from another who needed some advice about how to organize her classroom. Tomorrow, we will spend time setting up an Internet website that will be used by some of the 150 participants to take a distance-learning course. In a few weeks, one of us will travel to one of the sites served by students in the program to observe teaching, hoping to offer some insights to some of these young people about what they are doing well and how they can improve. A couple of summers from now, we will hood each of the individuals who entered the program this year, for they will have earned a master's of education degree from Notre Dame and an initial teaching license.

Although ACE originally focused on the southeastern United States, its service area expanded dramatically since 1994. In 2001, it stretches from Charleston, South Carolina, to Los Angeles, California. In addition, ACE has moved northward somewhat, with a group of six ACE teachers in Kansas City, Missouri. ACE is a national teacher service and teacher education effort, one that is also decidedly alternative teacher education.

In part, this book is a history of the ACE program. It is also a how-to text, intended to provide information to colleges and universities interested in developing their own service learning opportunities that link to teacher education. At the time of this writing, about a dozen schools are working with Notre Dame, attempting to develop their own ACE-like programs.

Most of the replicating institutions are Catholic colleges. This reflects that ACE was developed in a Catholic university context, Notre Dame, but also that the need to develop young teachers for the nation's Catholic schools is very great. The first decade of the 21st Century is promising that teacher retirements will far outstrip the supply of new teachers. With the decline in religious vocations, each year fewer and fewer religious are available to teach in Catholic schools. Because Catholic schools cannot pay teachers at the same level as public schools, teacher shortages are likely to hit Catholic schools particularly hard. Beyond numbers, of course, is the reality that teaching in a Catholic school is different from teaching in a public school. Moreover, secular teacher education institutions have done nothing to prepare teachers for the special needs and demands of Catholic school settings. In summary, there were multiple pragmatic reasons for Notre Dame to reenter teacher education, and especially for it to provide leadership in Catholic teacher education.

Beyond the pragmatics, however, there were also good conceptual reasons for Notre Dame to reinvolve with teacher education. Hence, the remainder of this introductory chapter is devoted to detailing some of the conceptual influences that were prominently on the minds of the founders and shapers of the ACE program from its inception in the middle 1990s to its present form. This brief survey of the conceptual foundations of the program will make clear that many perspectives had to be considered and balanced as ACE was conceived and mounted.

## THE THREE PILLARS

Since its inception, ACE has had three pillars: (1) The program develops teachers professionally and academically. (2) The program prepares its participants to live together in a supportive Christian community for the two years of the program. (3) The program fosters the spiritual development of its teachers so that they in turn can be better spiritual guides for their students. Of course, the three pillars are not stiff and independent but intertwine. For example, community life supports the individual members as they confront the challenges of beginning teaching. Community life is also the context where much of spiritual development plays out, with community members praying and sharing together. Similarly, part of the professional development of a Catholic schoolteacher is intended to foster spiritual development in individual students but also to nurture a caring community in the school.

Professional, community, and spiritual dimensions are difficult to separate in this program. Even so, we organize this chapter around the three dimensions, for some influences on the development of ACE seem more professional, some more spiritual, and others more connected to community.

## PROFESSIONAL FOUNDATIONS

A number of scholarly analyses pointed to the need for Catholic K–12 schools to be reinvigorated with a new generation of teachers, with an obvious source of teachers being American Catholic universities. In fact, there was a new awareness due to new scholarly analyses that Catholic schools have excellent track records with historically disadvantaged groups, making more obvious to universities such as Notre Dame that commitment to Catholic K–12 education was in the best interest of the nation. Teaching, and particularly teaching in Catholic schools, is a form of service that makes sense to many Notre Dame students, many of whom are products of the Catholic K–12 experience.

Notre Dame had to be aware of changing national teacher education standards as it developed its new program. Notre Dame faculty were determined to inform the new program with the extensive research on teaching that has developed in the past quarter century. The new program also had to be attuned to distance education, for

much of teacher education at Notre Dame would take place with professors and graduate students thousands of miles apart.

In the end, Notre Dame faculty were able to create a program consistent with much of the best thinking in contemporary teacher education. The perspectives that filled the minds of the ACE M.Ed.
developers are summarized in this chapter.

## Scholarly Analyses of Contemporary Catholic Education

In the 1990s, Catholic education received a great deal of scholarly examination (e.g., Hunt, Oldenski, & Wallace, 2000; Irvine & Foster, 1996; O'Keefe & O'Keeffe, 1996; Youniss & Convey, 2000;
Youniss, Convey, & McLellan, 2000). As a result, much is known
about the state of Catholic K–12 education at the dawn of the 21st
century.

There are fewer Catholic schools now than in the 1960s, which
was the peak period for American Catholic schools (e.g., McLellan,
2000). In the 1960s, many Catholic schools served urban areas that
were predominantly European immigrant populations, largely Catholic
populations. Forty years later, those neighborhoods are very different, with African American, Asian, and recent Hispanic immigrants
replacing European Americans, who moved to the suburbs when they
could afford to do so. The exodus of the predominantly Catholic European immigrants resulted in the closing of many urban Catholic
schools. Those that remained open now serve an ethnically and reli-
giously diverse group of students compared to 40 years ago (Lawrence,
2000; O'Keefe, 2000; O'Keefe & Murphy, 2000; Riordan, 2000).
Indeed, often the majority of students are non-Catholic in urban
Catholic schools (Polite, 2000), with local parents perceiving the local
Catholic school as a better school than the competing public schools.
Many urban parents living in poverty continue to believe in education as a route to a better life in America, and they view the Catholic
school their child attends as a lifeline to a better future. Of course,
they are correct, for minority children have done better in Catholic
schools compared to public schools (Irvine & Foster, 1996), and they
mature into adults who are grateful that the Catholic Church remains
committed to serving the inner-city poor, even students and their families who are not Catholic (O'Keefe, 1996).

When European Catholic families moved to the suburbs, Catholic
education did not move with them; there have been relatively few

Catholic suburban schools (Youniss, Convey, & McLellan, 2000). One explanation is that suburban public schools were much more attractive than the urban public schools left behind, able to offer much, given the tax base of support provided by suburban residential neighborhoods. A second explanation is that much of the historic anti-Catholic sentiment that had fueled the demand for Catholic schools in the first half of the century seemed to dissipate in the late 1960s, 1970s, and 1980s (e.g., Walch, 2000). In 1960, Americans elected a Catholic president; in the Vatican II decades that followed, American Catholics and Protestants felt more comfortable together, with both groups identifying more as Americans than as members of one Christian faction or another (Meagher, 2000). As part of that, suburban Catholics largely sent their children to public schools, where they studied side by side with Protestant students, far away from the urban centers now occupied by new immigrant groups.

Despite the decline in numbers of students in Catholic schools, the Church continues to support Catholic elementary and secondary education. For example, bishops and priests believe that Catholic education is important to the future of the American Catholic Church (Convey, 2000). Many religious congregations continue to sponsor schools (Mueller, 2000). Even so, since the 1960s, there have been substantial declines in the number of religious vocations, so there are fewer priests, sisters, and brothers to staff schools than was the case in the 1960s. Now, more than 90% of teachers in Catholic schools are lay teachers (Ristau & Reif, 2000). Although Catholic school faculty are more educated than they were in the 1960s, their education still lags behind public school teachers (Schaub, 2000). So do their salaries (Schaub, 2000), consistent with a general financial crisis in Catholic K–12 education, with many Catholic schools closing because of financial exigencies (Harris, 2000; Nelson, 2000).

Few teachers emerge from secular higher education with the theological background required to deliver a distinctly Catholic curriculum to students or with a complete understanding of the unique characteristics of Catholic schools compared to public and other private schools (Ristau & Reif, 2000). Most teacher preparation programs do not prepare teachers to view schools as both Christian and academic communities. Most do not prepare teachers to display publicly the integration of their faith and work for students, evangelize students as Catholic school teachers do, or encourage morality and ethical behavior at the level expected in Catholic schools (McClelland, 1996; McLaughlin, 1996; Traviss, 2000).

The ACE faculty and staff reflected a great deal on secular teacher education programs versus the ACE teacher education experience, which did much to motivate many of the most distinctive aspects of the teaching service and education program detailed in this volume. We recognized that knowledge about Catholicism and commitment to it vary with the amount of formal education in Catholicism (Galetto, 2000), and hence, we felt good about the fact that the people coming into ACE generally had extensive education in Catholicism. We also felt good that every one of our participants had a solid academic major in the liberal arts, humanities, sciences, business, or engineering, and hence, we were sending academically sophisticated teachers to the academically demanding institutions that Catholic schools are. We also believed that we could develop ACErs into educators who would be as good as the best coming out of any teacher's college, and in particular, be thoroughly Catholic educators. We drew on many academic resources for guidance and strength; several of these influences are covered briefly in the remainder of this chapter.

## CATHOLIC SCHOOLS AND THE COMMON GOOD

During the last quarter of the 20th Century, sociologists established that academic performance in Catholic high schools, particularly performance in core academic subjects (i.e., reading, math), was better than in public high schools (e.g., Coleman & Hoffer, 1987; Coleman, Hoffer, & Kilgore, 1982; Lee & Bryk, 1989), perhaps reflecting in part that students leave Catholic elementary schools achieving at a higher level than their public school counterparts (Hoffer, 2000). Yes, there are debates about whether the Catholic school advantage is small or large (Persell, 2000), as well as questions about which active ingredients in Catholic schools cause the superior achievements that have been obtained (Dreeben, 2000; Sørensen, 1996; Sørensen & Morgan, 2000). Even so, one motivation for enthusiasm about Catholic schools is that they are effective, especially for disadvantaged populations (e.g., Lee & Bryk, 1989).

One of the most important scholarly analyses of Catholic education ever produced appeared in book-length form in 1993. Anthony Bryk, a University of Chicago sociologist, and his colleagues published their landmark evaluation of the impact of Catholic high schools on students, *Catholic Schools and the Common Good*. This study by Bryk, Lee, and Holland (1993) was impressive and convincing social science, in part because it employed two contrasting methodologies to produce converging conclusions, conclusions that turned out to be very supportive of Catholic high school education. Bryk and his colleagues conducted extensive qualitative fieldwork in seven urban Catholic high schools: three single-sex and four coed high schools. They also did new statistical analyses of an important data archive, the *High School and Beyond* survey (National Center for Educational Statistics, 1982).

The statistical analyses were very revealing about some important differences between Catholic and non-Catholic high schools, predominantly public high schools. For example, the Catholic high schools were more academically oriented, more likely to offer advanced academic courses, and less likely to include vocational courses in their curricula. This translated into the vast majority of Catholic high school students being enrolled in academic tracks rather than vocational tracks. The academic-vocational split was much more even in the public high schools included in the *High School and Beyond* study.

Catholic high schools tended to be smaller (546 students on average) than public high schools (845 students). Indeed, there are few very large Catholic high schools, in contrast to the public sector. Size partially explains why Catholic secondary curricula are more focused on core academic subjects; there are not enough students in many Catholic high schools to support specialized electives. Size also partially explains the great sense of community in Catholic high schools; there are more personal social interactions between faculty and students in smaller compared to larger schools. The small size of Catholic high schools also contributes to students sensing that their teachers care about them. Furthermore, it permits a greater proportion of students to participate as leaders in the school. Perhaps it also accounts for higher job satisfaction among Catholic high school teachers than among public school teachers.

The field data were very revealing about the character of instruction in Catholic high schools (Bryk, 1996). Teaching is rather conventional. In fact, Bryk et al. (1993) described it as "ordinary" (p. 99). A good deal of testing and homework was observed, and academic standards were definitely high. The common academic core was seen as important for all students, and a goal was to encourage each student to achieve to her or his maximum with respect to that academic core. There was very little academic tracking in Catholic schools compared to public schools, reflecting the assumption in Catholic schools that learning of core academic content is important for all students. In Catholic high schools, the students are much more likely than in public schools to "all be in it together"—with all taking the same curricula and expected to meet high academic demands.

The students seemed very positive about the instruction they received, and, in general, they were engaged in class. The teachers worked hard; most teachers had multiple class preparations and many extensive extracurricular commitments to the school. Despite low salaries, which distressed some teachers, the faculty generally were satisfied with their work and found it psychically rewarding. Beyond teaching content, the teachers were very much interested in teaching values and promoting the personal development of their students, with that actually facilitated by the extensive contact permitted by the smallness of the school and faculty obligations to extracurricular activities. In turn, the students recognized their teachers as concerned to develop them as students and as persons. The mutual positive regard between faculty and students explained student engagement in and commitment to school. The teachers and students were part of a caring community, and it seemed to motivate student involvement in schoolwork and teacher willingness to work hard. Part of the community concept, of course, was shared religious experiences, including retreats and service experiences in the school and surrounding community.

The administrators in Catholic high schools seemed closer to students than their counterparts in public schools. In addition, Catholic high schools included ministers who are there specifically to attend to the personal needs of members of the school. Also, the teaching role in Catholic high schools definitely included a counseling component, with many teachers seeing themselves as much ministers as content-area specialists. Catholic high schools are full of dedicated and concerned professionals who see their work as vocation rather than occupation.

In short, Bryk et al. (1993; also, Bryk, 1996) painted a very favorable portrait of life in Catholic high schools. Catholic high schools are more personal and community oriented than public high schools. Bryk et al. (1993) determined that such support accounted, in part, for the high academic engagement observed in Catholic high schools. In turn, such engagement accounted for the achievement advantages of Catholic high schools relative to public schools. An especially interesting finding was that the differences in achievement between students from advantaged and disadvantaged groups was much smaller in Catholic compared to public schools. That is, students from disadvantaged groups are more likely to keep up with students from advantaged groups in Catholic compared to public high schools. This was an important finding, causing Bryk et al. (1993) to conclude that Catholic schools do much for the common good, with it more likely in Catholic than in public schools that students would complete high school—both students from advantaged and those from disadvantaged backgrounds.

## SERVICE LEARNING

ACE participation was seen as two years of service to Catholic schools, conceived of as value-added service, with the added value coming from the provision of high-quality teacher education to ACE participants. The first summer was to focus on the skills needed to mount and run a classroom; the second summer was to round out the teacher education experience, covering some of the foundations of teaching and taking up more advanced methods. The two years of teaching were also supervised in much the same way that student teaching is supervised.

Service learning as part of higher education was a popular approach for most of the second half of the 20th Century (Stanton, Giles, & Cruz, 1999) and a very important part of undergraduate education at the University of Notre Dame. A central belief is that important educational outcomes can be achieved by students providing some type of volunteer service.

The assumed outcomes of service learning are varied but include the following (Eyler & Giles, 1999): learning about other people, including the disadvantaged; developing an understanding of the perspectives of the needy; having the positive experience of helping others; learning how to work with others; growing spiritually; developing self-knowledge; developing leadership skills; developing interpersonal skills; applying what has been learned in formal classes; learning more (and concretely) about complex societal problems; developing critical thinking skills; becoming better citizens (i.e., knowing better what ought to be done, why it should be done, and how to do it; believing one can make a difference and developing commitment to do so). The ACE faculty and staff believed that two years of teaching in disadvantaged communities in the South probably would provide many of these benefits for ACE participants.

In particular, Notre Dame believed that the program would develop future educators and church leaders who would understand and be committed to Catholic schools more completely than they would without the ACE experience. Over the years, we have come to appreciate the depth of talent in our midst and to believe that a number of our program participants will do much to lead the Catholic Church, and Catholic schools in particular, in the 21st Century, with these individuals having the high intelligence required to tackle the enormous problems facing these schools in the new century. The ACE faculty and staff believe that much will be learned by ACE participants that will motivate them and prepare them to support and change Catholic schools for the better. We hope that we are educating them with a complete commitment to social justice, educating them to be leaders who are determined to lift those most in need. As academics, of course, we recognized from the very start that measuring many of the presumed outcomes of service learning would be challenging (Eyler & Giles, 1999).

We also recognized that the teacher education program not only had to mesh with service learning, since all the ACE students would be doing service, but it also had to be a model of service learning for teachers who are expected to provide service learning experiences for their own students. Contemporary Catholic schools typically include service learning experiences, seeing this as hands-on education in social justice and responsibility; some excellent social scientific evidence supports that perspective (e.g., Youniss & Yates, 1997). That so many schools are now including service learning experiences in their curricula has stimulated many educators to think hard about how students can provide service and learn from their service (Hoose, 1993; Lewis, 1995, 1997; Rhoads & Howard, 1998; Wade, 1997). The numerous resources available to inform K–12 teachers about how to do service learning increased the motivation of the ACE faculty and staff to assure that service learning be represented in the teacher education program they were developing.

## NATIONAL TEACHER EDUCATION STANDARDS

In 1997, when Notre Dame made the decision to mount its own teacher education program, there were huge changes in progress with respect to teacher education. Most of the changes were at the stimulation of the National Council for Accreditation of Teacher Education (NCATE). NCATE was calling for a fundamental shift in how the decision was made to grant a teacher a license.

The historic approach to teacher education was simply to have the teacher candidate take coursework distributed so as to cover the waterfront of knowledge and experiences expected of beginning teachers. This would be capped by a student teaching experience, which would be graded like a course and metered with academic credits. In recent decades, teacher education coursework has been complemented by standardized assessments of teacher knowledge.

In contrast to these traditional approaches to teacher education, NCATE proposed in 1997 that being granted a license would depend on performing as a teacher and documenting the performance with multiple forms of assessment, for example, a portfolio of teaching accomplishments and reflections on teaching. In addition, consistent with the standards movement sweeping the country in education, NCATE proposed new national standards for teachers, and each state was developing standards for the various types of teaching licenses. In doing so, the states were obligated to seek input from constituencies with great expertise in each area of teaching (e.g., professional associations dedicated to teaching, such as the National Council of Teachers of Mathematics). These various constituencies also proposed new standards to be incorporated into licensure patterns.

No institution would be given initial accreditation unless they could meet the new standards, including offering a capstone portfolio experience. Consequently, the ACE faculty and staff spent a great deal of time thinking about the emerging new standards in teacher education as well as about portfolio assessment and how it could be carried out in a program spread across the nation. As we did so, however, we were confident that we could meet the challenge of the new standards. After all, the ACE program requires two years of teaching, which permits plenty of opportunity to help young teachers become better teachers. We also were confident that we could amass the personnel resources required to help out young teachers in our program who might be struggling. In addition, the concerns with content mastery that were part of the new standards were no threat for a program enrolling no education majors. Our students all had completed at least one full undergraduate major other than education, and many students sported two majors. We had young people who knew the content they were going to be teaching.

We were especially confident because the new standards were emphasizing university-based teacher education programs as partners with schools, with the schools having substantial input to the teacher education experience. Since the inception of ACE in 1994, Notre Dame had interacted closely and collaboratively with diocesan school administrations in order to closely align their needs and the teacher education provided to ACE participants. The superintendents who had worked with Notre Dame were uniformly enthused about their experiences, feeling that Notre Dame had been responsive to needs generally ignored by other teaching education institutions, including the need to prepare teachers so that they would be impressive models of morality for students.

### ANALYSES OF CURRICULA AND INSTRUCTIONAL METHODS

Michael Pressley came to Notre Dame shortly after completing a book summarizing many of the social scientific analyses of education, including much of the research validating various curricular and instructional approaches (Pressley & McCormick, 1995). That book, like other analyses (e.g., Gagné, Yekovich, & Yekovich, 1993; Bruning, Schraw, & Ronning, 1993), documented that very much is now known about how students can be taught so they develop well as readers and writers and in their knowledge of mathematics. Much of the volume summarized theory and research carried out within an information processing framework, with this theoretical perspective stimulating many advances in curriculum and instruction in the past quarter century (e.g., ways of teaching beginning word recognition; developing comprehension skills; stimulating students to plan, draft, and revise recursively as part of writing; inculcating efficient and effective problem solving). The book also summarized the many advances in recent decades in understanding student motivation and how to maximize students' motivation to learn and participate in school. The research supported contemporary social interaction approaches to teaching, such as Vygotsky's (1978) and Bruner's (Wood, Bruner, & Ross, 1976) conceptions of apprenticeship and teacher scaffolding. The book also summarized the growing literature on the teaching of students with exceptionalities. It reviewed as well many alternative approaches to assessment, providing information about what is known about traditional measurements as well as contemporary approaches (e.g., portfolios).

This vast social scientific literature on teaching made obvious that a teacher education program could be crafted that was research defensible, one that taught students many procedures that were inspired by theory and tested in interpretable research studies. As the academic director of the ACE M.Ed. program, Pressley was determined that the program would be informed by the best educational scholarship. If it was, he believed it would fit well in a campus that is decidedly more research oriented with every passing year.

## MODELS OF MORAL DEVELOPMENT

For the past two decades, Notre Dame has been a center for theoretical and applied thinking about moral and ethical education, largely because of the presence of leading scholars in moral and ethical development, such as Clark Power and Dan Lapsley. Both Power and Lapsley identified strongly with the cognitive developmental theory of moral thinking developed by Lawrence Kohlberg (e.g., 1969, 1981, 1984), although both also developed expansive new conceptions in the fields of moral development and education (e.g., see Power, Higgins, & Kohlberg, 1989; Lapsley, 1996). Jay Brandenberger, with the Center for Social Concerns at Notre Dame, is also a visible advocate on the Notre Dame campus for moral development consistent with Kohlberg's vision. Not surprisingly, from the earliest conceptions of the teacher education program at Notre Dame, there was little doubt that cognitive and developmental theories of character, moral, and ethical education would play a prominent role in the program. Clark Power, in particular, was an important voice, consistently reminding that it would be sensible for a teacher education program at an institution like Notre Dame to have a strong grounding in moral development theory and research.

An individual external to the campus who would influence our thinking was Thomas Lickona (e.g., 1976). He began his career very much in the Kohlberg tradition, de-emphasizing direct teaching of moral and ethical positions in favor of opportunities for students to reason about and through ethical dilemmas. In recent years, however, Lickona's perspective broadened considerably, and as it broadened, so did its visibility, with his 1991 book *Educating for Character: How Our Schools Can Teach Respect and Responsibility*.

Lickona (1991) summarized the research literature documenting that many mechanisms can be used to promote the moral development of students, including the following:

- Teacher modeling of moral behavior and reasoning
- Guest speakers
- Storytelling and using literature illustrating great ethical themes
- Influencing students' television viewing, encouraging them to watch prosocial programming and avoid aggressive shows and other objectionable content
- Discussion of ethically controversial issues in the news
- Direct teaching of morality, including asking students to be more ethical in their conduct and explaining to them why they should behave ethically
- Mentoring and individually guiding students with respect to moral and ethical issues
- Cooperative learning and fostering cooperation in general
- Negative consequences for unethical conduct; positive consequences for ethical, fair, and altruistic behavior
- Connecting morality to the curriculum whenever it can be connected, which is often (e.g., during science units on ecology, during social studies units on community)
- Being idealistic, sending the message to students that it is both good and possible to live morally and responsibly
- Having high expectations that students can be moral and responsible, now and in the future
- Rejecting the perspective that ethics is simply a matter of personal opinion in favor of the perspective that there are ethical ideals that should be universal (e.g., respect for life and other people's civil rights)

During the first summer of the ACE program, Lickona provided a series of addresses to participants. They were well received, making clear to the ACE faculty and staff that ACE students wanted much about moral and ethical development in the teacher education curriculum. That Lickona so strongly identified with the direct teaching of morality in his presentations, in conflict with Kohlberg's formulations, provided plenty of grist for reflection among the program leadership about how to balance the faculty's preference for a more Kohlbergian moral education of ACE students versus a direct instructional approach.

During the second summer, Robert Enright of the University of Wisconsin talked with the ACE participants. Like the Notre Dame faculty interested in moral education, Enright began as a Kohlbergian. In recent years, he has spent much of his time researching the psychology of forgiveness. In particular, he is interested in developing interventions to make it easier for people to forgive others (Enright & Fitzgibbons, 2000). Enright's visit was received enthusiastically by faculty and staff, particularly those interested in moral and ethical development; in addition, many students could see that his work had the potential to be important to Catholic schoolteachers, who often are expected to play an explicit pastoral role in their classrooms and schools.

Finally, an exceptionally important development during the formative years of the ACE teacher education program was the hiring of Brenda Bredemeier and David Shields. They are experts in moral development in the arena of sports (Shields & Bredemeier, 1995). Like other moral developmentalists at Notre Dame, their starting point was Kohlberg, so there was high potential for points of contact with the teacher education faculty. Because many ACE participants include coaching as part of their responsibility during their two years of teaching in the program, it made sense to think hard about how to fold Bredemeier and Shields into the ACE teacher education effort.

### DISTANCE LEARNING

Part of the ACE M.Ed. instruction had to be offered over the Internet. This permits the ACErs to earn course credits during the school year, and it increases the technological savvy of ACE participants, which is a real desideratum. Although many of the Catholic schools hosting ACE participants do not have Internet access, some do. In the future, most American schools will use the Internet extensively. As ACE faculty and staff reflected on the emerging teacher education program, it was apparent that we had to prepare our students for the technological future of education.

### REPORT OF THE NATIONAL COMMISSION ON TEACHING AND AMERICA'S FUTURE

The final report of the National Commission on Teaching and America's Future, *What Matters Most: Teaching for America's Future,* appeared in 1997 as Notre Dame administrators contemplated their program. Many aspects of the Notre Dame program reflected conclusions in the report:

- The commission concluded that alternative programs can be effective if they offer streamlined and carefully crafted courses in learning theory, development, and teaching methods along with intensively supervised internships. Notre Dame's program included all these elements.

- The commission favored teachers with strong preparation in the content disciplines. That the participants in the Notre Dame program all had non-education majors was consistent with the commission's vision of the background knowledge required by a well-prepared teacher.

- The commission called for a year-long internship in an actual school. The ACE program provided two years of service in schools.

- The commission called for student teachers to have many more experiences with minority and disadvantaged students. That most of the schools served by ACE participants included substantial proportions of minority students assured that the ND program would meet this recommendation.

- The report called for mentor programs for beginning teachers. Each ACE participant is in a network of mentors, including a school-based teacher, the participant's principal, and clinical faculty in the program.

- The commission was concerned that provisions be made for low-wealth schools to obtain well-qualified teachers. ACE was set up to provide well-educated young people to needy Catholic schools at lower cost than the prevailing market.

- The commission cited the need for more technologically competent individuals in teaching. Because all of the ACE participants have some degree of computer literacy, the ACE teachers bring much computer know-how to their settings.

- The commission called for performance assessment of teachers. The ACE program is performance-based, with each participant preparing a portfolio of accomplishments as part of demonstrating proficiency as a teacher.

- Consistent with the commission's call for teachers to meet national standards, ACE participants are held accountable to both national and state teaching standards.

- The commission called for strong connections between coursework and practicum experiences. In the ACE program, at least one assignment in each course is intended to stimulate a direct change in the ACEr's teaching (e.g., when taking the course in liturgical music, students plan and carry out a musical experience with their students; when studying educational psychology, students plan and carry out a psychologically informed intervention).

- The commission called for teachers to be members of learning communities. ACErs are provided with multiple community layers, from the entire group of teachers, to their cohort (e.g., ACE VII), to their housemates, to other ACE teachers serving the same age or grade level, with many interactions among ACE participants over professional issues.

- The commission was concerned that well-qualified people stay in teaching. Every sign is that ACE is developing many career-dedicated teachers. The program is working hard to develop incentives and post-ACE opportunities that will make staying in teaching even more attractive.

In summary, the ACE M.Ed. program emerged consistent with cutting-edge, reform-minded thinking about teacher education. That the match between ACE and the commission's envisionment was so close did much to energize the ACE M.Ed. designers, especially during the period of time when the program was formally proposed to the campus and the state.

### TEACHERS FOR OUR NATION'S SCHOOLS

John Goodlad's *Teachers for Our Nation's Schools* (1990) was prominent in the thinking of many teacher education reformers in the middle 1990s, including the shapers of the ACE program. Not surprisingly, the ACE M.Ed. program had many of the characteristics favored in Goodlad's analysis:

- The proponents of the ACE program did much to cultivate the support of the central administration of Notre Dame, obtaining substantial commitment from the campus before proceeding forward with proposals to institutionalize the program.
- Groups of regular and clinical faculty who saw teacher education as a high priority were identified and organized.
- The program recruited participants with high literacy and critical thinking skills.

- The participants do a lot of actual teaching in real school settings as part of their program.
- The participants are immersed in the communities they serve, with opportunities to interact with diverse parents.
- Much reflection on practice is required as part of the program.
- Post-graduate opportunities facilitate the transition from the two-year ACE experience to other opportunities to teach and serve as educators.
- The program demands that the participants meet high professional standards rather than amass credits.

In short, the ACE M.Ed. program was intended to be consistent with the kind of alternative teacher training envisioned by Goodlad (1990).

All of the intellectual directions considered in this section were prominent in the thinking of Notre Dame administrators and faculty as they thought through the ACE program, with these diverse influences making clear that much academic reflection is required for developing a modern teacher education effort. The ACE approach, however, required more than academic conceptualization, for it also had spiritual and community pillars, dimensions not typical in teacher education.


## SPIRITUAL INFLUENCES ON ACE

ALTHOUGH IT WAS APPARENT from the earliest thinking about ACE that asking ACErs to follow Christ Teacher made sense, it took a while to flesh out exactly how that could be translated into the program. Similarly, although it made sense from the outset that the ideas in the *Catechism of the Catholic Church* should be incorporated into the program, the role of the *Catechism* in the program is evolving. As the ACE theological and faculty leadership reflected on the program, an important Catholic philosophy of education was published by Thomas Groome, *Educating for Life: A Spiritual Vision for Every Teacher and Parent* (1998). This work provided a further influence for shaping the spiritual dimension of the ACE program.


### CHRIST TEACHER

After completing one year of teaching in the ACE program (i.e., the first year of a two-year commitment to service in Catholic schools) and the second summer of coursework, each ACE participant receives a Christ Teacher medal. It portrays in miniature a piece of artwork by Ivan Mestrovic, who was the University of Notre Dame's artist in residence for several decades, resulting in many beautiful sculptures around the ND campus. Such an award is fitting since the title of teacher (i.e., rabbi) is the most frequent way of describing Jesus in the New Testament. On various occasions during their two years of teaching and participating in the program, ACE students are reminded that an overarching goal is for them to teach as Jesus taught, consistent with a perspective the Catholic Church holds with respect to all teachers working in Catholic settings (e.g., National Council of Catholic Bishops, 1972).

The founding leadership has a concrete reminder of this commitment on the campus (Scully, 1996). The ACE office is on the university's south quad. At the east end of that quad is O'Shaughnessy Hall, with an Ivan Mestrovic statue in front of it, *The Woman at the Well*, which depicts Jesus talking with the Samaritan woman (John 4:4–42). This is a dramatic teaching moment (see Galache, 1997, for an analysis, which informed what follows here). At first, the woman is mistrustful of Jesus, pondering why Jesus, a Jew, would ask her, a Samaritan woman, for a drink. The woman is also completely materialistic at the beginning of her conversation with Jesus, thinking that water, including the living water mentioned by Jesus, could only be obtained with a bucket, and Jesus, who is sitting on the edge of the well in the Mestrovic portrayal, clearly has no bucket. The Samaritan woman is also aggressive, challenging whether Jesus believes that he is greater than Jacob. She is selfish, demanding the living water from Jesus so that she will not have to come to the well again. But as the conversation with Jesus continues, the Samaritan woman changes. She comes to recognize that Jesus is a prophet, someone who is aware of everything she has ever done. She comes to believe in Jesus as a result of the conversation, her initial disdain yielding to an understanding of Jesus as Messiah and Savior of the world.

How was Jesus so effective with the woman? For his part, he presented himself in a way with which she could identify. What is so apparent in the Mestrovic statue is that not only is the Samaritan woman exhausted from hauling water, but Jesus is also physically tired as he rests on the edge of the well. Jesus begins the conversation, asking the woman for a drink, a request that Jesus must have realized would open up the pedagogical conversation he wanted to have with her. He gets her interest with reference to the "living water," which begins with the familiar concept of water but also is a bit different from the familiar. Gradually, he leads her to an understanding of living water. Throughout the conversation, he is honest with her, letting her know what he knows about her (e.g., pointing out that she has had five husbands). He responds to points the woman makes; for example, after the woman mentions worshiping on the mountain and in Jerusalem, Jesus makes reference to her comments as he points out that soon she will be worshiping differently. Through such dialogue, Christ succeeds in converting the woman; she is so taken that she leaves the water jar at the well, the jar that had been so much the center of her attention at the beginning of the conversation. The instruction provided by Jesus has gotten her beyond the water in the jar to a higher place.

As the ACE founders and staff encountered this statue, they thought about the need to prepare young teachers who could be powerful pedagogues, engaging children in teaching conversations that would transform their lives. Although no one involved with ACE expected to create teachers who are messiahs, all believed that young teachers could be developed who would shepherd young minds into literacy, numeracy, content competence, and spirituality.

## CATECHISM OF THE CATHOLIC CHURCH

An initial certification teacher education program teaches young people how to teach; it ordinarily does not have as its mission the teaching of content. For example, math methods courses develop knowledge of how to teach mathematics rather than knowledge of mathematics *per se.* Thus, although ACE teachers need to know how to teach religion, it would be expected that there would be little teaching of religion *per se.* Even so, there was a strong expectation that ACE teachers would teach positions consistent with the *Catechism of the Catholic Church,* which, in its most recent edition, is a 900-page volume. There was also a strong expectation that no ACE students would teach positions inconsistent with the *Catechism.*

The more we reflected on the *Catechism,* the more daunting it seemed to develop knowledge of it within a teacher education program. The *Catechism* covers a variety of topics in some depth, such as the meaning of the Profession of Faith, the Sacraments, life as vocation, and the nature of Christian prayer. Still, there was no doubt that these ideas needed to be developed in a program integrating Catholic spirituality with teacher preparation. We would have to think carefully about religious services connected to the program, retreat experiences, and places in courses where academically legitimate connections could be made to religious ideas.

At the time of this writing, ACE students begin their program of studies by reading a brief version of the *Catechism*. For many, this is only a reminder; for some, it probably is informative about ideas that were only vaguely understood previously. This provides background for understanding the many religious services and symbolic events that occur in the program, as well as for understanding religious experiences encountered in the Catholic schools served by the ACErs.

In addition, because of the community emphasis in the program, we wanted faculty and students to connect broadly, including with respect to religious ideas. This was challenging because not all faculty serving the program would be Catholic, and even those who were Catholic had little to no experience connecting their academic roles with Catholic thinking. The decision was to offer as much of the religious experiences of the program to faculty as they desired, doing everything possible to make such activities inviting. At the time of this writing, almost all ACE M.Ed. faculty participate in many of the religious activities of the program. Beginning with the summer 2001 ACE experience, any faculty member who wishes a copy of the briefer *Catechism* will be provided one free of charge.

Although it was hard to know exactly where to place the *Catechism* in the ACE experience, it seems to be finding its place and is a welcomed presence. An anecdote from summer 2000 comes to mind. As two ACErs took turns driving from Notre Dame to California, they also took turns reading aloud from the *Catechism*, reflecting on how the ideas in it might inform their teaching in the upcoming school year.

EDUCATING FOR LIFE

Although there is much philosophy, and even philosophy of Catholic education (e.g., Losito, 2000; Maritain, 1943), that people could reflect on when designing a teacher education program, one philosopher caught the attention of the creators of ACE more than any other. Thomas Groome (1981, 1996, 1998), a professor at Boston College, is one of the most visible and cited of contemporary philosophers of Catholic K–12 education. Michael Pressley, in particular, found himself reflecting often on Groome's thinking over the years of shaping the ACE M.Ed. program.

Groome's first major volume on the philosophy of Christian religious education (Groome, 1981) was an ambitious book, covering a variety of heady topics. For instance, a substantial proportion of the book was concerned with the purpose of religious education, about how education should promote the Kingdom of God, Christian faith, and human freedom. There was consideration of the social contexts of Christian education and a casting of religious education as a form of socialization. Groome argued extensively in the book that much of Christian education should take place through shared praxis, which is as "a group of Christians sharing in dialogue their critical reflection on present action in light of the Christian Story and its Vision toward the end of lived Christian faith" (p. 185). According to Groome (1981), much of faith develops through discussion with other Christians, discussions focusing on difficult issues.

In developing his perspective, Groome was influenced by developmental psychological thinking, particularly that of Piaget and Kohlberg, who believed that moral understanding increased by people dialoguing and critically reflecting on moral actions. Kohlberg especially believed that such reflections at their best were very much affected by certain universal moral principles (e.g., respect for life, civil liberties), much as Groome argued that shared praxis involves bringing the Christian perspective to bear on issues.

Groome (1981) concluded that all members of the Church are religious educators, that all members of the Church should be reflecting with one another over important issues in light of Christian understandings and positions. Groome expanded his inclusive vision of Catholic religious education in *Educating for Life: A Spiritual Vision for Every Teacher and Parent* (1998). The designers of the ACE program saw in this book a set of principles that we hoped ACE students would use in their roles as teachers.

Groome's purpose in writing *Educating for Life was* "articulating what amounts to both a philosophy of Catholic education and a 'Catholic' philosophy for educators—teachers and parents—regardless of their religious background or affiliation or, indeed, the social context of their educating" (Groome, 1998, p. 11). That is, Groome was trying to reach out to Catholic educators in particular, although he also believed that the Catholic perspectives he espoused would make sense for public school teachers, teachers in non-Catholic private schools, and many, many parents. In reading the book, we found ourselves in agreement. We found that the book did welcome everyone into his vision of Catholic education, which was Groome's intent.

At the heart of Groome's book are eight characteristics of Catholic Christianity that are relevant to a Catholic philosophy of education:

- Catholic Christianity has a positive anthropology. People are basically good, in God's own image.
- Ordinary and everyday life is sacramental. God can be seen in all things.
- Community is important. People are made for each other. We are each other's keeper. Teachers and parents need to commit to the common good, and when they do, they commit to the good of individual students.
- History and tradition are important, including Scriptures and Christian traditions followed by previous generations. This calls for broad education in the arts and sciences.
- Catholicism favors wisdom and reflection that encourage responsible decisions in life. In contemporary society, this includes the wisdom that comes from engaging individuals as whole people and engaging and including all people and the entire community in important discussions and reflections.
- Spirituality is important. People should seek holiness in life. Spirituality does much to promote the development and education of people.
- Faith demands justice, and emphatically, social justice; it also demands peace. Catholic social teaching is important (e.g., teaching students to honor the sacredness and dignity of people; teaching students the importance of contributing to the common good).
- Catholicity is a welcoming tradition. Students should be taught to care for everyone, work for the welfare of all, be open to all knowledge and wisdom, be in solidarity with all humankind, cherish roots, but reach out to all, and take initiative to care for others without borders (i.e., care for those outside one's own community).

Groome's philosophy is that education should encourage the building of community, welcome diversity, foster human dignity, nurture character, encourage justice, provide opportunities for service and care of others, encourage open and thoughtful and moral reflection, stimulate imagination, and provide for moral and spiritual foundation.

The spirituality pillar of the ACE program was informed by diverse inputs, from ones representing the doctrinaire Church to those representing more liberal thought. That diverse spiritual influences are required in such a program is apparent by reflecting on the spiritual practices that ACErs undertake voluntarily. Some pray the rosary and others attend Taize prayer services. Although many attend the folk choir Masses during the summer sessions, others prefer to attend the more traditional Sunday Mass at 10 A.M. in Notre Dame's basilica. Although the spirituality pervasive in ACE is a Catholic spirituality, there is diversity in the universality that is the Catholic Church, a diversity that is reflected in the ACErs and informs the program.

## COMMUNITY EMPHASES IN ACE

CENTRAL TO THE MISSION of ACE is the belief that schools should be communities of learners. When a school is a community, teachers and students understand better their commitments to one another. They understand better how to look after, care for, and promote each other. Thus, every aspect of the ACE M.Ed. program is permeated with the theme of community and the goal that graduates will leave the program committed to developing classrooms and schools that are communities of learners.

### SUMMER EXPERIENCE OF COMMUNITY

The role of community is developed in several ways within the ACE M.Ed. program. During the summer sessions, all the participants reside in the university dorms at university expense. Here they work and worship in supportive groups. They have e-mail for easy contact throughout the summer with faculty and staff. The university supports the faculty as part of this community by furnishing graduate apartments free of charge to national faculty members, and by providing meal tickets to the ACE staff and M.Ed. summer faculty, including the clinical faculty from the South Bend area schools, to encourage them to eat with the students. Faculty and students alike become a true community of learners (Goodlad, 1990).

### ACE M.ED. CURRICULUM AND COMMUNITY

Explicit attempts are made to immerse ACE participants in communities of learners as they take courses. First-summer students take two of their three courses with the same group of classmates, with about 25 students in a class group. Aspiring elementary teachers have their own section of Introduction to Teaching and also enroll in Introduction to Reading and Writing Instruction. Aspiring middle school teachers have their own section of Introduction to Teaching and also enroll in Introduction to Middle School Teaching. Aspiring high school teachers have their own section of Introduction to Teaching and also enroll in Introduction to High School Teaching. The instructors in these paired courses work closely together to find linkages between the courses, with a great deal of across-course communication. Professors in the paired courses encourage students to cooperate as they complete assignments and do the coursework. The two faculty and 25 students do all possible to be community members, cooperating to enhance each individual participant's experiences in the courses. Similarly, the human development and exceptionality courses for second-summer participants are linked, with one community focusing on elementary education, one on middle school teaching, and one on high school teaching.

ACE did not invent this community of learners model. The community linking of courses has a long history of successful implementation (e.g., Meiklejohn, 1932). This ACE M.Ed. approach to building communities of learners also is informed by a number of contemporary implementations of the community of learners model (e.g., Cross, 1998; Gabelnick, MacGregor, Matthews, & Smith, 1990; Palmer, 1997; Tinto, 1997a, 1997b; Tinto, Russo, & Kadel, 1994).

## LIVING IN CHRISTIAN COMMUNITY

Participants in ACE live in small communities of four to seven teachers. There are a number of reasons for doing so. An obvious one is economics. The participants are receiving very small stipends. By living together and pooling resources, they can afford a larger and more comfortable accommodation than they would be able to afford if each paid for her or his own housing. A second is that by living together, ACE participants can provide support for one another, for service can be very challenging (Stanton et al., 1999, ch. 9), especially beginning teaching (e.g., Dollase, 1992; Kane, 1991; Roehrig, Pressley, & Talotta, 2002; Ryan, 1970; Ryan et al., 1980).

A third reason for participants living together is to foster development of each other's spirituality through living in a small Christian community. Small, spiritually committed communities and support groups have been the subject of research (e.g., Pelton, 1997; Vandenakker, 1994; Wuthnow, 1994). Most of these groups do not involve the participants living together. There have been some analyses of how small, intentional, spiritually oriented groups work well (e.g., Wuthnow, 1994, chs. 5–6): small-group members often feel better about themselves, become more open and honest in their interpersonal communications, become more honest with themselves, develop a deeper love for other people, develop their abilities to forgive others and themselves, learn a great deal about how to serve others outside the group, deepen faith and religious commitment (e.g., feel closer to God, experience the Bible as more meaningful), better understand others' religious perspectives, learn how to share their faith with individuals outside the group, believe that more of their prayers are answered, and experience healed relationships with others.

Even so, the ACE faculty and staff worried about the functioning of ACE houses, for Wuthnow (1994, ch. 7) also documented problems within small communities. There can be disagreements between group members. Some members make little time for the group. Some members make others feel uncomfortable. In fact, the many potential problems cited by Wuthnow had a familiar ring to the ACE faculty and staff. Many of them had been experienced by at least one of the ACE houses during the early years of the ACE teacher education program.

On the other hand, the potential benefits of a small Christian community were ones that the ACE faculty and staff wanted for ACE participants. Wuthnow (1994, ch. 9) and others (Sofield, Hammett, & Juliano, 1998) have made progress in identifying activities that increase the positive functioning of small intentional groups. In fact, a lot can be learned about conflict management, forgiveness, communal decision making, faith sharing, intimacy, listening, and emotion management. Members of the ACE staff thought long and hard about just which of these functions could be developed in ACE participants, given the time and resource constraints. ACE faculty and staff are concerned to find the ways that will enable ACE houses to be constructive communities that foster the growth of the individuals in them.

In addition, the faculty, in particular, hoped that the experience in small intentional communities would affect positively an ACE participant's teaching, both in the short term and long term. A goal of the program is to understand the effect on a teacher's teaching if she or he has participated in an intense, spiritually focused, small-group living situation.

## SCHOOL AND LOCAL COMMUNITY

Emphasis on community stresses the power of participation in the school and local community (Bryk et al., 1993). We want ACE teachers and their students to look for ways in which their classroom community can strengthen service to their broader community, both school and local, through service learning projects or individual efforts.

The experience of and awareness of community is great in ACE. It begins with meeting and living with the members of one's ACE cohort. It continues as ACErs live and work with one another and with faculty at Notre Dame in the summers. Much of this is in preparation to live in community at the ACE sites and to develop classroom and school communities. The creators of this program wanted such a thorough community experience in order to develop graduates who have internalized commitment to community in their souls, who have come to believe that excellent educators habitually foster the common good as they live and work.

## PROGRAM UNITY

ACE IS AN EXPERIENCE that has been thought out from beginning to end. Although the various academic, spiritual, and community inputs at times could seem at odds, they have coalesced. The result is a program with unity. The academic program is increasingly spiritual and focusing on ideas about how community can be fostered; the academics and ACE teachers serving the program are intensely spiritual together; community members support each other's development as teachers and spiritual beings.

As this program developed, we became aware of many other alternative approaches to teacher education. As we did so, we came to believe that the work we are doing at Notre Dame is very cutting edge, an experimental mix of some of the best ideas in contemporary teacher education. For example, Alan R. Tom (1997) suggested five principles of conceptual design for teacher education. We are very respectful of all of them:

1. Our faculty are models for the ACE students (e.g., in cooperative learning experiences in summer classes and in Internet seminars) as they participate in the greater ACE community, including its spirituality.

2. The ACE M.Ed. experience is saturated with moral dimensions.
3. The ACE M.Ed. classes emphasize the development of pedagogical knowledge as a young teacher actually teaches. This is
   much more a constructivist approach to teacher education than
   a knowledge transmission approach.
4. With two years of teaching in the southern United States, ACE
   participants have rich multicultural experiences, complemented
   by much reflection about multiculturalism both in the formal
   curriculum of the program and during informal events (e.g., multicultural nights during the summer session).
5. The program constantly reflects on itself and renews.

   Tom (1997) also offered six structural principles. The ACE M.Ed.
program is generally consistent with the structuring reforms called for
by Tom:

6. Our academic coursework is compressed, occurring close in time
   when ACE participants will actually teach.
7. From day one in the program, we emphasize that ACE participants should not think about teaching as the way they were
   taught; rather, we emphasize best teaching practices as documented in research.
8. That ACE participants teach beginning with their first summer
   in the program provides great opportunity to integrate the theory and research covered in classes with actual teaching. The faculty are determined to do all possible to achieve such integration.
9. The full-time faculty play many roles in the program, rather than
   only offering courses in their particular areas of expertise.
10. The ACE participants go through the program in cohorts, so the
    experience is not isolated, as occurs in many conventional teacher
    education efforts.
11. Because the ACE M.Ed. program involves two years of actual
    teaching, we work with the students well into the early part of
    their career.

In short, the ACE M.Ed. program is consistent with Tom's envisionment of a principled and well-structured approach to teacher education.
   For many of us connected with the ACE experience, it seemed at
first an academic, spiritual, and community vortex. The more time we
spent in the vortex, however, the more we saw the pattern in the whirl
and the connectedness of the parts of this experience, the more we

saw the lovely orderliness to living as teachers who are developing academically, spiritually, and as community members. By the time you conclude this book, we hope you are convinced that both those who are ACE teachers and those who are ACE teacher educators grow as they participate in such a richly conceived program.

## REFERENCES

Bruning, R. H., Schraw, G. J., & Ronning, R. R. (1993). *Cognitive psychology and instruction.* Englewood Cliffs, NJ: Prentice-Hall.

Bryk, A. S. (1996). Lessons from Catholic high schools on renewing our educational institutions. In J. O'Keefe & B. O'Keeffe (Eds.), *The contemporary Catholic school: Content, identity, and diversity* (pp. 25–41). London: Falmer Press.

Bryk, A. S., Lee, V., & Holland, P. (1993). *Catholic schools and the common good.* Cambridge, MA: Harvard University Press.

Coleman, J. S., & Hoffer, T. (1987). *Public and private schools: The impact of communities.* New York: Basic Books.

Coleman, J. S., Hoffer, T., & Kilgore, S. (1982). *High school achievement.* New York: Basic Books.

Convey, J. J. (2000). Views of bishops and priests concerning Catholic schools: A ten-year perspective. In J. Youniss, J. J. Convey, & J. A. McLellan (Eds.), *The Catholic character of Catholic schools* (pp. 14–37). Notre Dame, IN: University of Notre Dame Press.

Cross, K. P. (1998, July–August). Why learning communities? Why now? *About Campus,* 4–11.

Dollase, R. H. (1992). *Voices of beginning teachers: Visions and realities.* New York: Teachers College Press.

Dreeben, R. (2000). Structural effects in education: A history of an idea. In M. T. Hallinan (Ed.), *Handbook of the sociology of education* (pp. 107–135). New York: Kluwer/Plenum.

Enright, R. D., & Fitzgibbons, R. P. (2000). *Helping clients forgive: An empirical guide for resolving anger and restoring hope.* Washington, DC: American Psychological Association.

Eyler, J., & Giles, D. E., Jr. (1999). *Where's the learning in service-learning?* San Francisco: Jossey-Bass.

Gabelnick, F., MacGregor, J., Matthews, R. S., & Smith, B. L. (1990). *Learning communities: Creating communities among students, faculty, and disciplines.* San Francisco: Jossey-Bass.

Gagné, E. D., Yekovich, C. W., & Yekovich, F. R. (1993). *The cognitive psychology of school learning.* New York: Addison-Wesley.

Galache, G. (1997). *Praying body and soul: Methods and practices of Anthony De Mello.* New York: Crossroad.

Galetto, P. (2000). Religious knowledge and belief of lay religion teachers in Catholic elementary schools. In J. Youniss, J. J. Convey, & J. A. McLellan (Eds.), *The Catholic character of Catholic schools* (pp. 124–141). Notre Dame, IN: University of Notre Dame Press.

Goodlad, J. I. (1990). *Teachers for our nation's schools.* San Francisco: Jossey-Bass.

Groome, T. H. (1981). *Christian religious education: Sharing our story and vision.* New York: Harper & Row.

Groome, T. H. (1996). What makes a school Catholic? In J. O'Keefe & B. O'Keeffe (Eds.), *The contemporary Catholic school: Content, identity, and diversity* (pp. 107–125). London: Falmer Press.

Groome, T. H. (1998). *Educating for life: A spiritual vision for every teacher and parent.* Allen, TX: Thomas More.

Harris, J. C. (2000). The funding dilemma facing Catholic elementary and secondary schools. In J. Youniss & J. J. Convey (Eds.), *Catholic schools at the crossroads* (pp. 55–71). New York: Teachers College Press.

Hoffer, T. B. (2000). Catholic school attendance and student achievement: A review and extension of research. In J. Youniss & J. J. Convey (Eds.), *Catholic schools at the crossroads* (pp. 87–112). New York: Teachers College Press.

Hoose, P. (1993). *It's our world, too!* Boston: Little, Brown.

Hunt, T. C., Oldenski, T. E., & Wallace, T. J. (2000). *Catholic school leadership: An invitation to lead.* London: Falmer Press.

Irvine, J. J., & Foster, M. (1996). *Growing up African American in Catholic schools.* New York: Teachers College Press.

Kane, P. R. (1991). *The first year of teaching: Real world stories from America's teachers.* New York: Walker.

Kohlberg, L. (1969). Stage and sequence: The cognitive-developmental approach to socialization. In D. Goslin (Ed.), *Handbook of socialization theory and research.* New York: Rand-McNally.

Kohlberg, L. (1981). *The philosophy of moral development: Moral stages and the idea of justice: Essays on moral development.* San Francisco: Harper & Row.

Kohlberg, L. (1984). *The psychology of moral development: Essays on moral development.* San Francisco: Harper & Row.

Lapsley, D. K. (1996). *Moral psychology.* Boulder, CO: Westview Press.

Lawrence, S. (2000). "New" immigrants in the Catholic schools: A preliminary assessment. In J. Youniss & J. J. Convey (Eds.), *Catholic schools at the crossroads* (pp. 178–200). New York: Teachers College Press.

Lee, V. E., & Bryk, A. S. (1989). A multilevel model of the social distribution of high school achievement. *Sociology of Education, 62,* 172–192.

Lewis, B. A. (1995). *The kid's guide to service projects: Over 500 service ideas for young people who want to make a difference.* Minneapolis: Free Spirit Publishing.

Lewis, B. A. (1997). *The kid's guide to social action.* Minneapolis: Free Spirit Publishing.

Lickona, T. (Ed.). (1976). *Moral development and behavior.* New York: Holt, Rinehart, & Winston.

Lickona, T. (1991). *Educating for character: How our schools can teach respect and responsibility.* New York: Bantam Books.

Losito, W. F. (2000). Reclaiming inquiry in the Catholic philosophy of education. In T. C. Hunt, T. E. Oldenski, & T. J. Wallace (Eds.), *Catholic school leadership: An invitation to lead* (pp. 59–68). London: Falmer Press.

Maritain, J. (1943). *Education at the crossroads.* New Haven, CT: Yale University Press.

McClelland, V. A. (1996). Wholeness, faith, and the distinctiveness of the Catholic school. In J. O'Keefe & B. O'Keeffe (Eds.), *The contemporary Catholic school: Content, identity, and diversity* (pp. 155–173). London: Falmer Press.

McLaughlin, T. H. (1996). The distinctiveness of Catholic education. In J. O'Keefe & B. O'Keeffe (Eds.), *The contemporary Catholic school: Content, identity, and diversity* (pp. 136–154). London: Falmer Press.

McLellan, J. A. (2000). Rise, fall, and reasons why: U.S. Catholic elementary education, 1940–1995. In J. Youniss & J. J. Convey (Eds.), *Catholic schools at the crossroads* (pp. 17–32). New York: Teachers College Press.

Meagher, T. (2000). Ethnic, Catholic, white: Changes in the identity of European American Catholics. In J. Youniss, J. J. Convey, & J. A. McLellan (Eds.), *The Catholic character of Catholic schools* (pp. 190–218). Notre Dame, IN: University of Notre Dame Press.

Meiklejohn, A. (1932). *The experimental college.* New York: Harper & Row.

Mueller, F. C. (2000). Sponsorship of Catholic schools: Preserving the tradition. In J. Youniss, J. J. Convey, & J. A. McLellan (Eds.), *The Catholic character of Catholic schools* (pp. 38–61). Notre Dame, IN: University of Notre Dame Press.

National Center for Education Statistics. (1982). *High school and beyond.* Washington, DC: Author.

National Council of Catholic Bishops. (1972). *To teach as Jesus did.* Washington, DC: Author.

Nelson, S. M. (2000). Black Catholic high schools in inner-city Chicago: Forging a path to the future. In J. Youniss & J. J. Convey (Eds.), *Catholic schools at the crossroads* (pp. 157–177). New York: Teachers College Press.

O'Keefe, J. (1996). No margin, no mission. In J. O'Keefe & B. O'Keeffe (Eds.), *The contemporary Catholic school: Content, identity, and diversity* (pp. 177–197). London: Falmer Press.

O'Keefe, J. (2000). Leadership in urban Catholic elementary schools: The reality and the challenge. In T. C. Hunt, T. E. Oldenski, & T. J. Wallace

(Eds.), *Catholic school leadership: An invitation to lead* (pp. 225–243). London: Falmer Press.

O'Keefe, J. M., & Murphy, J. (2000). Ethnically diverse Catholic schools: School structure, students, staffing, and finance. In J. Youniss & J. J. Convey (Eds.), *Catholic schools at the crossroads* (pp. 117–136). New York: Teachers College Press.

O'Keefe, J., & O'Keeffe, B. (1996). *The contemporary Catholic school.* London: Falmer Press.

Palmer, P. J. (1997, November–December). Teaching and learning in community. *About Campus,* 4–12.

Pelton, R. S. (1997). *Small Christian communities: Imagining future church.* Notre Dame, IN: University of Notre Dame Press.

Persell, C. H. (2000). Values, control, and outcomes in public and private schools. In M. T. Hallinan (Ed.), *Handbook of the sociology of education* (pp. 387–407). New York: Kluwer/Plenum.

Polite, P. C. (2000). Cornerstones: Catholic high schools that serve predominantly African American student populations. In J. Youniss & J. J. Convey (Eds.), *Catholic schools at the crossroads* (pp. 137–156). New York: Teachers College Press.

Power, F. C., Higgins, A., & Kohlberg, L. (1989). *Lawrence Kohlberg's approach to moral education.* New York: Columbia University Press.

Pressley, M., with McCormick, C. B. (1995). *Advanced educational psychology for educators, researchers, and policymakers.* New York: HarperCollins.

Rhoads, R. A., & Howard, J. P. F. (Eds.). (1998). *Academic service learning: A pedagogy of action and reflection* (*New Directions for Teaching and Learning, 73*). San Francisco: Jossey-Bass.

Riordan, C. (2000). Trends in student demography in Catholic secondary schools, 1972–1992. In J. Youniss & J. J. Convey (Eds.), *Catholic schools at the crossroads* (pp. 33–54). New York: Teachers College Press.

Ristau, K., & Reif, M. (2000). Preparing for the journey: Teachers for Catholic schools. In T. C. Hunt, T. E. Oldenski, & T. J. Wallace (Eds.), *Catholic school leadership: An invitation to lead* (pp. 129–140). London: Falmer Press.

Roehrig, A., Pressley, M., & Talotta, D. (2002). *The challenges of beginning teaching.* Notre Dame, IN: University of Notre Dame Press.

Ryan, K. (1970). *Don't smile until Christmas: Accounts of the first year of teaching.* Chicago: University of Chicago Press.

Ryan, K., Newman, K., Mager, G., Applegate, J., Lasley, T., Flora, R., & Johnston, J. (1980). *Biting the apple: Accounts of first year teachers.* New York: Longman.

Schaub, M. (2000). A faculty at the crossroads: A profile of American Catholic school teachers. In J. Youniss & J. J. Convey (Eds.), *Catholic schools at the crossroads* (pp. 72–86). New York: Teachers College Press.

Scully, T. R. (1996). We drink from our own wells. In M. L. Poorman (Ed.),

*Labors from the Heart: Mission and Ministry in a Catholic University* (pp. 209–220). Notre Dame, IN: University of Notre Dame Press.

Shields, D. L. L., & Bredemeier, B. J. L. (1995). *Character development and physical activity.* Champaign, IL: Human Kinetics.

Sofield, L., Hammett, R., & Juliano, C. (1998). *Building community: Christian, caring, vital.* Notre Dame, IN: Ave Maria Press.

Sørensen, A. B. (1996). Educational opportunities and school effects. In J. Clark (Ed.), *James S. Coleman* (pp. 207–225). London: Falmer Press.

Sørensen, A. B., & Morgan, S. L. (2000). School effects: Theoretical and methodological issues. In M. T. Hallinan (Ed.), *Handbook of the sociology of education* (pp. 137–160). New York: Kluwer/Plenum.

Stanton, T. K., Giles, D. E., Jr., & Cruz, N. I. (1999). *Service learning: A movement's pioneers reflect on its origins, practice, and future.* San Francisco: Jossey-Bass.

Tinto, V. (1997a, November–December). Classrooms as communities: Exploring the educational character of student persistence. *Journal of Higher Education, 68,* 599–623.

Tinto, V. (1997b, January–February). Universities as learning organizations. *About Campus,* 2–4.

Tinto, V., Russo, P., & Kadel, S. (1994, February–March). Constructing education: Increasing retention in challenging circumstances. *AACC Journal,* 27–29.

Tom, A. R. (1997). *Redesigning teacher education.* Albany: State University of New York Press.

Traviss, M. P. (2000). Preparation of teachers for the Catholic schools. In T. C. Hunt, T. E. Oldenski, & T. J. Wallace (Eds.), *Catholic school leadership: An invitation to lead* (pp. 141–156). London: Falmer Press.

Vandenakker, J. P. (1994). *Small Christian communities and the parish.* Kansas City, MO: Sheed & Ward.

Vygotsky, L. S. (1978). *Mind in society: The development of higher psychological processes.* Cambridge, MA: MIT Press.

Wade, R. C. (Ed.). (1997). *Community service-learning: A guide to including service in the public school curriculum.* Albany: State University of New York Press.

Walch, T. (2000). The past before us: Three traditions and the recent history of Catholic education. In J. Youniss, J. J. Convey, & J. A. McLellan (Eds.), *The Catholic character of Catholic schools* (pp. 176–189). Notre Dame, IN: University of Notre Dame Press.

Wood, S. S., Bruner, J. S., & Ross, G. (1976). The role of tutoring in problem solving. *Journal of Child Psychology and Psychiatry, 17,* 89–100.

Wuthnow, R. (1994). *Sharing the journey: Support groups and America's new quest for community.* New York: Free Press.

Youniss, J., & Convey, J. J. (Eds.). (2000). *Catholic schools at the crossroads: Survival and transformation.* New York: Teachers College Press.

Youniss, J., Convey, J. J., & McLellan, J. A. (Eds.). (2000). *The Catholic character of Catholic schools.* Notre Dame, IN: University of Notre Dame Press.

Youniss, J., & Yates, M. (1997). *Community service and social responsibility in youth.* Chicago: University of Chicago Press.

JOHN WATZKE
PATRICK DAUNT
RACHEL MORENO

# 6

# Field Supervision of ACE Teachers

This chapter will provide a description of the field supervisory model employed by the ACE program and its implementation. Field supervision is an integral part of the support provided to ACE teachers as they work in under-resourced Catholic schools in the southern United States. The two years of service in the program can be viewed as a two-year internship, albeit a demanding one, involving full-time teaching responsibilities during the school year. Consistent with the model of Christ Teacher, ACE teachers also are supportive members of their Christian community, both at home and in their professional activities.

The literature on learning to teach within a service-based model such as the ACE M.Ed. program is limited. Sources that summarize the research base in teacher development focus on four main settings: preservice teachers in practicum settings; preservice teachers in student teaching experiences; preservice teachers in professional development schools; inservice teachers during their first years of teaching (Dadlez, 2000; Feiman-Nemser & Remillard, 1996; Gold, 1996; Murray, 1996; Sikula, 1996; Wideen, Mayer-Smith, & Moon, 1998). The ACE program is unique in that it incorporates elements of traditional teacher education programs into a two-year, full-time teaching experience. Teacher development does not take place in a preparatory program or follow the completion of such a program. It is situated in the experience of teaching. This presents challenges to the supervision of ACE teachers that are not yet fully addressed in the professional literature.

Initial supervision of ACErs begins during their first summer session as they complete a practicum experience. This teaching practicum, combined with education coursework completed in the first summer, addresses initial teacher concerns of orientation to the profession of teaching, issues of classroom management, and emerging skills in the delivery of instruction (McDonald & Elias, 1980; Veenman, 1984). As the ACErs begin their first year of full-time teaching, field supervision supports these teachers as they struggle with issues of *self-survival* and the *teaching task* (Berliner, 1988; Burden, 1981; Carter, 1990; Fuller, 1969; Kagan, 1992; Katz, 1972; Odell, 1986). Beginning teachers initially tend to focus on self-survival: surviving in the classroom, receiving good evaluations by administrators, being accepted by peers, and feeling adequate in day-to-day teaching. This early focus on self-survival gradually shifts to a focus on the teaching task: the teaching situation (e.g., duties, materials, number of students), effective methods of instruction, and adequate delivery of instruction to meet learning objectives.

As the ACErs transition into their second year of teaching, supervision begins to focus on the teachers' increasing ability to recognize their own professional growth and the impact of their teaching on students' lives (Reeves & Kazelskis, 1985). This impact derives from the teachers' increasing awareness of diverse student needs and the ability to adapt the delivery of instruction to meet these needs.

Supervision in this programmatic model takes on a broader spectrum of teacher development than in traditional preparatory programs. The ACEr is quite literally both student and teacher. The ACE program's long-term collaborative support for teacher development models lifelong professional development. This is at the heart of best practices in teacher development (Wideen et al., 1998). The challenge of supervision in ACE is to serve the beginning teacher in preparation for a career in education while meeting the immediate needs of full-time teaching.

## SUPERVISION FOR PREPARATION AND TEACHING

THE SUPERVISION of ACE teachers initially focuses on the preparation for teaching before transitioning to full-time teaching. As early as the April before the first summer session, applicants who have been accepted into the ACE program participate in a weekend retreat designed to introduce them to the three pillars of ACE: professional education, community, and spiritual life. At this retreat, ACErs meet representatives from the various dioceses, schools, and the university staff. It is the beginning of a two-year supervisory process, with principals, mentor teachers, and university supervisors answering questions and providing information to ACErs through a variety of formal and informal activities. Formal supervision serving preparation for teaching continues through the first two-month summer session as ACErs complete a practicum teaching experience in South Bend Catholic and public schools. Supervision of full-time teaching begins in August as the academic school year begins.

## THE FIRST-SUMMER PRACTICUM

Participants are initially prepared for teaching during the first days of the ACE M.Ed. program. Their first week of class is an intense overview of the psychology of teaching, Catholic education in the United States, and basic classroom management. By the third week of the summer session, the ACErs are practicum teaching in South Bend summer schools. The major goal of the summer practicum is to provide each ACE teacher with an opportunity to prepare and teach lessons, and to reflect upon these experiences through guided analysis and supervisory feedback. During this experience, ACErs first receive formative evaluations from university field supervisors, who work with them and observe them during this first summer. In addition, master teachers from the South Bend area assist in supervision, observing, and reflecting with the ACErs about their practicum experiences. The ACErs also receive their first feedback from cooperating teachers during this summer session. The South Bend–based teachers provide much hands-on information about translating theory into practice. The ACErs are explicitly charged to use best practices in their teaching during these initial experiences. The faculty continually emphasize that ACErs need to apply the theory they are learning in their education courses to the real world of teaching.

Each new ACE teacher spends either four or five mornings per week in their practicum schools for five or six weeks, totaling from 50 to 80 hours of contact time with students. These teachers begin the process of reflective teaching by maintaining a daily reflective journal, implementing theories encountered in their summer coursework into their daily lesson planning, completing a reflective video analysis of one of their teaching episodes, and discussing their teaching with their cooperating teachers and the university supervisors.

Schools and programs cooperating in the summer program include three area public and one Catholic high school, one public middle school program, and two public and several Catholic elementary schools. Typically, no more than two ACE teachers are placed in one classroom under the direct supervision of a cooperating teacher. Some of the South Bend programs, especially at the high school level, are purely remedial. Several of these are part of highly sophisticated needs-based programs, which clearly define the areas of study for the pupils. Other South Bend summer programs are loosely defined enrichment programs, with a focus determined solely by the classroom teacher. A few of the programs serve both students who need enrichment and others who need remediation.

During this first summer, the university supervisors get to know the students they will be working with over the next two years. Additionally, the university supervisors make meaningful contacts with South Bend teachers and administrators, share teaching strategies and new information on teaching, and continue to develop their own pedagogical knowledge and skills to serve in supervision. The summer practicum helps to initiate a positive process of teaching, reflection, and supervision as the ACErs are inducted into the reality of teaching in schools. These novice teachers learn that teaching is very hard work, but they also learn, as they interact with their supervisors, that teaching takes place in a community of learners, one in which even the most senior supervisor in the program interacts with other classroom professionals to hone and enlarge skills. Once the summer session concludes, the ACErs prepare to report to their schools in the southern United States.

## The School-Year Program

Many ACErs begin teaching in their assigned schools the first week of August. Working with new teachers after the initial summer practicum is indeed a wonderful experience. They come to their classrooms in the South with a sense of professional ownership, bolstered by the growth they experienced during the summer of teaching in South Bend. For example, the ACErs often refer to students as their kids.

Upon arrival in the South, these new ACE teachers immediately confront how to arrange their new classroom physically, what displays and decorations to put up, and how to make it special. ACE teachers establish an emotional climate in their classrooms that reflects their individual personalities. The ACE teachers strive for success in their teaching from day one; they are motivated toward success and want to motivate their students. They are totally committed, although they also are immediately confronted with innumerable challenges, requiring many decisions by them.

Second-year teachers return to their schools informed by their first year of teaching and a summer of reflection on that first year. In many cases, dramatic breakthroughs occur during the second summer session, which are translated during the second year of teaching. There is a renewed commitment to best practices. Second-year ACErs regularly write in their journals about the enormous differences between their first and second years of full-time teaching, with commentary overwhelming that the second year of teaching is better.

## TRI-LEVEL MODEL OF SUPERVISION

A NUMBER OF ISSUES complicate supervision during the two years of full-time teaching ACErs complete during the program. In traditional teacher education programs, the university supervisor visits student teachers numerous times during a semester, with additional face-to-face contact coming from simultaneous coursework completed on campus. The distance nature of the ACE M.Ed. program has resulted in the development of a tri-level model of supervision designed to capitalize on the regular contact ACErs have with professional educators: the mentor teacher, the clinical supervisor (building administrator), the university supervisor.

### THE MENTOR TEACHER

The mentor teacher typically selected by the school principal or other appropriate administrator is a model veteran educator who exemplifies the attributes of a master teacher and often has graduate-level preparation in supervision, curriculum, or instruction. The mentor helps the ACE teacher to understand the philosophies, goals, policies, and needs of the local school, introducing the ACE teacher to the culture of the school and community. In an effective mentoring relationship, the mentor and ACE teacher develop a strong collaborative rapport. This permits the mentor to offer constructive criticism and guidance on classroom management, teaching strategies, planning, and continued professional growth. Ideally, such a trusting, positive relationship continues through the second year of the internship. The best mentors are attentive listeners and focused questioners.

Gentle advice and guidance from the mentor can help the ACE teacher avoid some of the early and common pitfalls of beginning teaching. Thus, the mentor teachers are especially asked to spend some time observing the ACErs teach at the start of the school year, then conferencing with them, providing written commentary on what has been observed. Each mentor is asked to complete at least two formal observations of the ACE teacher each semester during the two years. It is recommended that the first observation take place during the first month or two of teaching. The mentor is provided with observation report instruments that reflect the principles of the Interstate New Teacher Assessment and Support Consortium (INTASC). The INTASC principles are endorsed by most states and are the core professional standards for the ACE M.Ed. program. These observation reports are sent to the university supervisor according to a prearranged schedule.

Ideally, the first formal mentor-teacher observation follows several shorter, drop-by, visits to the ACE teacher's classes. Mentor teachers are asked to help the ACE teacher in learning how to use curriculum guidelines, grade-level competencies, planning books, grade books, and school and local resources. These initial visits are an ideal time to make sure the new ACE teacher is on track in these areas. Many mentors have found that these early visits are best facilitated by short notes to the ACE teacher commenting on the positives and, if needed, a few well-stated questions. A few mentors have developed a shared steno notebook for comments and questions. This collaborative notebook is passed back and forth between the mentor and ACE teacher, allowing each to write comments and questions.

Additionally, mentors also assist ACE teachers by identifying other teachers they might observe. Some mentors arrange for the ACE teacher's classes to be covered so that the ACEr can observe several teachers. The ACE program requires that first-year ACE teachers observe at least two other teachers during their second semester of teaching.

Mentors are provided with assistance and support from the local school administrator and the university supervisor. Appropriate observation strategies, forms, and mentoring approaches and techniques are shared in consultation with the university coordinator. The mentor is consulted in the evaluation process but is not expected to complete a summative evaluation of the ACE teacher.

In brief, the mentor teacher becomes a trusted supporter of the ACE teacher; models enthusiastic, professional behavior; helps interpret school experiences for the ACE teacher; serves as a sounding board for reflection and growth; provides guidance in the development of classroom management skills; offers assistance in planning; helps interpret curriculum and community expectations; regularly observes the ACE teacher's classes; confers with the ACE teacher at least weekly, but much more often in the beginning; assists in finding teaching resources; helps in orienting the ACE teacher to the school environment; supports the analysis and reflection on teaching by the ACE teacher; is a good listener and source of advice.

## THE CLINICAL SUPERVISOR

The school principal or building administrator fulfills an important role of support to the mentor teacher and ACE teacher in the ACE tri-level model of supervision. On a basic level, the administrator provides support to the ACE teacher as he or she would to any new teacher in the school. Providing the ACE teachers with appropriate policies, handbooks, and curriculum guides and generally orienting them to the school and community are typical forms of support. However, the ACE supervisory model asks that the administrator assume the role of clinical supervisor. This requires that he or she observe and confer regularly with the ACE teacher. Most principals observe and conference with the ACE teacher two or three times each semester.

The clinical supervisor has primary responsibility for completing the summative evaluations of the ACE teacher. Although most administrators have been prepared to supervise teachers, the clinical supervisor is trained in the use of the INTASC standards. This training comes from general question and answer sessions during the April retreat, on-site workshops delivered by the university supervisor, and general experience gained over years of working with ACE teachers.

The clinical supervisor keeps the university supervisor informed of the ACE teacher's progress, monitors the effectiveness of the mentor and ACE teacher relationship, and identifies areas needing the attention of the university supervisor. The university supervisor maintains communication with the clinical supervisor through phone and e-mail contact to arrange school visits and to set up formal times to meet during a site visit.

## Determining ACE Teaching Assignments

Determining the ACE teacher's assignment is one of the most critical decisions made by the building administrator who will directly act as clinical supervisor to the ACE teacher. Several factors need to be considered in this decision. The ACE program strongly recommends that a regular preparation time be built into the ACE teaching assignment. Daily preparation time of 40 to 50 minutes is typical. Principals are asked to limit the number of different preparations to no more than three at the secondary (high school and middle grades) level. If the ACE teacher is teaming or working in a departmentalized setting at the upper elementary level, administrators are asked to try to limit the number of different preparations to three or four.

The ACE program recommends that the new ACE teacher not be assigned extra duties, such as coaching, leading extracurricular teams or groups, or directing special programs, during the first marking period or first few months of teaching. Additional responsibilities can be added as the ACE teacher becomes settled and demonstrates the capability to assume more responsibilities. Administrators are encouraged to involve ACE teachers in the various school community activities but to limit formal or required duties at first so as not to overwhelm them during the first weeks. ACE teachers need time to acclimate to all the expectations of their new profession.

Principals confirm the beginning ACE teacher's assignment in early June, sending the ACE teacher the necessary teacher textbooks, curriculum guides, course outlines, and other instructional materials. Policy handbooks, discipline policy and school rules, and grading scales should also be sent to the ACE teachers early in the first summer. This enables the ACErs to use these documents in their coursework during the first summer and to become familiar with the school and instructional expectations. Ideally, ACE teachers prepare some future lessons and units as part of their summer coursework.

## Selecting a Mentor

The principal selects the mentor for the ACE teacher. The ACE program recommends that mentors have a minimum of three years of teaching experience and hold an advanced degree or specialized training in mentoring. Willingness on the part of the mentor is the first consideration. The ACE program discourages administrators from attempting to serve as mentors. Principals have too many other responsibilities, which naturally interfere with providing appropriate mentoring to the ACE teacher. In addition, principals are expected to evaluate the ACE teacher's progress periodically for both the Notre Dame program and the diocese. The roles of summative assessment and evaluation are incompatible with fulfilling the supportive responsibilities expected of the mentor teacher.

Selecting a teacher who wants to mentor and is capable of working with a beginning teacher requires selecting someone who is willing to spend the extra time needed to counsel, guide, listen, and assist. While it would be logical to have the mentor teaching in the same area (grade or subject), this may not be workable.

Selecting the mentor in the spring, immediately after the ACE teacher has been assigned to the school, permits the ACE teacher and mentor to communicate during the summer. This also permits the mentor to plan for the arrival of the ACE teacher. The first few days at the new school are crucial to the development and future success of the ACE teacher. It is recommended that the mentor be provided with a written description of the expectations of the ACE program well in advance of the ACE teacher's arrival. This includes the *ACE M.Ed. Handbook*, which is sent to each building principal. The ACE program recommends that a planning conference take place between the mentor teacher and principal to design a specific plan of action for introducing the ACE teacher to the school. The principal's guidance, monitoring, and assistance are important here if the ACE teacher is to have a positive beginning, and they are part of the principal's role as the clinical supervisor.

In brief, the clinical supervisor (principal or building administrator) serves as the school-site contact person for the university; assists the ACE teacher in acclimating to the school and community; observes the ACE teacher; conferences with the ACE teacher; monitors and supports the mentor teacher; completes the university summative evaluation each semester; and communicates with the university coordinator as needed.

### THE UNIVERSITY SUPERVISOR

The role of the university supervisor is to coordinate the experience of the ACE teacher by providing information and support in a liaison role with the clinical supervisor and mentor teacher. The university supervisor provides appropriate report forms, assessment instruments, and other administrative details as needed. A visitation to site schools includes observation of the ACE teacher, conferencing with the ACE teacher and mentor, conferring with school administrators, and providing requested support. The university supervisor is also available as needed in special circumstances. Regular contacts via e-mail, telephone, and mail are maintained with all three school-site persons (principal, mentor, and ACE teacher) so as to keep everyone informed of expectations, progress, and needs.

The university supervisor is responsible for assigning grades for the supervised teaching experience each semester. The summative evaluation reports from the school administrator, plus the input from the mentor teacher, serve as valuable guidance in assigning these grades. During the school year, ACErs are enrolled in a 3-credit course each semester for their teaching experiences (EDU 595 Supervised Teaching). ACE teachers are expected to keep the university supervisor informed of progress and experiences through regular communications and updates. They are also required to maintain a reflective journal of their experiences. These journals are considered private and are reviewed only by the university supervisor when the ACE teacher is visited.

The university supervisor examines the plans and teaching materials of the ACE teacher during classroom visits. Self-made units and lessons designed by the ACE teacher should demonstrate the educational theory, planning skills, and best practices taught in the methods course during the summer session and Internet courses during the school year. Additionally, first-year ACErs are required to videotape and complete a reflective analysis report each of the first two semesters. Mentors are asked to review the second semester video with the ACE teacher.

The university supervisor establishes a visitation schedule in conjunction with the appropriate school administrators, the mentor, and the ACE teacher. The purpose of the visit includes meeting with each of the involved supervisors, administrators, and the ACE teacher. Classroom visits to observe the ACE teacher are expected so that the university supervisor can facilitate professional growth and improvement. Each ACE teacher is visited once each semester. More frequent visits may be arranged in certain circumstances. The university supervisor, other M.Ed. faculty, and ACE staff are available for special situations where assistance is needed.

In brief, the university supervisor is the primary liaison or contact person for the supervised teaching experience; provides information regarding expectations and requirements; supports the supervisory activities of the mentor teacher and clinical supervisor; visits each semester to observe, conference, and consult with the ACE teacher; consults with both the mentor teacher and clinical supervisor; assigns semester grades for the supervised teaching experiences; provides special assistance when needed.

## ASSESSMENT OF PROGRESS

Assessment of the progress of the ACE teacher is accomplished through multiple sources of information and is based on performance and growth. Key input is the principal's end-of-semester formal evaluation. Principals are asked to evaluate the performance of the ACE teacher on more than 50 items, using a scale of Distinguished, Proficient, Basic, or Unsatisfactory. This end-of-semester assessment is organized into four domains of teaching, consistent with the INTASC principles: Planning and Preparation, Classroom Environment, Instruction, and Professional Responsibilities. Space on the evaluation instrument is provided for comments and suggestions for continued growth.

Just as critical in determining the semester grade is the university supervisor's assessment of work and materials. Teaching plans, self-made teaching units, and other teaching materials are examined when the university supervisor visits each semester. Journal reflections that describe successes, challenges, and highs and lows are reviewed during these field supervisor visits. ACE teachers also complete a self-assessment each semester, which is shared in the conference with the principal.

ACE staff members, who are experienced teachers, also visit host schools and communities to keep informed of ACE teachers' progress and involvement in the schools and diocesan communities. While the ACE staff are primarily concerned with the community and spiritual development of the ACE teachers, they also visit the classrooms and consult with the school administrators regarding progress, growth, and needs. M.Ed. faculty also occasionally visit the host schools to offer assistance and consultation. Both staff and faculty keep the university supervisor informed of their observations, support activities, and recommendations.

## THE CHALLENGES OF SUPERVISION
## FROM A DISTANCE

ONE OF THE BIGGEST CHALLENGES to the university supervisor in the ACE M.Ed. model is the distance between teaching sites, which limits the actual face-to-face contact with the ACErs in their schools. This distance is overcome in a variety of ways. First, the long-term nature of the program allows time to develop a working relationship with each teacher, beginning with the initial summer practicum, through two years of teaching and study. This relationship can be tailored to address particular needs of teachers based on their personalities, strengths and weaknesses, and issues particular to their teaching situation. Second, supervisors and ACErs use technology (the Web, e-mail, fax, phone) to stay in contact on issues and concerns during the school year. University supervisors are issued cell phones and laptop computers to facilitate contact while traveling between distance sites and the campus. Third, assignments in the form of written updates, video analysis, observations of other teachers, and reflective writing provide regular feedback to supervisors.

Fourth, visits to each site once a semester serve as a way of touching base with the ACErs on a variety of fronts (classroom teaching, participation and collaboration with school staff, progress toward teaching goals). Fifth, interaction with the principals and mentor teachers provides further insight into the novice teachers' experiences and areas of growth. Both principals, acting as clinical supervisors, and mentor teachers provide formal written feedback and evaluations twice each semester. Finally, ACErs are required to keep written weekly journals of their experiences. These journals offer an indication of reflection and growth that can be addressed by the university supervisor. Journal writing on the Web is currently being explored as a way of increasing contact with the experiences of the ACE teachers.

### WORKING WITH MENTORS AND ADMINISTRATORS

The university supervisor strives to develop a productive working relationship with the mentor teachers and clinical supervisors. In addition to the formal interactions during their visits to sites, the university supervisor hosts dinners with the mentors and school administrators to develop lines of communication and cooperative relationships. Often these informal relationships can be instrumental in the productive resolution of issues when they arise. During the April retreat, university supervisors make an effort to meet diocese representatives, principals, and teachers who have come to Notre Dame for the weekend to work with their new ACErs.

The time and support that mentor teachers offer to ACE teachers vary considerably. Some mentors are appointed more for their availability of time rather than for their exemplary teaching or ability to work with novices. Others are active in the leadership of the school, seasoned mentors, and excellent models of professional growth. When a school or diocese does not have a strong mentoring program for beginning teachers, the university supervisor can help to structure the mentor and ACE teacher relationship by making sure the mentor understands the goals of the program, the need for observation and support, and the importance of providing feedback to the ACE teacher. A *Mentor Handbook* has been developed that serves this purpose. The role of the mentor can take on considerable significance for the ACE teacher, especially when the ACE teacher is blessed to work with a mentor teacher who is caring, conscientious, and concerned about the ACE teacher's growth and welfare.

The principal is in the best position to address significant issues concerning the ACE teacher. Many principals are actively involved in helping these novice teachers develop positive relationships with parents and colleagues, understand the curriculum and the school milieu, and develop reasonable classroom management strategies. They also can adjust teaching loads and extracurricular responsibilities based upon their observations of the ACE teacher's performance and readiness. The university supervisor can keep abreast of these issues through regular contacts with the principals via telephone and e-mail.

## The Variety of Administrators and Mentors

While the vast majority of school experiences are positive for ACErs, some circumstances create challenges for the university supervisor. For example, there can be turnovers of principals and mentors just when the university supervisor has begun to establish a working rapport. The result is a whole new set of people who need to be informed of the program, expectations, and procedures. Frequently, it takes several contacts before new school administrators realize that the ACE program sends a number of people to check on the ACErs and communities, and that a number of members of the ACE family will visit classrooms headed by ACE teachers. In some cases, new administrators will assume that the ACE teacher has had four years of preparation in a traditional teacher education program, and they cannot understand why an ACE teacher might need some special assistance, especially during the crucial first few weeks. Some administrators are skeptical of this nontraditional approach at preparing teachers for Catholic schools and do not support the ACE teachers in many respects. The idea of "service through teaching" is a foreign concept to them.

More common is the principal who is reluctant to share with the field supervisor some of the trials and challenges the ACERs have been facing in their teaching. Some principals are quite adept at saying, "Everything is fine; the ACE teacher is doing a great job." However, classroom observation may reveal that everything is not fine, and that the ACE teacher is struggling. Too often this is a case of the mentor teacher not being available to visit the ACE teacher's classes to learn about these struggles, and the administrator not monitoring this relationship. The university supervisor must approach this administrator with extreme care and finesse if any progress and support are to be forthcoming.

The greatest challenge, perhaps, are principals who are reluctant to give any kind of affirmation to their ACE teachers, simply leaving them to wonder what kind of a job they are doing. Some ACE teachers are shocked to learn from their university supervisor that they, indeed, are doing a credible job of teaching. A few ACE teachers have cried when receiving positive feedback on their performance from the university supervisor. Such ACE teachers typically then share the doubts and anxieties they have been experiencing, because they have not received any form of compliment or encouragement from either their mentor or principal.

Weak mentors and principals are in the minority in the ACE program. The vast majority observe their ACE teachers, conduct meaningful evaluative conferences, and truly contribute to the ACERs' success and growth. Of the more than 100 schools where ACE teachers are placed, there are typically fewer than 10 where the proper on-site supervision is sorely lacking. Most principals understand the program, are willing supporters of it, and are willing to allocate the necessary energy and resources to enable the ACE teacher to be a success and a real contributor to the school community. Examples of this outstanding commitment include the many principals who regularly visit the classes of the ACE teachers who are struggling with classroom organization and management, often demonstrating how to accomplish certain tasks, and conferencing with the ACErs in an attempt to foster success. These principals' faith in the ability of the ACE teacher to learn how to do it is unquestioned. They are willing to do all things possible to empower the ACE teacher. On the whole, most principals understand the ACE program, respect it for what it is, and support and appreciate the contributions these young people make to their school communities. In fact, most administrators of ACE participating schools repeatedly request more ACE teachers.

### SUPPORTING MENTOR TEACHERS

The mentor teacher can be one of the most important individuals assigned to work with the ACE teacher. While these individuals receive only a nominal stipend for their efforts, they typically contribute significantly to the success and experiences of the ACE teacher. Many mentor teachers, however, do not have the time to do all that is required of them to support the ACE teacher. Financial support is offered from ACE to reimburse for substitute teacher expenses, so that the mentor can spend time observing and working with the ACE teacher.

Given their busy teaching schedules, it is often difficult for the university supervisor to spend a great deal of time with the mentors during the supervisor's visit to the school. Often, all that is possible is a consultation between classes or at lunchtime. This makes the initial inservice meeting during the first visit even more important. More positively, mentors will frequently contact the university supervisor through mail, e-mail, and telephone if the need arises. Most seek their principals for guidance and information while they try to support the ACE teacher. The majority are true mentors who serve as supportive colleagues and advisors.

### CHALLENGES OF SCHEDULING

Because the ACE teaching sites are spread throughout the southern and southwestern United States, it is not possible for the university supervisor to drop in to visit classrooms on a regular and informal basis. To aid in scheduling site visits, ACErs provide their class schedules, maps or directions to their schools, and school calendars within the first weeks of arriving at their schools. The fact that site visits are prescheduled means that the ACE teacher always knows when the supervisor will be visiting. Hence, the university supervisor might not see the real ACE teacher in action; the ACEr may be in best form only for the class periods when the supervisor is present. However, in most cases, the real ACE teacher is observed.

The university supervisor builds a profile of the teaching situation and performance based upon previous experience with the school, reflective writing assignments, journals, and conversations and evaluative feedback from the mentor teacher and clinical supervisor. Examination of previous lesson plans and teaching materials during the classroom visit also helps to determine if what is observed is atypical. The students of the ACE teachers also provide evidence as to what really happens on a normal day of class. Those ACErs who are struggling with classroom management, for example, will not be able to conceal this very long. Additionally, if the teacher does not normally plan thoroughly, fails to return student work promptly, or is generally disorganized, it is hard to hide this for even a few hours (e.g., someone will complain about not getting a paper back, the teacher will not be able to locate key props for classroom demonstrations, comments from the principal will note parental complaints in this area).

### Extracurricular ACE Teaching

Most ACE teachers have not learned to say no to their administrators when asked to perform extra duties and lead extracurricular activities. Catholic school principals are thrilled to have bright, accomplished young people who have the energy and rapport to work with students. Sometimes it is irresistible to the point that they ask the ACE teacher, especially in the first year, to take on more than is reasonable. This can lead to overload and result in the negligence of teaching responsibilities on the part of the beginning ACE teacher. It also can make it difficult for the university supervisor to schedule a post-observation conference with the ACE teacher to discuss progress. The university supervisor can be put into the awkward position of insisting that the load be reduced to protect the ACE teacher. When this is the case, additional pressure for reduced extracurricular responsibilities can come from other ACE staff.

## Dealing with School Values

While ACE teachers typically bring tremendous idealism, enthusiasm, energy, and a different set of experiences to a school community, they quickly discover the pressures of the school norms and local customs. They can experience subtle and not-so-subtle pressure from veteran teachers to be less enthusiastic and less committed to educational excellence. Many ACE teachers understand they are going to learn considerably from these experiences. There is a certain art to being able to survive in an environment in which one does not fully accept all that is the norm. This is where the support of ACE resources can really make a difference to the ACE teacher. Some ACE teachers find the support they need in their community. Other ACE teachers rely on the communications with university faculty members with whom they have maintained contact. Some use ACE staff or their university supervisor. Still others find someone in their school with whom to share their frustrations. Many ACE teachers are able to grow, serve, and become better persons through these experiences.

## REWARDS OF SUPERVISING ACE TEACHERS

THE REWARDS of supervising ACE teachers far outweigh the challenges. While a supervisor is required to be on the road and away from family, friends, and colleagues for up to 12 weeks each semester, the satisfaction in seeing a young teacher blossom into a quality educator is reward enough. It is an honor to work with these young people who so willingly give two years of their lives to serve in Catholic schools far from their homes. Some will choose to remain in Catholic education as teachers and future administrators. In fact, some choose to remain in the schools they served during their ACE years. ACE teachers have the attitudes and are the spiritual models that the Catholic Church wants to put before young people. Some ACE teachers have so influenced their students through their service that these students are now considering ACE for themselves.

The university supervisors have been witnesses to much outstanding teaching by the participants in the ACE program. These novice teachers have designed numerous public service activities for their students, directed countless spiritual retreats, and created caring classroom environments that permit students to share their fears and doubts about life, Christ, family, and future. The university supervisors have had the opportunity to influence this new generation of teachers. In doing so, they have met and worked with Catholic school administrators and teachers in 25 different dioceses, from Charleston to Los Angeles. As a result, they have grown as well, including in their own faith. Perhaps this is the legacy of the ACE university supervisor—to serve Catholic schools and, in doing so, to serve both the current generation of ACE teachers and the future generation being socialized into teaching who are now students in ACE classrooms.

## NEW DIRECTIONS IN SUPERVISION

As THIS CHAPTER is being prepared, two new initiatives are underway in the area of supervision. The first is a longitudinal study of stages of teacher development within the ACE programmatic model. This research will undertake the quantitative and qualitative study of teacher development for the improvement of supervision. The second is a restructuring of supervised teaching courses to include the participation of master teachers and reflective assignments in an effort to strengthen formative support across two years of teaching. These initiatives will serve to ensure that supervision continues to reflect the growing experience and knowledge of how best to serve beginning teachers in the ACE program.

## REFERENCES

Berliner, D. C. (1988). Implications of studies in pedagogy for teacher education and evaluation. In *New directions for teacher assessment.* Princeton, NJ: Educational Testing Service.

Burden, P. R. (1981). *Teachers' perceptions of their personal and professional development.* Paper presented at the annual meeting of the American Educational Research Association, Des Moines, IA. (ERIC Document No. ED 210 258)

Carter, K. (1990). Teachers' knowledge and learning to teach. In W. R. Houston (Ed.), *Handbook of research on teacher education* (pp. 291–310). New York: Macmillan.

Dadlez, S. L. (2000). *A Comparison of secondary professional development school and traditional teacher education graduates: Analysis of professional concerns and perceived problems.* Unpublished doctoral dissertation, University of California, Riverside.

Feiman-Nemser, L., & Remillard, J. (1996). Perspectives on learning to teach. In F. B. Murray (Ed.), *The teacher educator's handbook* (pp. 63–91). San Francisco: Jossey-Bass.

Fuller, F. (1969). Concerns of teachers: A developmental conceptualization. *American Educational Research Journal, 6,* 207–226.

Gold, Y. (1996). Beginning teacher support: Attrition, mentoring, and induction. In J. Sikula (Ed.), *Handbook of research on teacher education* (pp. 548–594). New York: Simon & Schuster, Macmillan.

Kagan, D. (1992). Professional growth among preservice and beginning teachers. *Review of Educational Research, 62*(2), 129–169.

Katz, L. G. (1972). Developmental stages of preschool teachers. *Elementary School Journal, 73,* 50–55.

McDonald, J., & Elias, P. (1980). *The problems of beginning teachers: A crisis in training.* Princeton, NJ: Education Testing Service.

Murray, F. B. (1996). *The teacher educator's handbook.* San Francisco: Jossey-Bass.

Odell, S. J. (1986). Induction support of new teachers: A functional approach. *Journal of Teacher Education, 37*(1), 26–29.

Reeves, C. K., & Kazelskis, R. (1985). Concerns of preservice and inservice teachers. *Journal of Educational Research, 78,* 267–271.

Sikula, J. (1996). *Handbook of research on teacher education.* New York: Simon & Schuster, Macmillan.

Veenman, S. (1984). Perceived problems of beginning teachers. *Review of Educational Research, 54,* 143–178.

Wideen, M., Mayer-Smith, J., & Moon, B. (1998). A critical analysis of the research on learning to teach: Making the case for an ecological perspective on inquiry. *Review of Educational Research, 68*(2), 130–178.

# 7

JOYCE V. JOHNSTONE

# Performance Assessment

## The Summative Portfolio

I n the development of the ACE M.Ed., the faculty were encouraged and challenged by the requirement for a standards-based, performance-assessed model. Traditionally, teacher candidates have been evaluated through credit and course counting in pedagogy and in content areas, through passing scores on the National Teachers Exam (or a state-developed equivalent), and through successful completion of student teaching. By the late 1980s, however, there was a movement toward teacher education reform with the establishment of the National Board for Professional Teaching Standards (NBPTS). Supported by the Carnegie Foundation, the NBPTS had as its purpose to establish standards for high levels of competence in the teaching profession, to assess the qualifications of those seeking board certification, and to grant certificates to those meeting the standards. To fulfill this requirement, the NBPTS created a framework for teacher assessment using portfolios. This evaluation of teacher performance involves a process whereby teachers plan, implement, and reflect upon their work with the goal of improving practice. Presumably, this improved practice should lead to improved student achievement. The NBPTS, however, concentrated its efforts on performance of experienced teachers who have a minimum of five years of teaching.

By the early 1990s, a second body known as the Interstate New Teachers Assessment and Support Consortium (INTASC) began working on standards for beginning teachers. The INTASC standards represented a common core of knowledge, dispositions, and performances that are essential to good teaching at the beginner level. More than 30 states, including Indiana, adopted the INTASC standards as the basis for their new performance-based license patterns. In 1998, the National Council for Accreditation of Teacher Education (NCATE) incorporated this performance evaluation of teachers based on INTASC standards into their revised standards for accreditation of teacher education programs.

In Indiana, the INTASC standards were adopted as the basis for the further development of content (math, social studies, English, foreign language, science) and developmental standards (early childhood, middle childhood, early adolescence generalists, and adolescence/young adult), following the NBPTS model of evaluating teachers as masters of presenting specific content to a particular age level. A high school math teacher, for example, would be judged on the INTASC standards or principles, the math content standards, and the adolescence/young adult developmental standards. The teacher education programs in Indiana were faced with the task of aligning the national INTASC standards and the state developmental and content standards with their curriculum and then assessing the performance of its candidates.

Notre Dame's ACE M.Ed. program was aligned with this new standards-based, performance-assessed system as the courses were being developed in the fall of 1997 and spring of 1998. However, we were still faced with developing a process for assessing performance. ACE participants had the advantage of two years of service as teachers over the course of the M.Ed. A portfolio of the ACE teacher's work giving a snapshot of the teacher's performance in relation to the standards of best practice (Lyons, 1998) was the vehicle chosen, at least as an initial trial for assessing performance. The capstone course in the curriculum would be EDU 596 Summative Portfolio Development, and the portfolio demonstrating performance on the standards would be developed in this course and serve in lieu of a master's thesis for the M.Ed. The faculty also wished to remain true to Shulman's (1986) view of a teaching portfolio as a structured documentary history of selected accomplishments substantiated by samples of student work. The first students under this newly created M.Ed. were accepted in June 1998 and would be expected to demonstrate performance before graduating two years later.

Three additional factors had to be considered at Notre Dame in this performance assessment. First, because the ACE program recruited graduates in the liberal arts, science, engineering, and business, all of the ACE students would enter this graduate program with a content major and then would need to demonstrate knowledge and performance for teaching that content or one closely related to it. We would not be counting courses and credits in that content area, however. This freed very competent mechanical engineers, for example, from demonstrating that they had 3 credits titled "analytical geometry" when they sought a math license. Their knowledge and performance as math teachers would be the basis of their evaluation. The second factor that had to be considered was that the ACE students are in residence on campus only during the summers, and therefore, although exhibition portfolios (Cambell, Cignetti, Melenyzer, Nettles, & Wyman, 1997) were very attractive to the faculty, it was not feasible for students to come to South Bend from their distant teaching sites. Lastly, the program accreditation standards demanded a system in which student performance was embedded within the larger assessment system for the teacher education program; therefore, the ACE teacher portfolios would serve as an important part of the program evaluation.

## DEVELOPING THE PORTFOLIO PROCEDURE

As classes began in the summer of 1998, the faculty knew that they had less than a year to develop a process and guidelines for EDU 596. ACE V, the first class entering the new M.Ed. program, would need orientation to this process in the summer of 1999. In September 1998, a performance assessment committee of 12 was formed. As director of Educational Outreach and accreditation coordinator, I chaired the committee. Two of the members, George Howard and Julie Turner, were faculty in the Psychology Department. Two members, Wendy Holthous and Al Stashis, were associate directors of ACE for pastoral formation. Seven were practicing master teachers who served as clinical faculty for our Internet courses during the 1998–1999 school year: Caryn Ellison in elementary education, Mary Beth Borkowski in middle school education, Mary Lou Derwent in mathematics, Karen McKibbin in science, Mary Nicolini in English, Jim Schmidt in social studies, and Gabrielle Aboud in foreign language.

The committee faced the following constraints: (1) the portfolio needed to speak for itself—students had to contextualize their teaching practices so that a reader far away could understand their practices and rationales; (2) the portfolio had to provide a way for the

ACE teachers to demonstrate performance on their required standards; (3) ACE teachers needed to demonstrate in the portfolios their performance on the entire conceptual framework (i.e., the three pillars of ACE, not just the standards); (4) participants must use evidence of current educational theory from their coursework to support innovative practices in their classrooms (McLaughlin et al., 1998); (5) the process had to be specific and provide formative feedback along the way; (6) the process needed to instill in ACE teachers that they not merely plan and perform their work, but that they inspect it and reflect on their instruction (Darling-Hammond, 1986); (7) the designing of the framework for the teaching portfolio had to be a theoretical act itself, with the criteria for reasonable portfolio entries reflecting the theory of teaching at Notre Dame (Shulman, 1998).

Throughout the 1998–1999 school year, the performance assessment committee met monthly (sometimes more often) to flesh out the EDU 596 Summative Portfolio requirements, as we wanted to give these to the students the following summer and have information sessions with them before they returned to their ACE schools in the fall. We read the literature, looked at examples, and reviewed our conceptual framework. Sometimes we met in small groups to discuss evidence or artifacts, reflection, and instructions and procedures, and often we met as a committee of the whole. By June we had designed the portfolio process and developed the summative portfolio guidelines handbook.

The team decided that for each of the 27 performance indicators, both the artifacts and the reflection would receive a grade of distinguished, satisfactory, or weak. A rubric in the portfolio handbook spelled out the criteria for each designation and specified the required scoring for an entire portfolio to be judged satisfactory or distinguished. In addition, it set the consequences and timeline if a portfolio was found to be weak. We then met the ACE V students twice in the summer of 1999 to explain the requirements. We also met with Pat Daunt and Rachel Moreno, the university supervisors for the ACE teachers, to coordinate requirements with the expectations for supervised teaching.

EDU 596 Summative Portfolio Development was offered for the first time in 1999–2000, corresponding to when the ACE students were required to complete portfolios. Our new challenge was how to grade the portfolios and who would read them. Following the work of Pamela Moss (Moss, 1992, 1996, 1998), we proposed an integrative approach to this task. As Moss (1998) argues, "to understand a teacher's decision to use a particular instructional strategy, or to respond to a student's work in a particular way, it is important to understand the larger context in which that decision was made. All this points to the importance of locating a particular performance in the preceding and subsequent context which surrounds it" (p. 204).

Moss goes on to advocate for a pair or team of readers, always including classroom teachers, to evaluate a candidate's entire set of performances using the articulated principles or standards as a framework to guide the gathering and analysis of evidence. She explains that through this integrative approach, individual biases can be challenged and controlled through debate, audit, and appeal. We formed, therefore, three teams of readers, each responsible for approximately 20 ACE teachers. Each team had a university faculty member (Johnstone, Turner, and Howard) and two practicing teachers, members of the clinical faculty. The nine team members met monthly as they constructed the process.

We knew that students would have questions as they worked with the guidelines to develop portfolio entries. We wanted all students to receive the same answers to the questions. Therefore, all questions were sent to me, the students and team members were put on a listserve, and as questions came in, I responded with the question and answer for everyone. Additionally, in order to provide the ACE teachers with formative feedback on the process, the teams required that the ACE teachers submit five portfolio entries by October 31, with the completed portfolio due on March 1. Each student's fall submissions were read by three readers and were given extensive feedback. These fall entries were returned to the students in early December. This process served the readers as a way to develop criteria for grading entries and provided an opportunity to judge inter-rater reliability.

The team of readers tried to be flexible and supportive. In one case, a student's school burned to the ground, with the ACE teacher's work in it, two weeks before the portfolios were due. The team offered the student alternative means of presenting his performance evidence, including videotaping himself explaining his artifacts. He was able to demonstrate satisfactory performance before the end of the semester. Also, during this first year, two portfolios were rated weak, and the ACE teachers, working with their readers, were able to revise their entries and submit a satisfactory product before the end of the spring semester.

The group of faculty and master teachers who had been involved in this first year of portfolio development would continue to revise and refine this process during the next year. We worked more closely with faculty during this second year.

## TYING THE PORTFOLIO TO THE CURRICULUM

THE SUMMATIVE PORTFOLIO, a collection of work across the span of the M.Ed. program, reflects how students have integrated academic, community, and spiritual development as teachers, consistent with the conceptualization of the program. It serves as the summative evaluation for the M.Ed. and coherently documents mastery of the INTASC principles and the standards beginning teachers are required to meet by the Indiana Professional Standards Board (IPSB).

From the first day of recruitment into the program, students are made aware of the conceptual framework of the ACE M.Ed., the three pillars of professional education, community, and spirituality. In April, prior to the beginning of the coursework in June, the students are given the M.Ed. program handbook and the standards that each teacher will be required to meet. A middle school math teacher, for example, has to document performance on the INTASC principles, the early adolescence generalist standards, and the math standards. A high school Spanish teacher must address the INTASC principles, the adolescence/young adult standards, and the foreign language standards. Also included in this handbook is a description of the portfolio process, the 27 performance indicators, and suggested artifacts for each. Within the first week of the program, the INTASC standards are explained, as well as the IPSB developmental and content standards.

The intent of the creators of the program was for every syllabus in every course to remind students of the conceptualization of the ACE M.Ed. program in terms of academic, community, and spiritual development as a teacher. Each course contributes to the academic development of a teacher, a teacher's understanding of community and educating in a community, and how individual spiritual and ethical development relevant to teaching in Catholic schools may occur in the context of the course. Every year, higher proportions of syllabi are coming into compliance with this intent.

In addition to reflecting on the three pillars, the syllabus for each course in the program is intended to specify how the content in the course is relevant to the IPSB standards. Progress is being made in meeting this intent. In each course, there is specification of potential portfolio entries or artifacts that might be developed in fulfillment of course requirements—or, at a minimum, how the course material might be used to refine existing portfolio entries and plan others. Every course requires, at a minimum, development or refinement of one or more portfolio entries as part of the evaluation in the course. That is, there is concern in courses that students make progress in meeting the standards with respect to the development of a portfolio of teaching.

Students received portfolio information beginning with the first summer they were enrolled. They began to organize artifacts and reflections that first summer. During the second summer, students met with faculty members assigned to the portfolio course to obtain initial feedback on the materials they organized. During the second year of the program, students enrolled in EDU 596, which is described as follows:

> EDU 596 Summative Portfolio Development (3): The professional portfolio entries developed throughout a participant's experiences in the program will be integrated into a coherent presentation. The portfolio will document how the participant has grown with respect to INTASC and IPSB standards and to the three conceptual pillars of the M.Ed. program: development as professional educators, increased understanding of how to promote community in education, and spiritual development that translates into effective spiritual and ethical development of students. Taken during the second year of supervised teaching, with completion expected before the end of the second year of teaching and not later than one year following the completion of the second year of teaching.

The portfolio experience emphasizes that teaching be reflected in planning, execution, and evaluation, which should be connected. The capstone document also is to have holistic integrity rather than be just a collection of individual entries. The expectation is that the portfolio be an autobiographical summary of the two years of teaching, and as such, be extremely well organized, well written, and scholarly. The portfolio is a way to document not only what the ACE teachers and their students did, but how the teachers thought and made decisions. It reflects what happened in the classroom, why it happened, what the teacher knows about the subject area, the students, and teaching, and how the teacher grew as a beginning teacher.

## PORTFOLIO STRUCTURE

For their portfolios, the ACE V teachers were asked to choose work that reflected growth as a teacher and that would provide examples of successful and best work. ACE students were also asked to submit examples of failed or unsuccessful lessons, along with reflections on how the lessons could be changed or improved. Each performance indicator, then, was accompanied by a reflection.

### Contents

The completed portfolio was a large 3-inch binder or a box with hanging files. It contained a table of contents and was divided into three sections: the teaching situation, evidence of growth and performance, and analysis of professional growth.

### Section 1: My Teaching Situation

The purpose of this section was to provide the contextual setting to the reader. It included (a) information about the school; (b) information about the teaching assignment (an explanation if the teacher changed assignments from year one to year two); (c) commentary about the class or classes. The teacher included any descriptive information that might be helpful to the reader, such as piloting a new textbook series or not having materials, or particular information about students.

### Section 2: Evidence of Growth and Performance

This section provided performance evidence of the standards and principles upon which the conceptual framework was built. Artifacts and reflections were organized according to specific performance indicators for the three pillars of the ACE program, with the first pillar, professional teaching, being subdivided into the four professional domains of teaching: planning and preparation, classroom environment, instruction, and professional responsibilities. These domains were found in the conceptual framework and in the semester evaluations used by the clinical supervisors. Following the four domains of teaching were two domains reflecting the other pillars of ACE, community and spirituality. Each of these six domains contained four to six individual performance indicators. For example, under Domain I (Planning and Preparation) of the teaching pillar was Indicator 1: Demonstrates knowledge of content and pedagogy. Under the spirituality pillar was Indicator 3: Fosters spiritual development in children.

For each of the 27 performance indicators, the ACE teacher listed the standards that were addressed, followed by an introduction to the artifacts, then the artifacts, and then the reflection referring back to the standards. Reflection was crucial for explaining why each artifact was significant and why it represented an INTASC, content, and developmental standard. In many cases, the reflection was more valuable than the artifact itself.

*Section 3: Analysis of Professional Growth*

This section documented ongoing assessments and required the ACE teacher to examine his or her performance across the two years. The ACE teachers included (in chronological sequence) observation and performance assessments by their mentor teachers, principals, and university supervisors on their teaching through February of their second year. Each of these observation and assessment instruments was designed around the conceptual framework, imbedding the INTASC and content standards. In light of what the ACE teachers learned from reflections on their teaching and what others said about their teaching, they then provided a self-evaluation. They explained general patterns they saw across the evaluations, as well as perceptions about strengths and weaknesses.

ACE teachers began the portfolio process with the advantage of a year of teaching under their belt. They examined what went right and wrong as well as what they still needed to know, continuing to do so during the second year of teaching.

PORTFOLIO ENTRIES

The portfolio process is best illuminated with examples. Consider the first performance indicator, "demonstrates knowledge of content and pedagogy." One ACE teacher, a middle school science teacher, chose three artifacts for this indicator. The first was a research paper he wrote for his Seminar in Science Education on the need to incorporate the history of science into the curriculum. The second artifact was an astronomy unit he wrote and used with his seventh graders that infused an historical perspective. The third artifact was a video-tape of his seventh graders conducting the trial of Galileo, dressed in 16th Century costumes. From their words and actions, it was clear that the students understood the Church's prevailing theory on the geocentric universe and Galileo's revolutionary theory of the helio-centric universe. They also demonstrated knowledge of church law and legal protocol of the 16th Century. In his reflection, the ACE teacher discussed the need to provide early adolescents with active learning experiences and opportunities for meaningful research, citing the INTASC, developmental, and content standards that supported this approach to teaching science.

Under Domain IV of the professional teaching pillar, Professional Responsibilities, is Indicator 2, "communicates with families." Many students provided as their artifacts examples of the correspondence they sent to parents, and they reflected on the usefulness of their correspondence in involving the parents in children's education. One ACE teacher chose a group of letters he sent to the parents of one of his children indicating his concern about the child's achievement. In the introduction to his artifacts, he explained that he taught in a small school on the Mexican border, and many of his children crossed the border to attend his school. On a questionnaire that this teacher asked each child to complete at the beginning of the year, a student, Marco, indicated that his parents spoke English. The ACE teacher therefore wrote letters to the parents in English, expressing his concern about Marco's progress and requesting a conference. He never received a reply. One day, while fretting about the lack of response, it dawned on him that maybe they did not really speak English. He asked Marco about this. Marco explained that although his parents spoke English, they were not fluent readers of English.

The ACE teacher wrote in his reflection:

Like Paul on the road to Damascus, I felt blinded by the truth. Was this an example of "cultural blindness" on my part? Am I truly insensitive to the vast differences in culture and language down here? This situation taught me that as a teacher one needs to gather even more information about parents, family situations, and so forth to be the best advocate possible for the students. You need to reflect on your own attempts to communicate and how they might be working or failing. . . . Only after I began reflecting and re-evaluating my choices was I able to truly foster productive parent relationships in an instance of diverse family and language situations.

These two different examples reveal the quality of selection and reflection that went into the development of portfolio entries. These examples reflected the judgment and openness to learning prevalent in the majority of the portfolios.

## EVALUATION OF THE PROCESS

THE EVALUATION of the portfolio process began immediately and on several fronts after the first cohort, ACE V, completed the portfolio in the spring of 2000. Michael Pressley had two of his doctoral students prepare an analysis of the process through surveying all students who had completed the process and interviewing the members of the portfolio teams. ACE V students reported that the process focused them as reflective practitioners and gave them a sense of pride and completion. Many enjoyed the flexibility and creativity the process allowed and appreciated the practical implications of having this tool for future teaching jobs. However, the majority also pointed out communications-related and feedback problems and a frustration with the timing of the portfolio. Several students felt overwhelmed and stressed out by the process.

The graders had positive and negative views of the process as well. Some found the work of the ACE teachers inspiring, believing the process allowed for creativity and flexibility. However, the subjectivity of the process bothered some, and the time pressures involved in grading the portfolio bothered almost everyone. Also, graders, who were grouped by developmental level (there were elementary, middle school, and high school teams), believed it would have been better to be grouped by content areas.

An ad hoc portfolio review team met in the summer of 2000, mainly to review and revise the portfolio guidelines given to students. I chaired this committee, which was composed of members of the portfolio team as well as eight members of the ACE V cohort. The committee made revisions to the guidelines and prepared for a portfolio information night with the ACE VI students who would be enrolling for the course in the fall. They also suggested that the information about the indicators and suggested artifacts be given to the new cohort of ACE VII students who were just starting their first summer. This was done.

Michael Pressley also appointed an ad hoc faculty committee in the summer of 2000 to review the process and content of the summative portfolio, as this serves as the M.Ed. thesis requirement. In the summer of 2000, the first year for summative portfolios, this committee was composed of chaired and tenured professors in arts and letters as well as an associate dean of the graduate school. This committee was charged to ensure that the M.Ed. summative project had parity with other graduate-level program requirements. The committee was generally satisfied with the portfolios, although there was some concern that the students could have related their teaching more to theory and research covered in the M.Ed. program.

During the fall of 2000, Caryn Ellison, the 2000–2001 Notre Dame Teacher-in-Residence, completed an analysis of the grading of the portfolios. For each of the 27 performance indicators, she computed the percentages of distinguished, satisfactory, and weak ratings for both the artifacts selected and the reflections. She also analyzed the course syllabi to determine the types of performance requirements used as course assessments, and this information was given to the faculty. In the spring of 2001, as the teams read portfolios, samples were selected for content analysis of relationship to the curriculum. The readers looked for coursework mentioned in either the introductions or reflections, for artifacts that came directly from courses, and for references to the research and literature. Sometimes a course did not seem to be relevant, and yet a year later, with additional teaching experience, a teacher recognized the value of what was taught and included work or reflection on what was learned in that course as a valuable tool in development as a teacher. Use of this information can be a helpful means of program improvement (Snyder, Lippincott, & Bower, 1999).

The portfolio process was a hybrid of the INTASC approach to performance assessment and the Praxis III approach. Praxis III is the self-reflective assessment tool developed by the Educational Testing Service (ETS) to supplement the quantitative standardized tests in Praxis I (reading, writing, and math) and Praxis II (the content specialist tests). The Notre Dame portfolio reflected the content validity inherent in the Praxis III approach and used the performance indicators described in Praxis III, which are based on the work of the teacher: planning and preparation, maintaining a classroom environment conducive to learning, instruction, and professional responsibilities. Notre Dame then added the section on community and spirituality to correspond with our conceptual framework. ETS, in developing the criteria for Praxis III, researched four main areas relating to content validity: job analysis, analyses of state regulation, research reviews, and expert panel reviews. Notre Dame's performance assessments represented that same content validity (Porter, Youngs, & Odden, 2001).

At Notre Dame during the first three years of the ACE M.Ed. program, we attempted to develop a culture consistent with Wolf's (1998) vision of a learning environment with intense expectations, care, and richness. This culture was based on the Deweyan teaching ideal of practice being constantly reflected upon and improved. Portfolio preparation must be viewed as serious cognitive work that involves collecting, categorizing, judging, comparing, wondering, and reflecting. A summative portfolio, however, was an overwhelming requirement. Sifting through three semesters of teaching artifacts and preparing reflective analysis of one's teaching proved staggering. While the experience provided a vehicle for clarification of ideas, philosophy, and teaching strategies, even having transformational potential, for busy teachers it also posed the danger of trivializing teaching— that is, picking out one lesson or assessment tool and purporting it to be best practice (Lyons, 1998).

After a comprehensive evaluation of the portfolio process, a committee of faculty serving the program decided on an alternative capstone evaluation capturing the performance of ACE teachers. A core part of the process, however, will be the development of portfolio-type entries over the entire two years of teaching, complemented by a presentation of a portfolio entry in poster form during the second summer of residence in the ACE M.Ed. program. The final words of this chapter are being composed the day after those poster presentations, permitting me to claim that our students made presentations about ambitious lessons, which were reflected upon in light of theory, research, and standards. They were great living, breathing, three-dimensional portfolio entries that were shared with other students in the program, ACE M.Ed. faculty, and local educators.

## REFERENCES

Campbell, D., Cignetti, P., Melenyzer, B., Nettles, D., & Wyman, R. (1997). *How to develop a professional portfolio.* Boston: Allyn & Bacon.

Darling-Hammond, L. (1986). A proposal for evaluation in the teaching profession. *Elementary School Journal, 86,* 531–551.

Lyons, N. (Ed.). (1998). *With portfolio in hand.* New York: Teachers College Press.

McLaughlin, M., Vogt, M. E., Anderson, J., DuMez, J., Peter, M. G., & Hunter, A. (1998). *Professional portfolio models.* Norwood, MA: Christopher-Gordon.

Moss, P. A. (1992). Shifting conception of validity in educational measurement: Implications for performance assessment. *Review of Educational Research, 62*(3), 229–258.

Moss, P. A. (1996). Enlarging the dialogue in educational measurement: Voices from interpretive research traditions. *Educational Researcher, 25*(1), 20–28.

Moss, P. A. (1998). Rethinking validity for the assessment of teaching. In N. Lyons (Ed.), *With portfolio in hand*. New York: Teachers College Press.

Porter, A. C., Youngs, P., & Odden, A. (2001). Advances in teacher assessments and their uses. In V. Richardson (Ed.), *Handbook of research on teaching* (4th ed.). New York: Macmillan.

Shulman, L. S. (1986). Assessment for teaching: An initiative for the profession. *Phi Delta Kappan, 69*(1), 38–44.

Shulman, L. S. (1998). Teacher portfolios: A theoretical activity. In N. Lyons (Ed.), *With portfolio in hand*. New York: Teachers College Press.

Snyder, J., Lippincott, A., & Bower, D. (1998). Portfolios in teacher education: Technical or transformational? In N. Lyons (Ed.), *With portfolio in hand*. New York: Teachers College Press.

Wolf, D. (1998). Creating a portfolio culture. In N. Lyons (Ed.), *With portfolio in hand*. New York: Teachers College Press.

# 8

JOHN STAUD

# BUILDING COMMUNITIES OF FAITH, HOPE, AND LOVE

"Our hearts are restless until they rest in you, O God." In his spiritual autobiography, *The Confessions*, St. Augustine generalizes profoundly to illumine a fundamental truth of the human condition. Augustine's insight relates to community life in ACE because we believe strongly that decisions to join ACE are best understood as the responses of restless hearts to be teachers in Catholic schools and members of faith-based communities.

Designed for college graduates who wish to give two years of service through teaching to under-resourced Catholic schools, ACE emphasizes community as one of its three pillars. During their service, ACE teachers live in small intentional Christian communities in which they are called to grow together, support one another, and challenge each other as they develop personally, professionally, and spiritually. The community pillar of ACE is certainly broader in reference and scope than each ACE house and includes (with increasing awareness) the larger ACE community as well as schools, dioceses, and the professional community of faculty and Catholic educators. When one considers the variety of stakeholders that the Alliance for Catholic Education comprises, "alliance" can be viewed as the prophetically chosen descriptor of the program. As the program has expanded across the South and into Texas, Arizona, and California, the

ACE community has grown beyond Notre Dame and its geographical focus to include places where our alumni live and work, the home institutions of summer faculty, and recently, other universities interested in establishing service through teaching programs similar to ACE.

This sense of community is vital to the program's success, and our understanding of community in ACE has certainly deepened as the program has evolved. Yet it is important to acknowledge that the development of Notre Dame's Master of Education program has been our focus over the past several years. One major achievement is the extent to which all three pillars of ACE have become increasingly integrated in the M.Ed. program. This is evident not only in the curriculum but in the commitment of the faculty, who during the summer eat lunch daily with the ACE students, often join them at nightly Mass, and stay in close contact through e-mail and telephone throughout the year.

Still, the principal experience of community in ACE is rooted in the life of each household. From the program's origins, it was deemed essential to send teachers out in communities for reasons practical and spiritual. In a chapter that seeks to explain why we emphasize community, what our vision of community entails, and how we strive to build vibrant ACE communities, the governing conception of community is, for the most part, the household of four to seven ACE teachers.

### WHY THE COMMUNITY PILLAR?

THE RATIONALES for establishing community as one of the three pillars of ACE range from the practical to the theological. To begin with the practical, economics alone dictate the prudence of pooling resources by having ACE teachers share rent, utilities, and other living expenses. With most ACErs living on less than $1,000 per month, communities of four to seven allow them to take advantage of the economies of scale. Dioceses are responsible for locating housing that is affordable, safe, and proximate to the schools that the ACE teachers serve. In most cases, rent is no greater than $200 per person each month. Housing situations include converted convents, houses, and town houses. Occasionally, apartments are large enough to accommodate communities of four. Though housing is sometimes less than ideal from some perspectives, most ACE teachers find it reassuring to know that they have a home in an unfamiliar city. Community living thus saves time, money, and uncertainty for the program's participants, allowing them to be more productive, especially at the outset, when the stresses of beginning teaching are most intense.

Another practical benefit of the ACE community model is immediate and daily professional and personal support. First-year teaching is particularly challenging, and our experience is instructive of the value of community for the participants' growth as teachers and, ultimately, the program's high retention rate (more than 98% complete the first year and more than 92% graduate in two years). ACE teachers depend on each other to lend a willing ear and to offer advice and reassurance as they grapple with the inevitable struggles that arise. A powerful sense of group solidarity bonds those who have lived together through what frequently becomes the most difficult year of their lives. Simply put, ACE teachers minister to each other personally and professionally. "As a first-year teacher, you can feel as if you are alone in your frustrations, your confusion, and your struggles," explains Matt Arsenault of ACE IV. "For someone who went into a profession hoping to contribute to society, it was difficult to feel like that work was unappreciated or unsuccessful. Community helped assuage those feelings. When you gathered at dinner, you heard that everyone else had the same struggles and concerns. It helped give you a bigger picture of a society outside your classroom. Your community gives you the strength to say that you need to work one day at a time."

Molly Davis, who taught in Tulsa, echoes Arsenault: "I can't imagine facing the teaching aspect every day without the support and wisdom from the others in community. It made me stronger as a teacher." To be sure, the pooled inexperience of a first-year group does not always yield perfect solutions, but this is why ACE offers a larger community of faculty, staff, and mentors, a multi-tiered structure of professional support. Writes Tom Perez of ACE II: "The best thing was having a support system when teaching was painfully hard and you really wanted to quit and get a high-paying job in the business world." Like most of his peers, Perez persevered and continues to teach three years after finishing ACE; in 2000, he was honored as educator of the year at Bishop Dunne High School in Dallas. Townsend Bailey also is grateful for his housemates in Pensacola: "It is nice to have a couple of fashion censors in the house. It saves me some embarrassment in front of my students."

ACE communities provide a social support system of particular value for the majority of ACE teachers undergoing the difficult transition from undergraduate life. "We're all new to the area, so we have people we can hang out with and not feel like a complete stranger to our new surroundings," says Trish Sevilla of her experience in Jacksonville. Most participants find themselves in regions far from home; they enter a city having essentially no social ties except for their respective faculties. "The best thing about our community in Dallas," observes Veronica Flores, "was that we were all new to the city and had to experience everything together—from teaching to cooking to driving." While dioceses and local alumni clubs generally offer tremendous hospitality, there is no substitute for the community as an instant social set, notwithstanding running jokes among the participants that the hectic nature of beginning teaching and graduate study defers until graduation the never-mentioned "fourth pillar of ACE—a social life." Most participants quickly realize that they will no longer have the time nor the energy to sustain the social life of a college senior. On the other hand, ACE is not a program of wallflowers. In most cases, the proximity of communities to each other (most are no more than a four-hour drive from another ACE house) provides an environment conducive to road-trips—a staple of ACE existence that flows naturally from its model of small communities concentrated in the South and Southwest.

Despite their value as support systems, ACE communities are meant to be much more. In fact, we invite ACE teachers to see their life in community as an important part of "voluntary displacement," the movement "to counteract the tendency to become settled in false comfort" (McNeill, Morrison, & Nouwen, 1983). Community thus serves two seemingly contradictory functions. On the one hand, it helps to foster the sense of displacement, for in choosing ACE one yields the choice of one's community members and the locale of one's service. Rightly understood, community fosters a spirit of openness to God's will, an openness that extends to the discernment and active response to God's call that lies at the heart of ACE. At the same time, community ameliorates the loneliness that can accompany the displacement of living far from family and friends and struggling with a new and difficult ministry. The program's focused mission contributes to the assembly of like-minded people with common motivations, shared values, and the oft-cited desire to be a part of something larger than oneself. Steve Camilleri of ACE I reflects: "You had a sense of purpose and mission; you knew that you were part of something good. As many would say, there was nothing better than coming home to dinner and knowing that the experiences you had that day could resonate with your community."

Camilleri's insight gestures toward the deeper theological reasons for ACE's emphasis on community, reasons ultimately grounded in the Catholic understanding of God as Father, Son, and Holy Spirit. The profound truth of this mystery is that God exists in relationships and that we are called to life in community. As ACE has moved to articulate its vision of community, we consistently return to this scripture from Paul for inspiration and example:

> Now there are a variety of gifts, but the same Spirit, and there are varieties of service, but the same Lord, and there are varieties of working, but it is the same God who inspires them all in every one. To each is given the manifestation of the Spirit for the common good. . . . For just as the body is one and has many members, and all the members of the body, though many, are one body, so it is with Christ. . . . If one member suffers, all suffer together; if one member is honored, all rejoice together. Now you are the body of Christ and individually members of it. (1 Cor. 12:4–27)

Most profoundly, then, ACE makes community one of its three pillars because, in the words of Thomas Groome (1998), "community is the primary context for 'being saved' and 'becoming human'" (p. 175). In his articulation of the great commandment, Jesus links love of God and love of neighbor; you cannot have one without the other. We are not just responsible for ourselves. Consider Luke's description of the early Christian community: "The faithful all lived together and owned everything in common; they sold their goods and possessions and shared out the proceeds among themselves according to what each needed. They went as a body to the Temple every day but met in their houses for the breaking of bread; they shared their food gladly and generously; they praised God and were looked up to by everyone" (Acts 2:44–47). While one feels a nostalgic longing even in this early account, living in Christian community remains a powerful way to spread the Good News, particularly in an age like ours that celebrates individualism and prizes independence. Indeed, as the Second Vatican Council reaffirms, community is central to evangelization, to bearing witness of the Good News to the world. Pope Paul VI (1975) eloquently connects the power of Christian community to evangelize individuals and, more largely, culture itself:

> Above all the Gospel must be proclaimed by witness. Take a Christian or a handful of Christians who, in the midst of their own community, show their capacity for understanding and acceptance, their sharing and life and destiny with other people, their solidarity with the efforts of all for whatever is noble and good. Let us sup-

pose that, in addition, they radiate in an altogether simple and unaffected way their faith in values that go beyond current values, and their hope in something that is not seen and that one would not dare to imagine. Through this wordless witness these Christians stir up irresistible questions in the hearts of those who see how they live. (n. 21)

Living in community thus challenges us to grow in love of others and of God. By practicing love, we become more loving. We may find it easy to love at a distance, much harder to love up close. "It is very hard to love someone you live with every day, every morning, every evening," writes Laura Eideitis of ACE IV. "Loving people in front of you is one of the hardest challenges in life." Life in Christian community reminds us that love is more than a feeling; it flows from a decision, a commitment to put others before ourselves, to think and act with their best interests in mind, to will the good for them.

In elucidating the various reasons for establishing community as a pillar of ACE, I began by distinguishing the practical from the theological. This distinction might imply a false dichotomy. For what could be more practical than a community of love to support new teachers and to energize their mission of service? In light of research about the efficacy of Catholic schools, an effectiveness linked in part to cohesive and caring school communities, ACE's focus on building community connects to its most evident mission. Our focus on community seeks to augment a signature strength of Catholic schools, namely, that they educate for the common good (Bryk, Holland, & Lee, 1993).

## TOWARD A CLEAR AND COMPELLING
## VISION OF COMMUNITY

ACE LEADERSHIP has resisted the temptation to insist on a monolithic model of community that would inhibit the freedom of individual communities to find their own way. Our caution in prescribing a uniform community model represents two important realities of ACE: first, its desire to learn from and adapt to the reflective experiences of its participants and, second, its sensitivity to community contexts that vary in size, composition, personality, and teaching assignments.

ACE communities range from four to seven members, and a model that works well for four may be impossible to achieve with seven.

Moreover, since its second year, ACE has really sponsored two types of households—those whose residents come from one cohort and those with a mixture of novices and veterans. Amid such different contexts, flexibility is essential, especially given the heavy demands of teaching, coaching and other extracurricular activities, and manifold responsibilities to the school community. Beyond differences in composition, differences in teaching assignments preclude the wisdom of a fixed model. In Baton Rouge, for example, everyone teaches at the high school level. In Dallas, everyone teaches at K–8 parish schools. In most cases, though, teachers from one community work in both elementary and secondary school settings. Those at the high school level typically have one or two free periods during the day and fewer preparations, but often more commitments in the afternoon and evenings than their counterparts in elementary and middle school. Elementary teachers may have a comparatively shorter school day, with less adult interaction, and potentially greater exhaustion at the end of the day, so that their needs and desires in community can differ from those who teach high school.

That there is not a model of community does not mean ACE lacks a vision of it. An ACE community should not be a collection of independent roommates living under one roof. Our challenge is to raise the bar or, more precisely, to encourage participants to raise the bar for themselves and each other. Unfortunately, sometimes not everyone in an ACE community feels accountable to the community life pillar. Although a university-based program like ACE can impose sanctions on certain behaviors that disrupt community, personality conflicts and negative attitudes require persuasion rather than regulations. In many situations, the ACE staff, most of whom are ACE alumni, respond as best we can to facilitate resolutions to community problems, often by challenging everyone to remember why they felt called to ACE in the first place. So the community itself must find a way to move forward.

What, then, is the vision of community put forth by ACE to its teachers? From its inception, but with deepening understanding, ACE espouses the formation of a community of teachers bonded by their commitment to follow Christ Teacher. ACE may be a new program, but it draws on the richness of the Catholic tradition. We have come of late to advance a vision of community grounded in the three theological virtues; our ultimate goal is to strive to build communities of faith, hope, and love. The theological virtues offer an inspirational model—simple, memorable, compelling, and open to specific outworking and enactment.

First, ACE households are called to be communities of faith. The Gospel is the foundation and inspiration of our mission "to go forth and teach." In the words of Laura Considine, who taught high school Spanish in Mississippi, "faith in action is what drew us to ACE in the first place." Our conception of a community of faith thus represents an explicit convergence of the three pillars of teaching, community, and spirituality. ACE teachers are called to be prayerful people, to develop their faith as individuals and as members of an intentional Christian community. ACE seeks to provide a variety of rich opportunities for prayer and faith sharing during the summer and on retreats. From the program's origins, the Eucharist has always been the central act of prayer and worship, the coming together of the community of faith. During the summer's daily Masses, and especially during the celebrations of Eucharist in which the entire ACE community convenes—Missioning Mass at summer's end and on the December retreat—the overwhelming sense of community not only signals God's presence but provides memories that inspire and sustain. This is important, for at their local sites, ACE teachers are expected to form prayerful communities, a sometimes difficult but necessary opportunity to grow as prayer leaders at home and school, apart from the rich liturgical offerings on campus or with the whole of ACE. As Considine intimates, prayerful ACE communities are also communities of action. Urged to see Christ in one another, indeed, in all people, members of the ACE community need to have faith in each other and build relationships of trust to invigorate their teaching ministry.

Second, ACE calls upon its members to forge communities of hope. In any context, but especially in a Catholic school, teaching is an inherently hopeful act. Working with children to transmit our knowledge, values, and faith inevitably looks toward the future; from a Catholic perspective, education is essential to building the kingdom of God. Hope connotes much more than mere optimism. Hope arises from the heart of the Gospel, literally the Good News. Far from inviting a complacent retreat from the world, ACE teachers seek to energize each other and their students to work for a more just and compassionate world. As communities of teachers, ACE households, ideally, stand as vivid reminders that we are instruments of grace. If the principal goal of Catholic education is to evangelize students and their culture, then the enthusiasm that characterizes ACE teachers is, to quote Notre Dame's president, Fr. Malloy, "a sign of hope to all of us." To be communities of hope, ACE households must be enthusiastic, joyful, accepting of struggles in school and at home. Both the local communities and the larger ACE community must be voices and witnesses against the cynicism and despair so prevalent in the postmodern age, one John Paul II has labeled a "culture of death."

Third, and most importantly, ACE communities must be communities that manifest love in a variety of ways. Love is at the center of ACE's mission, and people enter the program primarily motivated to give of themselves in service to others. Community is meant to uphold the mission of teaching, itself a profound act of love. Yet ACE's identity as a service program goes beyond the gift of self in the classroom and school to include the radical gift of self in Christian community. As a community of faith, we *see* Christ in one another. As a community of love, we are called to *be* Christ for one another. ACE communities, if they are to be communities of love, must be communities of forgiveness, for tension and conflict are inevitable. ACE communities must also avoid the temptation to become exclusive or insular. Instead, they must be inclusive communities that extend warm hospitality. Joe Villinski, who taught in Pensacola, speaks frankly about the relationship of community to the Christian life: "The greatest challenge of community is the greatest challenge of living: trying to be selfless. When your housemate comes home after a bad day when you've had a bad day, it takes the strength of Ruth to be present and give of yourself. Some might get by without huge fights or dissension, but ultimately, you're just bodies sharing a common space if you're not selfless. It's hard for recent college grads to do this, coming from a time when all they did was worry about themselves to a large extent." Villinski may single out his peer group, but emptying oneself is hard at any age.

## ACE'S EFFORTS TO BUILD COMMUNITY

Just as the program's vision of community has evolved over time, so too has our understanding of the preparation and practices necessary to help build communities of faith, hope, and love. What follows is a nonexhaustive summary of ACE's central action plan to form community from recruitment through graduation and beyond. Though our strategies have become increasingly self-conscious over time—particularly as they are informed by experience, the counsel of various constituencies of the alliance, and an outside consulting group—it is important to acknowledge that, like our vision of community, our action plan is anything but static. Our hope, of course, is that it continues to improve.

One thing we have stressed from the outset is the need to recruit and select people who are eager to live in community and have demonstrated success in living with others. All informational materials (video, website, and brochures) highlight the importance of community life for prospective applicants. Essay questions on the application invite reflection on all three pillars. We also ask applicants to obtain letters of recommendation from peers and dormitory rectors (ideally) or others who can attest to their ability to live and work well with others. Interviews also focus considerable attention on this theme. While anyone can have a difficult roommate situation in the past, we screen carefully for fitness and openness to community life.

A central tenet of ACE's philosophy of community is that its small faith-based communities ought to involve both men and women to reflect the experience of lay Christian life. The primary challenge is to form gender-balanced communities while matching individual credentials and grade-level preferences to the specific requests of the schools. Most ACErs find it reassuring to learn that their talents and the needs of the schools principally determine the composition of their local community, rather than any attempt to construct communities based on the personalities of the members. During times of discord or tension, they know that the reason for their coming together has everything to do with their mission, which is a powerful motivation to work out problems.

Establishing a sense of community actually begins with the recruitment and selection process. Each ACE cohort receives its own name (ACE VII, for example), so that they can begin to identify at once with the larger community of the whole program and the smaller community of their particular year. At the information session for new acceptances, we add another layer by revealing for the first time their small communities, known hereafter by location (Brownsville, for instance). These multiple group identities persist even after graduation and help to knit stronger community bonds, especially as cohort size has doubled from 40 to 80. Throughout the entire experience, we reinforce this sense of community through shared rhetoric, ritual, and activities. One example? Toward the end of each summer session, the new ACE T-shirt is unveiled (every year a different color) as all gather for the annual ACE photo on the steps of Bond Hall. Though this little ceremony might sound slightly corny, somehow it works, perhaps because it is only one of many social occasions intended to convene the whole group and foster a sense of identity—cookouts, parties, baseball games, bowling, and trips to the Lake Michigan beaches.

ACE also comes together to pray as well as play. Masses and retreats have always been the basis for community in ACE, as detailed in the chapter on spirituality. All retreats devote considerable time and attention to strengthen the ACE households of faith. The December retreat is illustrative, when most of Saturday afternoon is scheduled for community breakout sessions, each one facilitated by someone on the retreat staff.

A centerpiece of our community-building effort is a 1-credit course, EDU 550, the Integrative Seminar, which meets daily for the first week (new cohort only) and for 90 minutes one night a week during the summer (with both cohorts). The main purpose of EDU 550 is to deepen understanding of the integration of the three pillars of ACE. Thus, we have fashioned a document called the "community covenant," distributed at the first class meeting. Our choice of the word "covenant" instead of "contract" bespeaks our ultimate purpose. During the meeting, each community responds to questions, organized under four main categories: communication and commitment, spiritual life, social life, and household management. Through dialogue informed by readings and presentations across the summer, we expect each community to submit a completed community covenant by the final class. On the last page, they formulate a community mission statement and affix their signatures.

This document is but one of many ways that the ACE staff seeks to know well the people and communities in the program. Forming trusting relationships begins with recruitment and continues past graduation, especially as we seek to deepen our post-ACE initiatives. Notwithstanding the growth of ACE, we endeavor to establish relationships with all participants. Still, we gain focus and depth by dividing responsibilities for particular communities, as the associate directors and the director of pastoral formation and administration each serve as the primary contact for a different region. During the summer, staff members meet with each person in their region as well as their assigned communities to monitor their progress. During the academic year, this is continued with regular telephone and e-mail communication as needed, but once or twice a month minimally. We also conduct site visits early in the fall and spring. By day we meet with superintendents and principals and visit the ACE teachers in their classrooms; we spend the evenings (and late nights at times) eating and praying with the community. I sometimes joke with my hosts that our site visits often succeed before our arrival, for they frequently prompt honest and healing conversation in anticipation of our night together.

ACE has always emphasized the value of weekly community prayer, which can build intimacy and create an atmosphere of honesty, trust, and mutual love. However, regular prayer and faith sharing are often the first things to go when schedules fill up. To encourage persistence in common prayer, ACE provides a variety of spiritual resources: community subscriptions to *Living with Christ* and *Quest*, local chaplains appointed by the diocese or, better yet, discovered by the ACE household, and regular communication from the ACE office with ideas and materials for prayer, often in connection with the liturgical season. During the summer and on retreats, we structure opportunities for ACErs to lead group prayer. ACE also provides financial resources and consultation for each house to plan and to make one or two retreats each year. Our hope is that ACE teachers and graduates become prayer leaders for schools, parishes, and families.

Fortunately, even when weekly prayer falters, grace before meals invariably remains a fixture in ACE houses. Preparing and eating dinner together is probably the single most important feature of community life. We strive to make this practice habitual and comfortable by designating one night a week during the summer, usually Thursday, as community dinner night. Gina Velasco explains how dinner became the central ritual for her community in Corpus Christi: "Everyone was assigned a night to cook. A lot of the times we would talk with each other as we cooked. I loved this time together. It wasn't always happy. We had arguments and problems; sometimes we hardly spoke. But it was our time to relax and be together and regroup. Most nights, we would laugh until we cried; I loved it. I don't think any of us ever consciously thought about how much those dinners meant to us at the time. . . . It brought us together every day." On our site visits, the state of the community life is invariably revealed in the dinner by who helps, who talks and how, who listens and how, and who feels comfortable lingering.

Working together, whether reviewing the day's successes and failures around the dinner table or cleaning up the dishes and doing other domestic chores, is another sign of a healthy community. Like many faculty who teach in the program, I find the spirit of professional collaboration among ACE participants quite moving indeed. Whether it be late nights at a campus computer cluster or at an ACE house, people habitually extend themselves for each other to help them become better teachers. (This is certainly modeled by the staff and faculty, who dedicate enormous energy to their students through individual conferences, daily lunches, nightly Masses, and in many cases, frequent communication throughout the academic year.) In ACE households where such generosity goes beyond the professional dimension to include the mundane realm of cleaning and cooking, the sense of community is typically palpable. Few things build community like mutual labor—one reason that ACE graduates strongly advise new houses to establish chore charts to hold everyone accountable.

Kate McCann of ACE IV indicates the importance of shared work and play to sustain personal and community energy. "Sometimes you didn't feel like you were drowning quite as much when someone else was up late doing lesson plans or correcting. My community definitely reminded me to take time to have fun, whether it was playing football in the street or our ongoing men vs. women pool tournament." The experience of those who have completed ACE underscores the value of community play, even if fun must be scheduled. Just as we urge ACE communities to build weekly prayer into the calendar, we also invite them to set up a regular time for social events at which all members participate.

Spending weekends with nearby ACE communities also is a popular and unifying part of ACE culture. Gina Velasco extols "our road trips to Mission, Texas. If we hadn't hooked up with them, my ACE experience would not have been nearly as fulfilling. They are wonderful, fun, incredible people, and I cherish every moment we spent with their community." True, some ACErs go overboard and exhaust themselves through constant travel, but so important are these community visits that we included two houses in Los Angeles to forestall a sense of disconnectedness from the rest of ACE. When Phoenix became a late addition to our expansion that year, we promised to fly the Phoenix group to L.A. one semester and bring the L.A. houses to Arizona the next in order to help form a regional identity.

Though simple living is not an explicit feature of ACE's vision of community, successful households typically find ways to avoid being consumed by the distractions of modernity, such as television, telephone, video games, the Internet, and alcohol. Kate McCann offers an anecdote that exemplifies the lessons of simple living from her service in Charlotte. "During Lent our first year, we decided that we were going to try to clean out our cupboards a bit and live very simply. We bought only the essentials for the last several weeks of Lent. It was an exercise in making due with what you have, and we got pretty creative. We also had to come together in our commitment to it, and for as much as it frustrated me that we didn't have lots of prayer nights, there was a real spiritual element to being able to do this. I was the one who was least excited about doing it, and yet I'm very grateful that we did. It's something I'll always remember."

## CHALLENGES TO COMMUNITY: OPPORTUNITIES FOR GROWTH

COMMUNITIES OF ACE TEACHERS, though established and enjoined to be "the light of the world," do not always burn brightly. While every year presents its own set of problems, most issues can be grouped in one or more of these categories: time, transition from college life, money and materialism, personality conflicts, divergent expectations and experiences of community, romantic relationships, and complacency. Exploring these challenges to community and the responses of the faculty and staff illustrates the dynamic process of building communities of faith, hope, and love in ACE.

Time, or its limited availability, consistently ranks as the number one obstacle to the successful ACE household. "I sometimes feel that everyone wants something of me, whether at school or home." This is a common refrain among ACE teachers, particularly during the first year. Dan McCue of ACE V speaks for many in his assertion of how hard it was to "make time for my community members when it seemed I had no time for myself." Their busy schedules often leave little time for group activities or even time to spend relaxing together. As Colleen Hogan Shean recalls her service in Mobile: "The greatest challenge of community was finding enough time to feed the many facets of community. There was never enough time in the day to pray enough, cook enough, or talk enough because of our overwhelming commitment to the students. The majority of our time was spent in the classroom, as it should have been."

That the demands on their time come mainly from competing goods within the mission of ACE can make equilibrium difficult to find or maintain. There are always lesson planning, grading, telephoning parents, and extracurricular involvement. Coaching, in particular, can keep many ACEers away from home well into the evening and on weekends, causing them to miss dinners, activities, and perhaps most importantly, the informal hanging out that is so essential to get to know others and deepen relationships. At its worst, community moves from being a support system to an additional demand on time, one more thing to do, one more task to check off the list or put off till tomorrow before crawling into bed.

The first summer acculturates the ACE teachers well to the problem of time. By the end of June, most of the new cohort are exhausted from maintaining a schedule that typically runs from early morning to well past midnight. "I tell my friends that I'm in an emotional, spiritual, and intellectual boot camp, and I love it," says Paola Gaine, who teaches in south central Los Angeles. Happily, Gaine's positive stance toward this demanding rhythm of life is ultimately shared, if not quite so effusively, by most of the participants. However, her image of the boot camp captures well the reality of the first summer, given all the first-year ACE teachers need to learn and do. In recent years, the faculty and staff have tried to minimize stressful situations as much as possible by adjusting program schedules and staggering course deadlines. Still, 10 credits, a morning practicum, and two retreats are packed into eight weeks, along with community building activities and regular evening liturgy.

Part of the transition to post-college life for many involves taking additional responsibility for personal finances. Though no one opts for ACE for economic gain, money matters can and do introduce tension in community. From one perspective, the graduate stipend is fairly generous in the context of the fully funded master's degree. Still, there is limited disposable income. Community challenges related to money can arise from several situations. ACE households sometimes contend with jealousy or its opposite, the temptation to self-righteousness, toward friends and acquaintances pursuing more lucrative fields. Friction can also build among community members over expenditures (brand name or generic?), budgets, and the sharing of valuable possessions such as cars and computers. Probably the most common form of nascent materialism involves allocating space in the ACE house. In mixed communities, the veterans usually get first choice of bedrooms. In single-cohort communities, rooms are often alternated from one year to the next. Every year, however, we help to facilitate a solution for a few communities in which someone claims, "I know it might seem fair for me to share a bedroom, but I really need my personal space. I'll be a better teacher and community member if I have a room of my own." We always attempt to invite the household to pursue a resolution that everyone can accept.

Personality conflicts are also part of community life in ACE, with escapism not a viable option, though some try it for a time by closeting themselves in their room or spending evenings at work and weekends on the road. Prevention through open communication is our first and most important tactic. To that end, we administer the Meyers-

Briggs personality inventory during the summer, which, through its descriptive lexicon, initiates conversations on personality type among each household. We ask each community to discuss the results with particular emphasis on how they respond to stress. When persistent personality conflicts emerge, ACE offers considerable support (regular communication, household retreats, extra site visits from ACE staff, local resources) to help the community resolve its problems. ACE encourages its participants to embrace with honesty and charity the challenges of communal living, to see them ultimately as opportunities for growth. To this point, ACE has not needed to reassign participants for community problems that have reached an impasse. Still, it is possible that community life within a house could become so difficult that alternative housing arrangements might need to be considered and enacted. In such cases, the leadership of ACE reserves the final right to determine alternative arrangements, even including a review of the participant's continuation in the program.

Even in households with compatible personalities, different expectations for community can lead to tension and fissures within the group. A specific example involves community meals. Some enter ACE expecting to eat dinner as a group one or two nights a week; others envision a household that comes together at table almost nightly. Resentment, worst when unspoken, can poison the spirit of trust when some members suspect that others lack commitment to community or when others feel suffocated by those who require, in their minds, endless sharing and processing. In these situations, gossip can be quite destructive. When community members talk about each other behind their backs, whether in community or, worse yet, in their professional circles, the ensuing distrust can be difficult to repair. Readings and workshops in conflict resolution and confrontation are important features of the summer program; however, we also recognize the value of a more clearly articulated vision of community in ACE and clearer guidelines for establishing successful communities. The ACE staff and faculty also spend substantial time listening and facilitating solutions.

ACE encourages its members to maintain and continue to form strong relationships outside the household. To do otherwise not only would be to recommend insular communities, but would be downright impractical, for ACE teachers are in an age group where romantic relationships are common. They can introduce friction to community life, however. Hours spent on the phone and numerous weekends out of town can pull one or more members away from community. Sometimes, the household essentially expands with the regular weekend guest. Occasionally, members of the same house fall in love with each other. All of these scenarios pose a different set of challenges. Here our response resembles that to many other perennial community issues—preparation and mediation in a prayerful context. In terms of preparation, one night of the integrative seminar is traditionally devoted to issues of friendship and intimacy from a perspective that melds Christian theology and developmental psychology. Mediation typically involves the ACE staff in a pastoral role, listening and advising with sensitivity to individual and community concerns.

In the end, perhaps the most difficult challenge to community is complacency during the second year in the program. "Why push it at this point? We only have a few months to go?" This sentiment, occasionally expressed by those in their last semester when the temptation toward apathy is greatest, can be more pernicious than hostility. We try our best to draw upon ACErs' leadership potential to get them to realize that they are called to summon the courage needed to tackle problems new and lingering, that to do less is to succumb to the path of least resistance. Conflict takes energy, but conflict can be a sign of hope. A community willing to risk conflict to move forward is more in keeping with the spirit of ACE than a community that devolves into a group of individuals who tacitly agree not to push it any longer. Sr. Joan Dixon, a clinical supervisor known and loved for her refreshing candor, once upbraided a complacent household for boasting that they never quarreled. "You all don't even care enough about each other to fight," she told them. According to Jenny Monahan, who taught in Charlotte, the struggles offer surprising rewards: "The best thing about my community was our collective willingness to work through our difficulties and to learn from each other's differences. I learned more about myself and about relationships and about valuing the differences in other people because we didn't always get along than I might have had we never encountered any problems."

## MOVING FORWARD IN COMMUNITY

In an effort to strengthen the community pillar of ACE, we have done our best to listen, reflect, discuss, and implement new ideas. Because of the inherent complexity of interpersonal relations, I suspect that community life will always be a work in progress for ACE. Programmatically, we have moved forward in the clarity of our vision, our understanding of its evangelizing potential, and our responsiveness to its challenges. One of the humbling joys of my work is to observe the growth in faith, hope, and love among the ACE teachers—humbling because the program flourishes mainly due to the grace that animates them to serve their students and each other. We are all aware of the admonition to "perform random acts of kindness." Community in ACE enjoins its members to go much farther—to practice habitual acts of kindness as the only authentic response to follow Christ Teacher. Typically, participants in the ACE program do go much farther, as this closing story from one ACE teacher illustrates:

> To date, I may very well be the only ACE teacher to have contracted head lice from one of her students. I'd have to say that was one of the most challenging experiences during my time in ACE. There's something completely disconcerting about having head lice, and it doesn't help when your school is in such a hysterical state about it that you can't tell anyone that the nurse found a few on your head, too. I've never wanted to be home with my mom like I wanted to during that whole experience. During that mess the community member that I clashed with the most was the one that volunteered to help. Faithfully this person searched my head and picked out lice eggs. Yes, there was a running commentary and lots of itching and scratching jokes, but I was at his mercy, and he completely went beyond the call of duty to help. It is something I will never forget. It really made me think about who will be there for you when things are difficult—sometimes it's the people you least expect. It was a real lesson in true community for me. This person really walked with me through a pretty challenging and disconcerting time.

### REFERENCES

McNeill, D., Morrison, D., & Nouwen, H. (1983). *Compassion: A reflection on the Christian Life*. New York: Doubleday.

Groome, T. (1998). *Educating for life*. Allen, TX: Thomas More.

Pope Paul VI. (1975). *Evangeli Nuntandi*.

Bryk, A., Holland, P., & Lee, V. (1993). *Catholic schools and the common good*. Cambridge, MA: Harvard University Press.

LOUIS A. DELFRA
TIMOTHY R. SCULLY

# COME AND YOU WILL SEE

## SPIRITUALITY IN ACE

We in ACE like to tell the story of how ACE began: how a nonexistent program with a nonexistent office, a nonexistent faculty, and a nonexistent budget invited a group of unknown, and unknowing, students to join in a largely inchoate, yet inspiring, vision to transform Catholic education by following in the steps of Christ Teacher. As Sean McGraw and Tim Scully have recounted in an earlier chapter of this book, they hung up some catchy posters inviting interested members of Notre Dame's senior class to show up at a Tuesday evening information meeting. As the date of that meeting approached, one fairly crucial question was on Scully and McGraw's minds: if anyone does in fact show up, what exactly are we going to tell them?

Perhaps the surest sign of the presence of the Spirit in the initial formation of ACE is that, although nothing formally existed, they were able to come up with a series of answers to this question: dare them to be teachers; invite them to head to the warm and exotic Catholic "mission" territories of the South; ask them to live with one another in an intentional faith community, to develop their prayer life, to do something intensely meaningful with their lives. Surely, different aspects of this invitation caught the attention of different people in that room. Indeed, perhaps even more extraordinary than the fact that 200 seniors attended the initial meeting is that over 100 decided to apply to ACE—whatever ACE was! Forty of these applicants became the first ACE teachers. Hundreds more have since followed in their footsteps.

This story of mysterious invitation and response has played out over and over again throughout the history of our Church. The Gospel of John records the very first time that this story of Christian invitation unfolded:

> The next day John was there again with two of his disciples, and as he watched Jesus walk by, he said, "Behold, the Lamb of God." The two disciples heard what he said and followed Jesus. Jesus turned and saw them following him and said to them, "What are you looking for?" They said to him, "Rabbi" (which translated means Teacher), "Where are you staying?" He said to them, "Come and you will see." So they went and saw where he was staying, and they stayed with him that day. (John 1:35–39)

At first, these followers have no idea who or what they are following. Hesitantly, cautiously, they walk behind this enigmatic figure, until finally he stops and asks them the very question that is burning, yet largely unarticulated, in their own hearts: "What are you looking for?" It is really their question, not Jesus' question, and so it is not surprising that they have no ready answer for him. So they simply address him, "Teacher"—that is, "Teach us what it is we are looking for." They ask him, "Where are you staying?"—that is, "Can we come and see what it is that beats so wildly within our hearts?" Jesus' answer, of course, as always, is "Yes! Come and you will see."

Do we dare be so bold as to juxtapose our small efforts in the ACE program with John's record of Jesus' call of the first disciples? Yes! Because if this ACE program means anything, from a spiritual perspective, if ACE has any spiritual foundation, it can only be in this: *in ACE, we believe we are called to an encounter with Christ Teacher, and it is the Holy Spirit who is calling people, as the Spirit called the first disciples, to this encounter.*

Many motivations and forces drive the ACE program and its teachers and staff: a spirit of service, the ideal of helping needy children grow and learn, premium graduate-level teacher training, community life with one of the most dynamic, talented, committed, and fun groups of young disciples anywhere. As we have discovered, it is not difficult to allow any one of these powerful and benevolent forces to be the driving force of our life in ACE. Yet spirituality is the central pillar of the ACE program, and we need to challenge ourselves more and more to realize what this means: that the deepest driving force in ACE, and in each of our teachers' lives, the one that gives all the other forces their ultimate meaning and life, is the call of Christ Teacher to "come and see," and the ensuing encounter of our teachers and our community with this Christ.

## THE ACE TEACHER

WHO ARE THESE ACE teachers? What motivates them? Though this is a thoroughly heterogeneous group, a few broad characteristics come readily to mind. First, when one walks into a roomful of ACErs, one is inevitably struck by their *enthusiasm*. Take Steve Camilleri, for instance. That first spring semester, before a structured program yet existed, Steve was one of the 40 seniors who was mailed an acceptance letter from ACE. The letter acknowledged that little yet existed in terms of faculty, placements in the South, time commitment, or just about anything else. Somehow, some way, they would be teachers if they accepted ACE's offer, but they did not need to sign the enclosed contract for another month or so, when more details would be in place. The night after mailing the acceptance letters, McGraw and Scully were attending a student social on campus when in burst Steve, bounding across the room, waving a signed contract, and yelling, "I heard you guys would be here! I want to be your first teacher!"

ACErs have been largely, even overwhelmingly, successful in their lives, succeeding in school, jobs, athletics, art, music, and many other activities. Now they are bound and determined to succeed at becoming Catholic schoolteachers. They arrive conspicuously endowed with determination, zeal, generosity of spirit, and volunteerism. They are contagiously hope-filled and idealistic about the job they are undertaking.

This is not an unproblematic dynamic, for we know with nearly absolute certainty that at least one thing is going to happen to these new disciples and teachers in their first months on the job: they will fail, and fail often. Many of them have not frequently, perhaps ever, tasted failure before. Thus, ACE's spirituality needs both to tap into the incredible energy and commitment of these new teachers and, at the same time, to prepare them for the inevitable difficulties and failures they will meet as beginning teachers.

As one comes to know these ACE teachers more deeply, a second set of characteristics reveals itself, falling broadly under the heading of *leadership*. Jen Ehren, Notre Dame's Class of 2000 valedictorian from the College of Science, is about to become a chemistry and physics teacher in Biloxi, Mississippi. Dave Hungeling, by all accounts one of the most charismatic student body presidents Notre Dame has ever had, is now on his way to teach a twelfth grade class in government at St. Joseph's High School in Jackson, Mississippi. Pete Miller, co-captain of Notre Dame's varsity basketball team, is preparing to teach history and coach basketball at St. Jude's High School in Montgomery, Alabama. Michael Downs, winner of the Class of 2000 Notre Dame Distinguished Student Leader Award, is about to begin teaching middle school religion in Austin, Texas.

These are the risk-takers and leaders of the senior class. A large majority, as undergraduates, have been resident hall assistants, studied abroad, played varsity athletics, or edited the school newspaper. This too is problematic. Who takes the lead in a community full of leaders? Is there enough room for true and effective cooperation? Are people able to listen empathetically to others? Do we recognize those in our community who are hurting or somehow marginalized? Are these leaders willing to learn how to lead others to Christ? Again, ACE's spirituality needs to inspire and transform the potent leadership inherent in this group of young teachers into the future leaders in our Church and in Catholic education. At the same time, our spirituality must also transform leadership into service: "those who wish to be first, must serve the rest."

One final, broad, but deeply defining characteristic of this group of ACE teachers is that they are called, in a profound way, to a *life of service*. Every teacher in our program has an undergraduate transcript that includes service in a multitude of forms. The *New York Times* wrote about Erin Lillis, of ACE VII, who helped begin a remarkably successful Great Books reading program for the homeless of South Bend. Maria Freiburger of ACE IV, while acquiring her anthropology degree, began an annual service-learning project in Nairobi, Kenya, that continues to send Notre Dame anthropology majors to East Africa today. Sean Byrne, Max Engle, and Steve Dotsch coordinated the PULSE Program in downtown Boston to place more than 300 college students in service positions in over 45 inner-city service agencies.

To a person, the ACErs include among their motivations for participation in this program the desire to give back out of the gifts they have received. Most of them view their years of service not merely as a job or an activity, but as a vocation. Thus, ACE's spirituality needs to provide increasingly rich opportunities for these teachers to experience and articulate their identity and their service within the story of the Gospel, the Eucharistic sacramentality of the Church, and the deep traditions of the Catholic faith.

At the same time, most of these teachers do not have a vocation to religious life (though each year, several have decided to enter religious formation). Many of the current structures and formulations of the Church are, explicitly or implicitly, formed under the assumption of religious life. This situation is changing, yet there is still much work to be done. ACE's spirituality needs to call its participants to a deeper life of prayer, a deeper sense of vocation, relationship, and community, a more Gospel-centered, Eucharist-centered, and Christ-centered life of service. It must do so, however, in a form and a vocabulary that fits the life experience and lay vocation of these ACE teachers. These are some of the challenges and opportunities that lie before us as we seek to strengthen the spirituality of ACE.

## THE MODEL OF CHRIST TEACHER

WHO IS THIS Christ who invites these incipient disciples to "come and see"? We in the ACE program have come to see that Christ reveals himself primarily as Christ Teacher. We are beginning to understand more deeply, and integrate more pervasively into our community and spirituality, several concrete and specific characteristics of our Master Teacher. We elucidate five key characteristics here.

First, *Christ came to know intimately and to love unconditionally those he taught.* The passage from John's Gospel that we used to open this chapter ends with an easily overlooked sentence, but one beautiful and compelling in its intimacy: "So they went and saw where Jesus was staying, *and they stayed with him all that day.*" The very first act that Jesus performed with his disciples was to invite them to spend all day with him. What happened that day? We do not know exactly, but clearly a deep and abiding friendship began between Jesus and these first disciples. Later, in each of the Gospels, Jesus *names* his 12 closest friends, sometimes even giving them new names. Anyone who has taught, or been a student, knows the power and the intimacy of the moment when a teacher calls a student by her or his name for the first time. "My teacher knows my name!" A whole sacred and sacramental relationship has begun to unfold!

The second characteristic of Christ Teacher that comes to light in our program is that *Jesus taught with a definite and unmistakable passion*. Jesus spoke to his disciples in such a way that they not only decided to spend the rest of that first day with him, but eventually dedicated the rest of their lives, and their deaths, to him as his disciples. Moreover, the very first thing these disciples did after spending the day with Jesus, as John records, was to grab their friends and bring them to Jesus. "Andrew was one of the two who heard John and followed Jesus. He first found his brother Simon and told him, 'We have found the Messiah!'" (John 1:40–41). Jesus' teaching was so compelling because there existed no gap between his teaching and his action. If he taught about the importance of prayer, then he prayed. If he talked about the importance of sharing, then he shared. If he taught that the greatest love was to lay down one's life, then he hung from the cross. Christ Teacher captured his disciples by teaching, and living, in a challenging and deeply compelling way. He taught with authority.

So, too, we challenge the members of the ACE community to lead compelling lives, realize and share their gifts, grow out of their self-centeredness, work hard, pray hard, and play hard, and lay their lives down for one another and for their students. We ask our faculty and staff both to teach and to model this.

The majority of people who apply to ACE first became excited about the program by hearing about it from a current participant. They heard that they will be taken seriously; that the faculty and staff will take a personal interest in their professional and spiritual lives; that their gifts will be drawn out and laid at the feet of others who need them; that they will be challenged to teach and, more importantly, to live as Jesus did, before a community of peers and a community of students that hunger for genuine, compelling, Christ-centered love. We follow the advice of Frank O'Malley, a revered former Notre Dame English professor, who said, "A teacher must enter into the life of his student, and demand to be engaged."

Third, *Jesus' teaching ministry is not primarily about transmitting information, but about changing lives*. When Jesus was ready to turn his worldly ministry over to Peter before his ascension, he appeared to Peter on the shore of the lake. During this encounter, Jesus asked Peter one question, and he asked it three times. The question does not elicit from Peter a recitation of facts about Jesus' teachings or ministry, but is rather, simply, "Do you love me?" The heart of Jesus' mission, and so the heart of our mission, is to transform our students' lives into lives of love of God and one another.

The fourth characteristic reflected in the ACE program is that *Jesus as Teacher enjoyed great success and persevered through great failure in his teaching ministry*. He touched some of his listeners so deeply that they spent the rest of their lives following him. Others routinely tried to have him killed! One thing, however, remains clear throughout the Gospels—regardless of the reception his teaching received, Jesus never stopped teaching.

It is difficult to overstate the importance of our ACE participants coming to know, and learning from, Christ Teacher in this fourth characteristic. Within one month, often sooner, of their entry into their classrooms, every ACE teacher will experience both the utter elation of realizing they have reached a student's mind and soul in some way, and the paralyzing shock of an intentional spitball splattering above their head as they deliver a lesson. As these novice teachers journey more deeply into their first semester of managing an entire classroom on their own, translating their university education into terms meaningful to a much younger group, and losing almost every moment of personal freedom to lesson plans and grading, the failures can seem to outweigh the successes. The spirituality of Christ Teacher—who through the consolation of prayer and friendship, and a single-minded perseverance in his mission through both successes and failures—is deeply resonant with and essential to our ACE community.

The fifth characteristic borne out in the ACE program is that *Jesus prayed constantly*. Because we teach toward a supernatural end—to transform our students' lives into lives of love—and because we need God's grace and consolation toward this end, we can identify readily with this fifth characteristic of Christ Teacher. He prayed constantly. He prayed alone, he prayed with his friends, and he prayed with those he taught. He prayed in petition, he prayed for discernment, he prayed in desolation, he prayed for consolation, he prayed in thanksgiving. As always, he taught others to do the same. This fifth characteristic of Christ Teacher sheds a revealing light on what we in ACE are about, for our need to pray reveals both the supernatural end of our work and our utter dependence on God to achieve this end.

Over the course of their two years in ACE, we strive to give these new disciples the opportunity to encounter Christ more deeply and more fully. We want them *to come to know Christ*—in the Eucharist, in the Gospels, in one another, in their students, and in the deepest longings of their own hearts—and, in doing so, *to become Christ*, as teachers. We want them to know that Christ desires, needs to take their enthusiasm, their leadership, their hunger for service, their countless gifts, even their limitations, and transform them into revelations of his love, for them and for their students. This is the transformation to which each of the ACE teachers is invited to enter.

## THE 12 STEPS OF ACE SPIRITUALITY

To HARNESS and more effectively embody and communicate the key themes related to Christ Teacher, we have devised a 12-step program, a series of 12 retreats and key spiritual periods over the course of the ACErs' two years in the program. This is a program, and a spirituality, that is still in the process of taking shape, and hopefully, in some ways, always will be. What follows is our initial endeavor to describe, and sometimes prescribe, ACE's 12-step journey in response to Christ Teacher's invitation: "Come and see."

### 1. THE APRIL RETREAT: COME AND YOU WILL SEE

Eighty people, nearly all college seniors in the later half of their final semester, gather on a Friday night in a gathering space on Notre Dame's campus, in order to spend one of the last weekends of their college lives on retreat. These members of the newest ACE class enter sporadically in groups of five to 10. Each is returning from a dinner with three to five other new teachers with whom they will live for the next two years in an intentional faith community in an unfamiliar city in the southern United States—and whom they most likely did not know until they sat down together for dinner that evening. They were joined by the superintendent of the southern diocese where they will be teaching, along with a few principals and teachers from their future schools who were able to make the mid-semester trek to Notre Dame. Sitting at the table with one's future family and bosses, none of whom one knew before and none of whom one got to choose—now *this* is a spiritual experience! In fact, this dinner, their first official activity as members of ACE, highlights the key spiritual dynamics of this weekend.

How can a dinner—unstructured, unpredictable as it may be—serve such a spiritual purpose? Recall that Jesus' first act with his new disciples was simply to spend the day with them. From the first, ACE's spirituality tries to emphasize that it is in the encounter with the other that we begin to encounter Christ. Thus, we begin as it seems Jesus began: we bring these new disciples together and invite them *to tell their story* of who they are and how they got here, and *to encounter others* as they share their stories too.

Storytelling is prominent during this first retreat weekend. The retreat is divided into three parts that correspond to the three pillars of the program—professional education, community life, and spirituality. We ask these new disciples to articulate for themselves, and share with one another, what their own expectations of and experiences with these pillars have been. When did you decide to do ACE? How did you tell your parents you were going to be a teacher? What people and experiences led you to this decision? What have been your experiences of community? What were experiences with roommates like? How did you pray growing up? How did you pray in college? In your ACE community, and as a Catholic schoolteacher, how do you hope to pray? In short, we try to create dynamics in which these ACE teachers *encounter* one another through the stories of their lives. These stories and these lives are the essential material of ACE's spirituality, because it is precisely *in their daily lives* that Christ seeks to encounter them.

We in ACE use this first retreat to lead these newest disciples to become more aware of, and to begin to share, the desire of their hearts. As they begin to try to understand that which beats inside of them with so much wonder and curiosity, and anticipation and some fear, we in ACE try to echo Christ's first invitation: "Come and you will see."

### 2. JUNE RETREAT I: SO THEY WENT AND SAW

As the new ACE teachers gather again on Notre Dame's campus for the beginning of their summer program, they are at once leaving a known and often comfortable way of life and embarking upon a new and relatively unknown journey. The classroom they have come to know and master is about to invert itself in a radical way. In a few short months, they will leave the security of their student desks and will teach students for the first time. It is this dynamic of *transition* that frames the spirituality of our second retreat.

On this second retreat, which formally opens the summer training session, we invite the ACE teachers to begin to take on a new and concrete identity—to become Catholic schoolteachers in the community of ACE at the University of Notre Dame. Again we structure the sessions of the retreat according to the three pillars of professional education, community, and spirituality. This time, however, we are much more explicit, sometimes even heavy-handed, about the demands that the coming journey will place on them. The M.Ed. faculty presents the considerable academic requirements of the master's program. The ACE staff addresses the teachers' new identity as public role models and witnesses, as more explicit representatives of the Church. The daily demands of community life and a deepening life of prayer are introduced.

Structured group discussions center around daily realities that the ACE teachers will soon encounter. What commitments will you make to one another in community? How will you stay accountable to those commitments? How will you address one another when an issue is bothering you? When will you eat together as a community? What types of personal possessions will be shared? When will outside guests be welcome in the community? How will you decide when to pray? How will you decide what format prayer will take? At what point in the year will your community take a retreat, and who will organize it?

These may at first seem rather mundane, even unspiritual themes. Yet we have come to realize that not only are these things at the heart of the ACE teachers' new identities in ACE, but also that in wrestling with how other people answer them differently, the ACE teachers enter into a crucial *spiritual transition*. For in wrestling with these dynamics, they begin to surrender their old, perhaps self-centered (at least, college-centered) ways of being, and begin to take on a new identity. Eighty former college seniors begin to be formed into a community of Catholic schoolteachers, and at a Eucharist during this weekend, as the ACE teachers don their new ACE T-shirts in a circle around the altar, we read from Paul's First Letter to the Corinthians: "As a body is one though it has many parts, and all the parts of the body, though many, are one body, so also Christ. . . . Now, you are Christ's body." (1 Cor. 12:12, 27)

### 3. July Optional Retreat I: Deepening the Encounter with Christ

On a fund-raising trip for ACE in Jacksonville, Florida, where we also happen to have an ACE community, we invited the ACE teachers to Mass and a barbecue on the beach the evening we would be in town. Before they arrived, we cooked up some burgers and brats, made some pasta salad and a few sides. After Mass, we put out our spread and invited the group to eat. As we sat down, one of the teachers (a former varsity athlete, with a corresponding appetite) eyed the table of food and, completely matter-of-factly, said, "This really looks great. But before we get started, I just need you to know: *I need more! I always need more!*"

From that moment, we knew that we had a new catchphrase in ACE. For, as we began developing our retreat program, it immediately became clear that someone always needed more, that merely an opening and closing retreat at the beginning and end of our extremely intense and demanding summer was not enough, spiritually, for many of our teachers. So we began to offer an optional weekend retreat or two in the middle of the summer on the shores of Lake Michigan, which 20 to 30 teachers normally attend.

We have tried various themes on these weekends and have discovered that the ACErs who come on this retreat are so exhausted at this point, and so spiritually hungry, that just about anything speaks to them, as long as it is Christ-centered, renourishing, refocusing, and relaxing. Amidst plenty of free time simply to unwind and have fun together on the beach, we structure a series of talks, and daily Eucharist, around Scripture passages where Christ reveals himself more fully to his disciples. Perhaps we will have them reflect on Jesus' question to his closest friends, "Who do you say that I am?" (Matt. 16:13–20); or on the constant companionship Jesus promises, particularly in the midst of challenging times, through a story like the calming of the sea (Luke 8:22–25).

A perfect Gospel for this retreat is the story of Jesus' Transfiguration. The disciples have become weary, if not disheartened, from following Jesus. Some of them, his closest friends, seem to gain life almost completely from their growing friendship with him, and on a mountaintop, he is revealed to them as he really is, as the Son of God. Here in this mysterious yet intimate encounter is complete renourishment for these disciples. At the end of the ACE retreat weekend on Lake Michigan, with several busy weeks ahead, the teachers resonate easily with Peter as he exclaims: "Lord, it is good we are here. Let's set up some tents and stay for awhile!" Jesus, however, focused on the mission at hand, leads them back down the mountain, as he leads these ACE teachers away from the peaceful shores of Lake Michigan and back into the daily business of this adventuresome, sometimes wearisome, journey. Most importantly, however, these disciples return with a renewed focus, a rekindled spirit. They have needed more, and they have been fed.

### 4. Missioning Liturgies I: Go Ye Forth

At the end of an extremely busy summer, we conclude this period of intense formation with a couple of important, and much needed, closing ceremonies and celebrations. After the last morning of classes, ACE spends the afternoon at the beloved Lake Michigan dunes, culminating in a sunset prayer service. Later that night, after a final charge by the ACE staff, the entire community gathers at Notre Dame's Grotto for the Blessing and Missioning of the Communities. One by one, each community is called forward to receive a community candle, a symbol that they will take with them to their new homes in the South, and around which they will gather to pray throughout the year. From these lighted community candles, each ACEr lights a smaller, individual taper. With the perimeter of the Grotto aglow in flame, we read the words of Jesus from the Sermon on the Mount: "You are the light of the world. . . . Your light must shine before all, so that, seeing your good works, all may give praise to your Father in heaven" (Matt. 5:14–16). Then the communities, one by one, and from different points in the circle, offer petitions to our Blessed Mother, Notre Dame. "The community of Charlotte, North Carolina, prays that we might be the light of God to our students and to one another throughout this year." "Montgomery, Alabama, asks for the strength to be faithful and challenging witnesses to the Gospel to those whom you will entrust to us." "Brownsville, Texas, *ora que Jesus guarde nuestra comunidad, nuestro testimonio, y nuestros alumnos, y que sea la inspiración en todo lo que hagamos este año.*" "Atlanta, Georgia, prays . . ." "Baton Rouge . . ." "Phoenix . . ." "Los Angeles . . ." A now renowned celebration, moving in its enthusiasm and fellowship, follows in the faculty club.

In the morning, we conclude our summer with a Missioning Mass, to which we invite an ecclesial leader of the American or global Church to preside. The recognition that the mission of these ACE teachers is ultimately connected to the larger evangelizing mission and teaching authority of the Church is a crucial one for our ACE community. An abiding, enlivening identity with the Church is very necessary, but not uncomplicated, for young lay disciples today. So it is important that we continue to forge a deepening relationship between these young people and their Church. It is, after all, the Church they will live in, draw nourishment from, and in turn nourish for the rest of their lives. As these new disciples are sent off to teach, we commission them with the same words that Christ commissioned his first disciples, the mission that the Church has carried on to this day: "Go forth and make disciples of all . . . and know that I am with you always" (Matt. 28:19–20).

### 5. Semester Site Visits: The Companionship of Jesus

In mid-September, one to one-and-a-half grueling months into the ACE teachers' service in their classrooms in the South, ACE staff members make a site visit to each local ACE community. During these visits, we have witnessed the spectrum from teachers already close to the top of their game to teachers who have already been stripped of much of their confidence. Community life, too, can range from a group of people who have already begun to find a rhythm with one another to houses where much unspoken tension hangs heavy among them. Some houses have prayed regularly together; some have yet to discuss it.

Obviously, then, many different needs, demands, opportunities, and challenges face the ACE staff and each teacher and community during these September site visits. From a spiritual perspective, the encompassing reality that we communicate is this: it is Jesus who calls them to this work, the same Jesus they began to encounter as Christ Teacher during the summer. Even more, this Jesus understands precisely what they are experiencing, and seeks to walk with them in intimate companionship through it. Perhaps a helpful Gospel to frame this visit is Luke's fourth chapter, the beginning of Jesus' public ministry. Here, in the span of perhaps no more than a couple of hours, Jesus unleashes the exhilarating power of his teaching ministry. Unrolling the scroll of Isaiah, he announces "a year acceptable to the Lord . . . and the eyes of all in the synagogue looked intently at him" and all were amazed at his teaching (Luke 4:16–22). Yet, later that same day, after Jesus challenges these same people to grow out of their self-centeredness and more deeply into the love of God and others, "They rose up, drove him out of the town, and led him to the brow of the hill . . . to hurl him down headlong" (Luke 4:29).

Here, in the successes and failures of the ACErs' first months of teaching, lies an incredibly rich opportunity for these new disciples to come to know the deep humanity, and thus intimate companionship, of Christ, and to risk discovering the strength and consolation to be found in persevering in the friendship he offers. At the same time, building on the community pillar of ACE, there lies here also a powerful opportunity to teach these new teachers to turn to, and accept, *one another* as sources of God's grace, encouragement, and strength. Theirs really is the experience of the early Church, trying to learn how to live with one another, often under very stressful circumstances. It is amazing how many passages from the Acts of the Apostles, or Paul's letters to the early Christian communities, parallel the situations of the ACE communities. The beginning of Paul's Letter to the Philippians has become one of the most frequented by our staff on these visits:

> I give thanks to my God at every remembrance of you, praying always with joy in my every prayer for you, because of your partnership for the gospel from the first day until now. And I am confident of this: that the one who began this good work in you will continue to bring it to completion until the day of Christ Jesus. (Phil. 1:3–6)

Despite the adversity that these teachers have encountered, in fact because of it, an amazingly rich opportunity presents itself at midsemester for these communities of teachers to enter more deeply into the heart of the Christian life, and to recommit themselves to their calling. It is an opportunity born out of the deep need of these teachers for affirmation, companionship, and support on their journey, and their deep capacity to be sources of this necessary encouragement and grace for one another in community.

### 6. December Retreat I: The Costs and Joys of Discipleship

Around the first of December each winter, the phones at the ACE office at Notre Dame begin to ring with increasing regularity. It is the annual onslaught of the first-year ACE teachers wondering, or downright complaining, about the wisdom of scheduling a required four-day retreat in the middle of one of the busiest times of their school year. This yearly ritual marks the beginning of ACE's Annual Pilgrimage and Retreat to the Gulf Coast in Biloxi, Mississippi.

It is the beginning because this weekend has become for our community a genuine Advent experience. A genuine Advent experience, as the Old Testament prophets tell us, begins in dryness, in darkness, with the barren "stump of Jesse" (Isa. 11:1). As the phone calls indicate, we do not need to work hard to introduce this spiritual reality to our first-year teachers. Of course, at the same time that Advent begins in exhausted barrenness, the deepest movement of this season is that precisely out of such darkness has come a great light, out of the stump of Jesse comes the shoot of David, out of dryness comes a wellspring of living water.

In this spirit, one of the most dynamic and enlivening scenes of the ACE year occurs on Friday night, the opening night of the retreat. Over the course of about a four-hour period, from all over the southern United States, groups of four and five teachers straggle into the Gulfport Retreat Center, stooped beneath suitcases full of lesson plans, text books, semester exams, and a weekend change of clothes. As they drop their suitcases in their rooms, slowly, steadily, the gathering room fills with the voices of teachers and old friends reunited. They are exchanging stories of the adventure of getting to Biloxi, or war stories from their first semester in the trenches. They are seeing their own fatigue and frustration, and glimmers of success, self-discovery, and hard-earned maturation mirrored in the familiar faces of peers and friends. Slowly, but unmistakably, the mood changes. They are laughing. They are embracing. Knowingly or unknowingly, they are celebrating. Little by little, this once empty gathering hall has become filled with the joy of reunited friendships and a reunited community four months dispersed on a common mission. When all have gathered, we celebrate the Eucharist, and this tired group of disciples rises up in song, in prayer, in fellowship—and is nourished again by the promised Savior of Advent.

The majority of first-year teachers have just experienced the most challenging five months of their lives. Thus, the key spiritual dynamic of the weekend is, first, to free up these teachers to articulate, and be affirmed in, the difficulties and adversities they have faced—*the costs of discipleship*—and, second, to reaffirm in the midst of these challenges all that God is accomplishing through them—*the joys of discipleship*. To do so, we focus on the basic Advent question: "Where do you see the Incarnation, God's presence, in your life?"

We first focus discussions of these two spiritual dynamics—the costs and the joys of discipleship—on their teaching ministry. Hopefully, at some point on this weekend, each ACE teacher realizes that the success of their ministry ultimately lies, not in their own efforts, but in God's grace. After one particularly grueling complaint session, the homilist at one of our Eucharists opened: "Hey! I got some news for you. This ain't up to you! Your success as a teacher does not ultimately depend on your own efforts. It's all up to God! So stop walking around like the world is on your shoulders!" There was an audible sigh of relief amongst the ACErs. This spiritual reality is at the very heart of the mystery of the Incarnation and our Advent retreat—that God's grace is at work in the very midst of all of our human limitations. The ACE teachers need to accept that they are no exception to this spiritual rule. One of the most re-enlivening movements of this retreat is when ACErs begins to realize that, contrary to what they had come to believe, God's grace is powerfully at work in their students' and their own lives, through their teaching.

The weekend also addresses the dynamic of the costs and joys of discipleship *in community life*. After a Gospel-centered motivation on Christ's call to a communal life of service to one another, such as Jesus' washing of the disciples' feet (John 13:1–20), focused on the reality that discipleship must extend beyond our students to the peers with whom we serve, there is a presentation from one of the ACE communities on their areas of growth and challenge as a community throughout the semester. Each community is then paired with a retreat staff member and engages in a candid discussion and assessment of their communal life. This is a very powerful, often liberating, time on the retreat, as conflicts and affirmations that have gone long unspoken are shared in honesty and in a spirit of growing together in discipleship. These sessions are often a time of heartfelt reconciliation among community members. In fact, after this session ends, we conclude Saturday afternoon with the sacrament of Reconciliation. The sacrament is entirely optional, and so it is a deeply moving scene to see these young disciples, unburdened, lined up 10 or 15 people deep at each station, awaiting to receive reconciliation, conversing and sharing deeply and laughing with one another as they wait in line, often for over an hour. As the sun sets behind Mississippi's Gulf Coast, we share dinner together, and the Algiers Brass Band, a soulful jazz quartet from New Orleans, fills the retreat center with music, and the ACE community lets loose in celebration and reunion.

Our December Retreat traditionally falls around the Feast of Our Lady of Guadalupe, and we close our retreat on Sunday by celebrating this feast, all the more relevant due to our increasing service in Hispanic schools. In its recounting of Mary's appearance to the Mexican peasant Juan Diego in the midst of famine and disease and European conquest, this is a quintessentially Adventine story. The certain assurance of God's presence among us, even in the midst of apparent dryness or weariness or failure, is a central message of the ACE

December Retreat. As the ACE community has done at Notre Dame's Grotto at its time of missioning, we again ask Our Lady to inspire and nourish our lives of service as we prepare, and return to the classroom to prepare our students, for the birth of Christ.

### 7. June Retreat II: The Return of the Disciples

Having completed their first year of teaching, the ACE teachers return to Notre Dame for a retreat during the first weekend in June. As these teachers straggle back to the Notre Dame campus from their sites throughout the South, the Gospel that comes most readily to mind is the return of the 72 disciples from their first mission:

> "The seventy-two returned rejoicing, and said, 'Lord, even the demons are subject to us because of your name.' Jesus replied, . . . "Nevertheless, do not rejoice because the spirits are subject to you, but rejoice because your names are written in heaven." (Luke 10:17–20)

This passage is relevant to the spiritual state of the returning ACErs insofar as, upon the disciples' return, Jesus refocuses their spiritual attention *not so much on what they did or did not accomplish, but rather on their growing friendship with him.* Only through Christ have they accomplished anything, and in fact have accomplished everything, their own salvation: "rejoice because your names have been written in heaven." This is an incredibly important reality for these newly returned teachers to grasp: all that unfolded this past year did so in God's providence and for the purpose of leading them, and their students, to their salvation.

Characteristic of the first-year ACErs' experience is that of ACE III's Colleen Knight on returning from her classroom in Fort Worth, Texas. Colleen tells the story of her student Jack, a seventh grader in her religion class, who gave her an extraordinarily difficult time throughout the year. Colleen's class focused on social justice, and "treating others as yourself" did not seem to rank high in Jack's life at this point. Toward the end of the year, Colleen organized a day of service for her seventh graders at the Catholic homeless shelter in Fort Worth. Colleen was confident that most of her students possessed the maturity, eagerness, and discipline to participate effectively in the day. Yet the thought of Jack set loose in such an unstructured setting filled her with pure dread. She prepared Jack's detention slip ahead of time, and the class set out for the shelter. As the morning passed without disruption, Colleen allowed herself to relax for a moment, until she realized she did not see Jack. Just as the reality set in that Jack probably had escaped for an afternoon of recreation in downtown Fort Worth, Colleen caught sight of a group of homeless children in the dining room, and Jack was in the middle of them, serving them seconds of food and drink. He was talking with the kids, particularly engaged by one who was his own age, asking them questions, laughing with them, pouring them cups of water. He remained with them until they left. Later that week, Colleen received the following note on her desk:

> Dear Ms. Knight, I know that you have impacted me in a way I'll never forget. I learned what it is to live by your values and morals. You have showed me how to love those who can be very difficult to get close to. You have taught me to help others, even when I'm not obligated to. You've taught me how important it is to look at life as our most important blessing. . . . These things will be with me forever. Thank you. I'm glad you were my teacher. Signed, Jack.

Here, encapsulated in Colleen and Jack's story, is the spiritual reality we hope to bring into focus for the returning ACE teachers: beyond their expectations and realizations, God has worked wonders through them in their classrooms and communities this year. The ACErs may not have been perfect, they may have made plenty of mistakes, but through their humanity, God spoke to his children through them, and God did so more often than they think.

We have found it helpful to return to a Gospel passage we have used once before, during the summer and before they began their teaching assignments. The passage begins with Jesus' question to his disciples, "Who do you say that I am?" (Matt. 16:15). The ACErs can now answer it in light of all that has unfolded this year. Hopefully, they, like Colleen, are beginning to see the ways that Christ has touched the lives of others through them. When they are able to do so, it becomes an extremely renourishing and motivating beginning to the second summer.

Finally, given that these now second-year ACErs are about to take on a leadership role within the community for the new first-year ACErs, we take this passage from Matthew's Gospel one step further. Immediately following Peter's confession of Jesus as the Messiah, Jesus for the first time begins to tell his disciples that he must suffer and die, and be raised again. Peter rebukes him, saying, "God forbid, Lord! No such thing shall ever happen to you" (Matt. 16:22). In response, however, Jesus begins to explain to his disciples the very heart of his Gospel message:

> Whoever wishes to come after me must deny himself, take up his cross, and follow me. For whoever wishes to save his life will lose it, but whoever loses his life for my sake will find it. (Matt. 16:24–25)

We now challenge our teachers to respond to Jesus' challenging invitation. Yes, Jesus says, I will work through you, as you have seen, but in order to do so fully, you must die to yourself, and accept all of me, and that includes the cross, giving your life away for others. We ask them now to take a servant-leadership role in the ACE community, mentoring and guiding the newest members, the entering class. On Sunday, as the retreat closes, the new first-year teachers join us for Eucharist and lunch. When they encounter these second-year ACErs, will they catch a glimmer of Christ Teacher?

### 8. July Optional Retreat II: Whoever Gives Their Life Away Will Find It

To date, we have not held separate July retreats for the first- and second-year teachers. All have attended the same retreat, and it has basically followed the framework of July Retreat I. There are definite advantages to having a mixed retreat, particularly in terms of community-building and mentorship opportunities between the two classes. At the same time, the second-year teachers are in a different space—professionally, in community, and spiritually—by this second summer. From their feedback, it is clear that we are being invited to provide them with a retreat that challenges them to journey still more deeply into the story of the Gospel.

The main question that we introduce to the second-year teachers on this retreat is, "Why take up the cross?" Whether or not they are able to articulate it, the second-year ACE teachers have already begun to answer this question, as it has appeared to them in various forms during their first year of teaching. Why, in the midst of five lesson preps per night, do Jane Feliz and Tom Jacobs take on the added responsibility of starting a senior retreat program at Bishop McGuiness High

School? Why, in her first year of teaching an over-enrolled fifth grade class, does Ann Marie Tomley decide to begin a Rainbow Program for abused children at Our Lady of Prompt Succour? Why, with hardly enough time at night to prepare the next day's lessons, does Zac Budzi-chowski create a lacrosse program and Tom Kessler rewire the school's computer clusters for increased capacity, at Resurrection High? Sure-ly, there are many reasons and motivations for taking up such crosses. Yet, ultimately, there is only one answer they give—love. "I love my students." "I love what I'm doing." "I do it out of love."

Simple enough. Does not Christ teach us, time and time again throughout the Gospels, that this is at the very heart of the Christian life, to lead a life of love? As we often recount on this retreat, when Jesus' followers asked him, "Which commandment in the law is the greatest?"—that is, "What is at the very heart of our lives?"—Jesus had a simple, two-fold reply:

> You shall love God with all your heart, with all your soul, and with all your mind. This is the greatest and the first commandment. And the second is like it: You shall love your neighbor as yourself. (Matt. 22:37–39)

Do our teachers realize that what they have begun to do during their first year—loving their students in concrete ways—is nothing less than to begin to respond to Jesus' greatest commandment, to the deepest longing of their hearts? This is the question in which we hope to engage them in this second mid-summer retreat.

Michael Himes, a former professor at Notre Dame and a master teacher and preacher, gave a series of talks to our ACE teachers a few years ago in which he challenged them to see their lives as teachers as responses to God's invitation to turn their lives increasingly into lives of self-gift. We know that God is love. There are many types of love (eros, friendship, etc.) but Himes underscored that God is "agape," which alone of the loves seeks nothing back from the one loved. God is, in other words, *pure self-gift*. We know, too, that we are made in the image and likeness of God. Thus, we are made in the image and likeness of agape, self-gift. If we return, then, to the Gospel passage that we used on our previous retreat—"whoever gives their life away for my sake will find life"—we see that this is not so much an ethical imperative, or a rule of conduct, but simply a description of the way things are. We are made to be self-gift, so that the only way to become who we are meant to be is to give ourselves away.

The second-year ACE teachers have already entered into this reality, this way of being, in an incredibly concrete way during their first year of teaching. What we hope to do on this retreat is to help them become more explicitly and consciously aware that this journey of self-gift on which they have embarked—of giving their lives away in service to God and others—is Christ's journey, the journey to the heart of the Gospel. There is no deeper reality for us to discover! This is why the Eucharist is the central prayer of our community. "This is my body, given away for you." "This is my life's blood, poured out for you." The Eucharist is Christ's total self-gift to us, and we receive this self-gift so that we can give our lives away too. We hope that more and more our ACE community will realize that this experience of giving our lives away to others is a whole way of life, the life of the Gospel. It is, in fact, a whole way of beholding the world, and we hope on this retreat to deepen this vision within our community, that we might live it more fully and be able to impart it more fully to our students and those with whom we live.

### 9. Missioning Liturgies II: Do You Love Me?

For the second-year teachers, the second summer is the last time their entire ACE class is gathered for an extended period of time. As the summer progresses, their focus again turns to a new year of school, a new set of students, perhaps a new community (if first-year teachers have been added to their community and graduated members have left). They have one year of hard-earned experience behind them—not a lifetime's worth, to be sure, but one year more than they had at this time last summer. They generally look forward to the upcoming year with much eagerness, and some beginning-of-the-year anxiety. They also think more about "What will I do when ACE is over?" This question of continued *vocation* will be primary throughout this second year.

The last few days of the second summer session are not a structured spiritual retreat. Rather, the days are organized around a series of missioning events: a day at the dunes, the missioning of the communities at the Grotto, and the Missioning Mass as our closing activity. As we found the beginning of the ACE teachers' spiritual journey to be well marked by the beginning of John's Gospel—"Come and see"—so we find the closing of their time at Notre Dame to be captured by the close of John's Gospel. Jesus is preparing to leave his disciples and to send them out into the world to do his work, to take up their cross and follow him. Certainly, the disciples experienced many of the thoughts and emotions that the second-year ACErs are experiencing at the end of this summer: an experience of leave-taking; of being sent forth to do work for which they have been well prepared and to which they have committed, but which still holds much uncertainty; of feeling the question well up within them, "What do we do next?" The end of John's Gospel gives us the following story, one mysterious yet poignant, as a paradigm of how Jesus responds to their experience and leads them forward.

> Jesus said to Peter a third time, "Simon, son of John, do you love me?" . . . Peter said to him, "Lord, you know everything; you know that I love you." Jesus said to him, "Feed my sheep. Amen, amen, I say to you, when you were younger, you used to bind your own belt and go where you wanted; but now you will stretch out your hands, and someone else will bind you and lead you where you do not want to go." . . . Then Jesus said to him, "Follow me." (John 21:15–19)

To the questions in his disciples' hearts, Christ Teacher answered with another question: "Do you love me?" Three times he repeats it, as if to drive home the point that their journey is only this, one of more and more turning themselves over to him in love. As his disciples hear themselves say again and again in deepening commitment, "Yes, you know I love you," then Jesus' answer comes: "Feed my sheep." "Tend my sheep." "Feed my sheep." "If you love me, take care of my people." Jesus' answer to our ACE teachers is, "If you love me, give yourselves over to the students who sit before you this year. Take care of them. Feed them. Nourish them. And what you shall do next will become clear to you." Of course, he does not say this without a caution: "If you give yourselves over to this journey, be open to be led where you did not think you would go. Come, follow me."

It is a strange and wonderful message with which to mission his disciples, a message at once reassuring and challenging, exciting and unsettling, filled with love and filled with risk. Yet is this not precisely the journey that lies ahead of the ACE teachers? Their immediate mission is clear: love concretely the students before you. Tend them and feed them. Who knows where it will lead?

At the close of our Missioning Mass, one by one the second-year teachers are called by name and come forth to receive a medal of Christ Teacher, with the inscription: "To make God known, loved, and served," words inspired by Fr. Basil Moreau, founder of the Congregation of Holy Cross, which sponsors the University of Notre Dame. These words frame the mission on which the ACErs are sent, this year to be sure, but also for the rest of their lives, each in his or her own way.

### 10. DECEMBER RETREAT II: FRESH EYES OF FAITH

The annual December Retreat brings together first- and second-year ACE teachers. The general structure is that of December Retreat I: the gathering and Eucharist, the theme of Advent, the community sessions and Reconciliation service, the Saturday-night jazz celebration, Our Lady of Guadalupe, and the closing Sunday Eucharist. This overall structure holds for the second-year teachers as well. Yet, obviously, in one very significant way, the second-year teachers are in a different spiritual space than their first-year counterparts; namely, with their graduation from ACE now just five months away, the question more forcefully arises, "Where are we being led next?" Therefore, we hold most of the main spiritual talks of the weekend in parallel, first- and second-year sessions (with the exception of the community discussions), with the second-year sessions focusing on this question: "Where are we being led?"

As has come to be revealed clearly in the lives and decisions of the second-year ACErs, this is a question that they answer *according to their vision of what has been unfolding in their lives.* If they see God at work in their lives, and experience success, peace, and joy in the work they do, or on the other hand, if they perceive failure or discontent in their lives, then they will have radically different answers to the question, "Where are we being led?" The first step we take on this December Retreat is simply to spend some time recollecting what has transpired over the previous year and a half, looking at these experiences through the eyes of faith and with the help of one another, and beginning to discern a vision of what seems to be unfolding in our lives, where the Holy Spirit seems to be leading.

We remember one of the teachers in our ACE IV class, Michelle Lavigne, a sixth grade teacher at a predominantly Hispanic school, Our Lady of Perpetual Help, in Dallas, Texas. One of Michelle's great gifts is her insistence in setting the highest standards for her work, and her single-minded drive to attain these standards. This same drive made her a stand-out runner on Notre Dame's cross-country team and an honors graduate in psychology. She naturally entered her first year of teaching with the same attitude of perfection. Five months into her teaching career, however, it was becoming overwhelmingly, even painfully, clear to Michelle that she was not attaining the high standards in her classroom that she had set for herself. Every day, she saw a student not grasping a lesson, or an activity not yielding the results she had anticipated. By the time she arrived in Biloxi for her first December Retreat, she was all but convinced that she needed to quit teaching and begin again in another vocation. This was only natural; in fact, it was the sensible conclusion for her to reach, *given her present vision* of herself and her work.

Who could tell where the Spirit was leading Michelle at this point? Perhaps teaching was not for her. At the same time, the Spirit seemed to have led her to ACE and to Our Lady of Perpetual Help. The ACE faculty and staff encouraged her to finish the year, with the promise of the professional, emotional, and spiritual support she would need to do so. Besides, when we contacted her principal and mentor teacher in Dallas, they indicated that Michelle's school and her colleagues were overjoyed at the energy, commitment, zeal, and competence that she was bringing to their school community. She made mistakes, of course, but nothing out of the ordinary for a first-year teacher.

As her local mentors in Dallas, the ACE staff, and her own community members encouraged Michelle throughout her second semester, and in particular, relentlessly held up before her the good that was being accomplished in her classroom and her students' lives through her teaching, Michelle began to find her stride. Day by day, she focused on the positive and life-giving things that were unfolding in her class. She learned to see her perfectionism as a gift insofar as it motivated her to be an effective and creative teacher, but a potential hindrance insofar as it made her focus on negative outcomes in the midst of so many positives. Most importantly, however, Michelle came to a deepening realization that God was at work in her as a teacher, if she chose to see it. She came to see that, somehow, through her gifts, God was touching the lives of her students through her.

By the time Michelle arrived in Biloxi for her second December Retreat, she had become as effective a teacher as we have had in ACE. When we began the first session for the second-year ACErs on "Where are we being led?" Michelle spoke of how grateful she was for where God had led her over the past two years, at what God had accomplished through her in her classroom, particularly this second year.

She announced, to the gaping mouths of all who had remembered her first six months in ACE, that when ACE ended, she would either be remaining at her school in Dallas for a third year, or accepting an offer to teach second grade at St. Peter's School in Massachusetts. As was the case at Michelle's first December Retreat, this was the natural outcome; in fact, it was the sensible, faith-filled conclusion for her to reach, *given her present vision, through fresh eyes of faith,* of God's work through her. Michelle continued her teaching career and today is pursuing a graduate degree in school counseling.

Michelle's story illustrates the theme of the second-year ACErs' December Retreat, "Where are we being led?" We invite them to discern a vision of their lives, through the eyes of faith, to discern what God has been accomplishing in their lives. Such discernment may or may not lead one to a future vocation in teaching, and that is not the point. The point is that if the ACE teachers can see where God has been working in their concrete, daily lives in the past, they might be able to see where they are going. It seems that when the ACE teachers are able to do this, and truly "rejoice in all God has done," they are led to a spiritual openness to both their past and future that is beautifully captured by Dag Hammerskjold when he prayed in his diary *Markings,* "For all that has been, thank you; for all that will be, yes!"

The second December Retreat also covers "Strategies for Continuing Lives of Service in the Church." We present to the second-year ACErs general and specific questions and strategies for planning their next steps after ACE graduation. Most are being led to continue a career in teaching, whether short-term or long-term. Several each year are led to professional schools in law, medicine, and business. Some are called to administration in Catholic schools or other Catholic organizations, like the National Catholic Education Association or the Urban Catholic Teacher Corps at Boston College. Some, too, are being led to further service at the international level, with ACE graduates having served as teachers in Africa, Bangladesh, and Chile. A few each year are called back to Notre Dame in some capacity; a community of 22 ACE graduates currently resides and works on or around campus. Some are being led to marriage, and a few each year to religious life. Some are being led to continue life in community, and several informal post-ACE houses have sprung up in cities like Atlanta, Boston, Charlotte, Chicago, Portland, and Washington, D.C. Each December Retreat includes recent ACE graduates who share their stories of how they are being led to sustain and nourish a life of service after ACE.

Sometimes, groups of three or four second-year ACErs will see a common path open before them: to live and teach together in a particular city, to begin an overseas teaching mission, or to realize together that, at this point, they have no clue what to do! Whatever the outcome, and there are as many as there are ACE teachers, we hope these soon-to-be ACE graduates come to experience on this retreat a deeper sense of what God is accomplishing through their lives, and where God may be leading them. We invite them to do so together, in an explicit context of prayer, faith sharing, and the Eucharist, as a community of disciples and friends.

### 11. COMMENCEMENT: ENDING—AND BEGINNING AGAIN

We face several challenges in integrating the ACE commencement weekend into the 12-step spiritual journey we have been outlining. The ACE teachers complete their second-year of teaching sometime in May. From their sites in the South, they scatter throughout the country, because, due to logistics, there is no immediate formal close to their service in ACE. Their commencement ceremony at Notre Dame, and the conferring of their master's degree, will not take place until the end of July.

Thus, when this community of disciples gathers again, for the last time, at their commencement, they have been dispersed and apart for almost two months, a significant gap in the continuity of their ACE experience. Furthermore, much happens during this commencement weekend, which includes the presence of their families and guests, scattered arrival and departure times, and the like. A retreat would be impossible. At the same time, given the nature and culture of ACE and its participants, the weekend can be infused with a spiritual focus if we as a community decide that is what we want and need. It will take a conscious and focused effort to accomplish this, and, admittedly, we have not been particularly successful at creating such a focus yet.

In fact, if anyone has been successful at beginning to cultivate a spirituality to this weekend, it has been the ACE graduates themselves. At our very first ACE commencement weekend, after the Graduation Mass and commencement ceremony, the ACE graduates decided, as a class, to gather in one of the dormitory chapels for a final chance to share their faith and their journeys, and to pray together as a community. It is not hard to imagine the depth and intensity of this faith gathering as this group of teachers and friends and disciples brought some closure to all that had transpired in their lives over the previous two years.

As we talk with the graduates on this weekend, they express deep gratitude for all that God has done in their lives, as well as hope about where the Holy Spirit is leading them. They do not want this commencement to signal an end to their service. Instead, most see the graduation as another missioning. The Christ Teacher medal that these ACErs received before they began their second year of teaching emblazoned their vocation: to make God known, loved, and served. Regardless of the career path to which each of these graduates is being led, many of them feel deeply that Catholic education is a vocation for a lifetime, a vocation to which they are willing to devote their lives in some capacity. They want to be "educators in the faith" and supporters of Catholic education for life.

At the closing Graduation Mass, just as at the Missioning Mass, each ACE teacher is called by name, one at a time, to come forward and receive a medal of the Madonna and Child. It is a particularly appropriate symbol with which to send off the ACE graduates. Throughout their two years in ACE—at the Grotto service on Missioning Weekend, at the celebration of Our Lady of Guadalupe on the December Retreat, in countless of our prayers—the ACE community has seen in Notre Dame, Our Lady, a call to nourish and bring to life her son Jesus in the lives of those who were entrusted to them. The campus of Notre Dame— its dorms, its classrooms, its dining halls, its playing fields and gathering places, its chapels and Grotto—has physically and sacramentally marked important moments over the past two years of learning how to walk in the footsteps of Christ. The bestowing of the Madonna medal to each ACE graduate by name is a call to accept a lifetime vocation of nourishing the life of Christ, especially through Catholic education. Also, it is an invitation to us to see Notre Dame as a place to gather, in the years to come, in continued fellowship, commitment, and common mission to support and promote Catholic education, and to renourish in our own lives our call to be Christ Teacher.

## 12. POST-ACE INITIATIVE: BREAD FOR THE JOURNEY

"And so they came and saw." As John's Gospel records so simply, this was the half-befuddled, half-courageous response of the first disciples to Jesus' invitation, "Come and see." So simple an invitation; so simple a response. Yet how filled with mystery, with unforeseen adventures, challenges, and opportunities beyond all belief! It is the greatest adventure in all human history, and it plays itself out again and again in each age of the Church, and in each Christian's life. It is the adventure into which we in ACE believe we have been invited, and even as the two-year experience of the first ACE teachers ended, we felt the insatiable call of the Spirit stirring up the new graduates of our program, and us along with them, to enter into the adventure yet again, even as our first adventure seemed to come to a close.

What was it that Andrew and John experienced that first afternoon with Jesus that so radically changed their lives, that led them so energetically to enter into adventure after adventure with Jesus throughout their lives? Andrew, the first disciple to come and see, gives us perhaps the ultimate answer to this question as he bursts forth from Jesus' home that first afternoon, in contagious excitement and anticipation, to find his brother Peter and share the news with him. When he finally comes upon Peter, he breathlessly exclaims our answer: "We have found the Messiah!" This is what happened to the first disciples that afternoon; this is what we believe, in sincere humility and utter excitement, is happening to us in ACE: we are encountering the Messiah, Christ Teacher. We, like those first disciples, somehow will never be the same again. One ACE graduate after another has spoken of the longing that has been stirred up in their hearts to lead meaningful lives of prayer, relationship, vocation, and service to God's people, to continue a life in and with and as Christ Teacher so powerfully encountered during their time in ACE.

Indeed, in concrete ways, they have *become* him. Like Christ Teacher, they have known intimately and loved unconditionally their students. They have taught with a remarkable passion and authority. They have changed their students' lives, and the lives of many others in their communities. They have enjoyed success and persevered through failure. They have prayed and taught others to pray and have become works of prayer themselves. They have lived the life of Christ Teacher as revealed to us in the Gospels. In doing so, and most powerfully through celebrating the Eucharist, they have become him, become his very presence in the world in the ever-unfolding mystery of the Incarnation. It seems true, what we have begun to see in the lives of our ACE graduates: they will never be quite the same again!

Thus, the pressing question for our ACE community becomes: as the ACE graduates go forth from their two years of teaching, how do we sustain and nourish this *lifelong* call to encounter Christ, and to become him for others? For our graduates, the years after their service in ACE are busy ones, regardless of the career paths they choose.

There is significantly less structure in terms of peer support and opportunities for prayer and fellowship. Many graduates feel isolated from others who seek to incorporate an explicit life of faith and service into their daily lives. Meaningful ways to continue to pursue the encounter with Christ, and friends with whom to pursue this encounter, can seem scarce. As a program, too, we are faced with complex challenges. In particular, as our graduates spread to almost every geographic region in the country and beyond, communication and gathering become increasingly difficult. The heterogeneity of the group, their spiritual needs and ambitions, and the circumstances of their lives make comprehensive, one-size-fits-all opportunities nearly impossible.

The spiritual hungers that ACE graduates experience upon leaving the program grow out of the spiritual movements that have taken place during their two years in ACE. Namely, they seek a deeper life of prayer, a deeper sense of their life's work as vocation, a more Gospel-centered, Eucharist-centered, and Christ-centered life of service and relationship, a lifelong commitment to Catholic education according to their individual circumstances and careers.

In July 1999, after our first three ACE classes had graduated, the ACE staff hosted our first post-ACE retreat on Notre Dame's campus. The staff planned the retreat largely on our own, without extensive input from the ACE graduates themselves. We did not invite a core group of graduates to the weekend but allowed the three graduated classes to self-select who would attend the retreat. Attendance was lower than expected, and the focus of the retreat was not as responsive to the diverse circumstances of our graduates as it needed to be. We learned some important and helpful lessons from this first retreat weekend and have begun a reinvigorated Post-ACE Initiative.

We gathered several graduates together for a second post-ACE weekend retreat in March 2000, where we invited a team of consultants to listen to the stories and needs of these post-ACErs as they strive to continue their lives of faith and discipleship. As a program, it seems clear that, given the diverse circumstances and needs of our graduates, the Post-ACE Initiative will need to focus on *organizing several different clusters of opportunities* for the ACE graduates. Such opportunities include different service initiatives in the field of education; regular prayer, fellowship groups, and retreats in different geographic regions; means of inner-connectivity among the post-ACE community, via the Internet and the like; and a regular post-ACE retreat on

Notre Dame's campus. We will need a Post-ACE Initiative coordinator as a full-time member of the ACE staff.

This much we know with certainty: as we have tried to do from the beginning of the ACE program, we will energetically and creatively respond to where the Spirit is leading our graduates and our entire community, which now seems more like a movement than a program. Whatever the concrete particulars of the Post-ACE Initiative over the coming years, it is clear that the Spirit is calling this wonderfully gifted group of disciples to grow, beyond their two years of service in ACE, more deeply in their identity as disciples of Christ Teacher, and in diverse ways, to become Christ in their Church and world. We feel deeply called as a community to continue to respond wholeheartedly to the Spirit's next invitation to "come and see."

### THE WORK OF THE SPIRIT

ONE CHARACTERISTIC of the spirituality of the 12-step program we have just described and prescribed (see Table 9.1), and of Christ Teacher, is crucially important: we all must realize and embrace that this spirituality is very much a *work in progress*. From the beginning to the present, the ACE program has clearly been a work of the Spirit, who, as Christ warns, "blows where She wills." This spirituality and these 12 steps have an essentially organic quality to them. They have grown out of the real-life experiences of our ACE teachers and graduates, and our community's attempts to respond pastorally to those experiences. This organic encounter and response must continue to be the way of our journey, in order for this spiritual movement to continue to grow in vigor and freshness and relevance.

We continue not to be sure where all of this is leading us. We are also extremely excited that this is the case! We believe that the Spirit is leading us into a powerful, effective, and deeply relevant lay spiritual movement, with a deep identity in Christ Teacher, through Our Lady's intercession at Notre Dame. We know that the ACE community will continue to respond with great zeal, creativity, and commitment to the needs and talents of one of the most talented groups of young leaders and teachers in the Church today.

Thus, we have the courage and hope to pray St. Paul's prayer for the budding new community of Christians at Philippi: "May the God who has begun this good work in us, bring it to completion" (Phil. 1:6).

**TABLE 9.1**

*The 12 Steps of ACE Spirituality*

| The 12 Steps | Time of Year | Key Spiritual Themes/Dynamics |
|---|---|---|
| 1. Come and You Will See | April Retreat (Senior Year) | To encounter one another and to hear in one another's stories Jesus' invitation to discipleship. |
| 2. So They Went and Saw | Beginning of Summer Program June Retreat I | To begin to be formed, through ACE's three pillars, into an intentional faith community of Catholic schoolteachers. |
| 3. Deepening the Encounter with Christ | Mid-Summer Optional Retreat I | To be renourished in the midst of the summer program by encountering the friendship of Christ in a more deeply intimate way. |
| 4. Go Ye Forth | End of Summer Missioning Liturgies I | To close our summer by celebrating the fellowship of our new ACE community and by commissioning our teachers into the evangelizing mission of the Church. |
| 5. The Companionship of Jesus | Semester Site Visits | To reaffirm the constant companionship of Jesus, especially through prayer and community, as the ACErs encounter the hardships of first-year teaching. |
| 6. The Costs and Joys of Discipleship | December Retreat I (Advent) | To articulate the challenges of discipleship through the first semester and to be opened to the work of God's grace in our gifts and limitations. |
| 7. The Return of the Disciples | Beginning of Second Summer June Retreat II | To give thanks for the work of God's grace in the first year and to be challenged to give our lives over still more as leaders for the new class of ACErs. |
| 8. Whoever Gives Their Life Away Will Find It | Mid-Summer Optional Retreat II | To live our lives of discipleship more intentionally in response to Christ's call to be like him, total self-gifts to others. |
| 9. Do You Love Me? | End of Summer Missioning Liturgies II | To celebrate the completion of our second summer and to introduce the central theme of the second year: the lifetime vocation to lead lives of love and service in concrete ways. |
| 10. Eyes of Faith | December Retreat II | To recognize where and how God has been present in our lives and ministry in ACE, in order to discern where God is leading us beyond our two years of service. |
| 11. Ending—and Beginning Again | Commencement Weekend End of July | To celebrate commencement in a spirit of thanksgiving and to commission our graduates as lifelong supporters of Catholic education. |
| 12. Bread for the Journey | Post-ACE Initiative | To provide inspired, effective, and relevant clusters of opportunities for our ACE graduates to lead Christ-centered lives of vocation, relationship, and prayer. |

In 1994, ACE began with 40 teachers under the direction of co-founders Fr. Timothy R. Scully, CSC *(third row, far left)*, and Fr. Sean McGraw, CSC *(first row, far right)*.

The first gathering of the ACE teachers is the April retreat. This annual retreat brings together the newly selected teachers with their future principals, superintendents, and community members. Fr. Scully, ACE teachers, administrators, and faculty celebrate the first April Retreat.

In their first summer, ACE teachers spend their mornings in the local Catholic and public schools as the classroom teachers of record. Under the guidance of master teachers, ACErs are able to observe and utilize best practices. Here, Ellen Butler takes advantage of local resources during a class field trip.

In the afternoons, Notre Dame Master of Education courses provide research and theory to reinforce experimental learning. First-year teachers are able to learn from the experience and discussion of their second-year colleagues. Here, David Wartowski shares his experiences with other middle school teachers.

With one year of experience, the second-year teachers focus on their professional development in the second summer, while also tutoring exceptional students of the South Bend area. Here, Molly Bates assists her summer-school student in computer mastery.

ACE teachers are challenged to incorporate all three pillars of the program (professional teaching, community, spirituality) into their summer experience. The Los Angeles communities offer a prayer of thanksgiving before sharing their weekly community meal.

ACE teachers strive to bring innovative and creative lessons to their students. At St. Anthony's School in Atlanta, James Brightman incorporates current events into his middle school history course to provide his pupils with a broad worldview.

Throughout the school year, ACE teachers receive a great deal of professional support. Mentor teachers, field supervisors, and ACE staff members offer constructive criticism and feedback. Here Sr. Lourdes Sheehan, RSM, Director of ACE from 1994 to 1996, offers some words of advice to John McGuire during her site visit to Jackson, Mississippi.

In their classrooms, ACE teachers serve as role models, caregivers, and educators all in one. Aimee Seiler enjoys a few hugs from her students in Fort Worth, Texas.

During the academic year, ACE teachers live in communities of four to seven members. These small Christian communities commit to serving, praying, and learning from one another over their two years together. (*Back row:* Ryan Blaney, Lisa Rodriguez, Malin Steans. *Front row:* Mark Leen, Jim Steffan.)

ACE communities provide the necessary foundation for success in all three ACE pillars. Teachers eat together, share their stories, and build an active prayer life. Here with their chaplain, the Mission, Texas community prays in the comfort of their home.

As willing and enthusiastic participants in their new communities, ACE teachers quickly become involved in extracurricular activities, including coaching, clubs, and parish youth groups. These avenues provide a unique opportunity for ACErs to learn about their students outside the classroom environment. Here, Scott Reis, ACE V, discusses the outcomes of the sectional meet with his cross-country runners from Charlotte Catholic.

Although some travel to see one another in the first semester, ACErs officially reunite after their first 18 weeks of teaching at the annual December Retreat. This Advent celebration brings teachers and staff together to discuss the joys of teaching. Here, Nick Hurt welcomes fellow classmate, Chris DellaPorta.

John Staud *(far right)*, Director of Pastoral Formation and Administration, facilitates a discussion with ACE English teachers *(from left to right)* Mariaelena Raymond, Patrick Burns, and Chad Barwick.

Fr. Scully, CSC, concludes the weekend with the celebration of the Eucharist. With renewed energy and commitment, ACE teachers return to their comunities and students to complete the school year.

ACE teachers work to fully integrate their faith into home and classroom. Here, Sarah Karr and her second grade students in St. Petersburg, Florida, share in prayer and some laughter before lunch.

Through internet courses and multiple observations, ACErs receive helpful feedback for continued improvement. Here, Joe Joy of Our Lady of Fatima in Birmingham, Alabama, guides his second-grade students through phonics.

ACErs find ways to weave fun into one curriculum. Here, Jen Ryan dances with her fifth graders during the Christmas show at Blessed Katherine Drexel–Sacred Heart School in Lake Charles, Louisiana.

ACE has been richly blessed by generous individuals and foundations. ACE established, with the support of a benefactor, the Laura Bush Scholarship, which provides tuition for deserving students in Texas. President and Mrs. Bush, along with Fr. Malloy and Fr. Scully, presented the first scholarship to Jorge Muruaga of Dallas in May 2001.

Following the guiding example of Christ the teacher, ACE participants are sent forth to humbly serve. Here, Dan Adams prays with his community during the candlelight Grotto service.

After two full years of teaching and learning, ACE teachers graduate with a Master of Education. Here, Fr. Edward Malloy, CSC, president of the University of Notre Dame, celebrates the Baccalaureate Mass with the greater ACE community.

Throughout the eight years, over two-thirds of ACE graduates have remained in education. Here, Andrea Ray accepts her diploma and hood from Academic Director, Michael Pressley.

As ACE continues to evolve, service to our neediest Catholic institutions remains the core mission. Here, Clare Deckelman at St. Jude High School in Montgomery, Alabama, provides the patience and Spanish fluency her pupil needs to excel.

ACE has grown to serve 14 states in 30 different communities across the southern and southwestern United States. Here, the 160 ACE teachers celebrate with faculty and staff Summer 2000.

PART **III**

# RESEARCH ON THE ACE MODEL

ecause Notre Dame is a research university, the founders felt that research on the program was essential, aspiring to research that would inform both the greater teacher education community as well as the creators of the program about issues that ACE amd the M.Ed. program should confront. It was apparent from the first cohort of ACE that the experience was challenging, consistent with a recurring conclusion in the teacher education literature that beginning teaching is filled with challenges. The two chapters in this section detail research projects that examined the challenges by ACE teachers, documenting that the ACErs are not only challenged but also resilient.

# 10

ALYSIA D. ROEHRIG
MICHAEL PRESSLEY

## THE CHALLENGES OF BEGINNING TEACHING IN ACE

The first summer of ACE is very intense, divided between the academic pressures of a 10-credit load, the demands of getting to know the other new members of ACE and future housemates, and a stimulating array of spirituality experiences. Even so, every September, the ACE faculty and staff always hear the same message from a number of ACErs: the summer was nothing compared to the workload during the school year. ACErs typically arrive at their schools before 8 A.M., and many school days continue into the evening as ACErs take on coaching and other extracurricular activities. Once an ACEr heads home, dinner with the community demands reflection with one another, which is time well spent, but time nonetheless. Then, there is lesson planning, which can take a young teacher several hours a night.

Is the beginning ACE teacher's life any more demanding than the life of a typical first-year teacher? Probably not. Virtually everyone who has studied the beginning teaching experience has concluded that it is filled with challenges. In a famous analysis of teaching, Lortie's (1975) *Schoolteacher: A Sociological Study,* the point is made that the beginning teacher is "fully responsible from the first working day . . . and performs the same tasks as a 25-year-old veteran" (p. 72). Additionally, the first year of teaching is a year of learning to teach. Many beginning teachers, however, find the experience overwhelming and do not return for a second year (Boser, 2000; Olson, 2000).

The developers of the ACE program very much want to prepare ACE teachers for what is ahead of them, to give them every advantage possible. To do that, the program developers needed to understand as completely as possible the particular challenges faced by beginning ACE teachers. In this chapter, we describe what was found in the several years spent examining the ACE program with respect to the teaching challenges ACErs encounter.

## RESEARCH ON THE CHALLENGES OF BEGINNING TEACHING

A GOOD STARTING POINT for anyone setting out to study the challenges confronted by beginning teachers is a review paper published in 1984 by Veenman, who began his article with a discussion of the "reality shock" often experienced by beginning teachers. Young teachers have many more responsibilities and duties than aspiring teachers ever imagine. The first year can be very emotional; it can result in massive change of attitudes (e.g., about students and self). The main thrust of the Veenman (1984) analysis was to review the findings across the existing examinations of the challenges of beginning teaching.

Most of the studies reviewed by Veenman involved beginning teachers completing questionnaires about their first year of teaching. The data proved to be very orderly, with Veenman able to group the challenges reported by teachers into 24 categories. Those categories were (from most frequently reported to least frequently reported) as follows: classroom discipline, motivating students, dealing with individual differences, assessing students' work, relations with parents, organization of classwork, insufficient materials and supplies, dealing with problems of individual students, heavy teaching load resulting in insufficient preparation time, relations with colleagues, planning of lessons and school days, effective use of different teaching methods, awareness of school policies and rules, determining the learning level of students, knowledge of subject matter, burden of clerical work, relations with principals and administrators, inadequate school equipment, dealing with slow learners, dealing with students from different cultural and socioeconomic backgrounds, effectively using textbooks and curriculum guides, lack of spare time, inadequate guidance and support, and large classes.

In addition to Veenman's overarching analysis, there have been a variety of case studies of beginning teachers assembled in the literature (Dollase, 1992; Kane, 1991; Kowalski, Weaver, & Henson, 1994; Ryan, 1970; Ryan et al., 1980; Shapiro, 1993), with these documenting that every beginning teacher faces challenges. The challenges on Veenman's list often occur in the beginning teacher's world, but so do some other challenges. Thus, a starting point for the study reported in this chapter was reading the case studies that were already available. In fact, 571 specific teaching challenges emerged in the analysis of the cases. Most, however, were specific instances that fit into the 24 Veenman categories. For example, for Veenman's category "dealing with individual differences," the following individual differences were reported as challenging by beginning teachers: immature students, transient students, angry students, overly tired students, depressed students, very shy students, students who are social misfits, hard-to-reach students, students with AIDS, abused students, students who are hurt by life, low-ability students, gifted students, emotionally disturbed students, students from disorganized and dysfunctional homes, students who are already parents of children themselves, and students affected by the demands of poverty.

As the ACE researchers examined the long Veenman list and the longer list of specific challenges, there seemed to be some overarching themes to the challenges. These themes suggested five general causes of the challenges confronted by first-year teachers: (1) aspects of the young teacher's self, (2) aspects of the students, (3) professional expectations and demands, (4) other adults in the school, and (5) factors outside the school. These five sources of challenge and the particular types of challenges associated with them are summarized in Table 10.1.

By the completion of the review of the literature on the challenges faced by beginning teachers, we had many questions. First, did ACE beginning teachers really face more than 500 different challenges during their first year of teaching? Second, many ACE teachers related how much easier the second year of ACE service was compared to the first year. Hence, we wondered, would there be a substantial drop in the number and seriousness of challenges during the second year of ACE? The only way to find out the answers to these questions was to study the ACErs and their challenges directly, with the expectation

**TABLE 10.1**

*Five Sources of Beginning Teaching Challenges*

| | |
|---|---|
| *SELF* | *PROFESSIONAL* |
| Lack of knowledge about teaching/ curriculum | Classroom discipline |
| | Assessment |
| Induction and mentoring issues | Classroom management |
| Conflicts with school culture | Resource issues |
| Personal life issues | Nonteaching, school-based demands |
| Gender/sexual challenges | Planning lessons and school days |
| | Classroom instruction |
| *STUDENTS* | Induction and mentoring issues |
| Misbehavior | |
| Motivation | *OTHER ADULTS IN SCHOOL* |
| Individual differences | Relations with parents |
| Teacher-student communications | Relations with teaching colleagues |
| Diversity issues | Induction and mentoring issues |
| Gender/sexual challenges | Conflicts with school culture |
| | Relations with principals/administrators |
| | Gender/sexual challenges |

*FACTORS OUTSIDE THE SCHOOL*
Personal life issues
Outside community issues

that such an investigation would provide a great deal of information about how to address beginning teaching challenges in the ACE M.Ed. program.

## WHAT CHALLENGES DO ACERS CONFRONT?

WE STUDIED THE CHALLENGES confronted by ACErs using several different methodologies. In this chapter, the focus will be on only one part of the data, however. The entire volume of a related book is dedicated to describing both the survey and interview phases of this study and provides a number of detailed case studies written by ACErs (Roehrig, Pressley, & Talotta, 2002). The study included a questionnaire tapping all 571 of the potential challenges of beginning teaching that were reported in the case studies of beginning teaching in the literature (i.e., Dollase, 1992; Kane, 1991; Kowalski, Weaver, & Henson, 1994; Ryan, 1970; Ryan et al., 1980; Shapiro, 1993). Samples of ACErs in their first and second years of teaching completed the questionnaire. Respondents were asked to indicate how often each of the challenges occurred, rating on a scale from "never" to "every day or almost every day."

Much was learned from the responses to this questionnaire. First, challenges were frequent for ACE teachers. First- and second-year teachers reported between 49 and 440 different challenges occurring during their school year (mean = 207.58, SD = 90.90). That is, on average, ACE teachers reported they experienced more than one unique challenge daily or almost daily. Even more striking was that the ACErs reported on average, collapsing across items, 23 different challenges a day. Then, there were 31 challenges reported as occurring at least once a week and another 53 occurring at least monthly, according to the ACErs. The ACErs are immersed in challenges. Perhaps the one bit of good news is that more than half of the 571 challenges were reported as occurring only a few times a year or less.

The second-year ACErs had slightly fewer challenges than the first-year ACErs on average. Male and female teachers did not differ in the number of challenges reported. High school teachers reported being slightly more challenged than elementary and middle school teachers. In short, systematic differences in the numbers of challenges reported were not great in this study; the generalization that first- and second-year teaching is challenging seemed to hold across the sample of ACE teachers.

One of the most interesting findings in the study was that every one of the 571 challenges tapped by the survey was reported by one or more ACE teachers. That is, beginning teachers often confront many and diverse challenges. Even so, many challenges were rated as occurring only once a year, if at all (i.e., 173 of the 571 challenges were so rated when collapsing across teachers). Also, only a small fraction of the 571 challenges on the survey were reported as experienced frequently by ACE teachers. Table 10.2 lists the 30 challenges that were reported as occurring at least a few times a month on average by the ACE teachers. What is obvious from this table is that what often challenges ACE teachers is the students. Students sometimes misbehave, lack motivation, and have diverse characteristics that can challenge the teacher. Even the "professional" challenges in Table 10.2 relate to students, including the challenges of discipline, classroom management, and planning so as to meet each student's needs. The results summarized in Table 10.2 are collapsed across the first- and second-year ACE teachers, male and female teachers, and across elementary, middle, and high school teachers.

In general, the differences in frequently encountered challenges were small as a function of teaching experience within ACE, teacher gender, and educational level taught. One difference was noteworthy, however. High school teachers indicated low student motivation as a frequent challenge much more than did elementary or middle school teachers. Thus, high school teachers more than elementary and middle school teachers reported that their students did not accept responsibility for their own failures, showed little energy or enthusiasm in class, found the material being taught irrelevant, did not share the teacher's work ethic, complained about homework, and were apathetic, bored, and uninterested.

An interesting finding was that more able and less able ACE teachers (as rated by their field supervisors) reported somewhat different challenges. The less able teachers reported having more difficulty with students and with fellow teachers than did the more able teachers. In contrast, the more able teachers worried more about their teaching, for example, reporting challenges with having enough planning time.

Although none of the challenges listed in Table 10.2 seems too serious, some were considered serious if they happened frequently (e.g., students do not do assignments or are mean). The list of 571 challenges did have some that certainly would be very serious if they happened (e.g., student suicide). Because young teachers need to be alerted to serious challenges they might possibly face, there was a thorough analysis of the reported challenges to identify serious issues that might affect the beginning teacher.

Notably, most of these challenges involved students. In short, students who cause serious problems are frequently encountered by beginning teachers. Something else that emerged from this analysis was that the beginning teachers often do not have the time for all students who need help or even time enough for themselves, with such lack of time perceived as a serious challenge by beginning teachers.

Some challenges would be very serious even if they occurred only infrequently (e.g., student suicide). ACE teachers reported a number of these very serious challenges as occurring either infrequently or moderately frequently (see Table 10.3). Fortunately, none of these very serious challenges occurred frequently. That is, very serious challenges can occur in the first or second year of teaching, although many of them are unlikely to happen at all, or happen only once a year or so at most.

**TABLE 10.2**

*Challenges That Occurred at Least a Few Times a Month*

*SELF*

   *Lack of Knowledge of Teaching*
      Encountering a situation teacher education did not prepare one for

   *Personal Life Issues*
      Not having any spare time•

*PROFESSIONAL*

   *Classroom Discipline*
      Finding a balance between being in control and being too autocratic

   *Classroom Management*
      Students leave the classroom messy
      Individual students are disruptive or uncontrollable*

   *Planning Lessons and School Days*
      Not enough time to teach each student as much as needed*

*STUDENTS*

   *Misbehavior*
      Students who are inattentive
      Disruptive student hyperactivity
      Students sitting inappropriately (e.g., sprawled over or sitting on desk)
      Students who are tardy
      Students talking too much

   *Motivation*
      Students do not do assignments/homework*
      Students do assignments/homework late
      Students do assignments/homework haphazardly
      Students turn in sloppy work

   *Individual Differences*
      Students who are immature
      Students who are angry
      Students who are overly tired
      Students who are social misfits
      Students who are mean*
      Students who are hard to reach
      Low-ability students
      Gifted students
      Students living in disorganized/dysfunctional families*
      Students with short attention spans
      Students with vastly different abilities
      Students with special education needs*
      Students with problems understanding material
      Students who watch too much TV
      Students who are rude/disrespectful*

*Considered serious if it happened frequently.

**TABLE 10.3**

*Serious Challenges That Occurred Infrequently or Moderately Frequently*

---

*PROFESSIONAL*

*Classroom Management*

Person enters room without authorization and will not leave*

Having to make moral compromise to keep peace with students*

Student disappears from classroom (teacher cannot find a student who is supposed to be there)*

*STUDENTS*

*Discipline*

Having to administer corporal punishment*

Pressure by principal (or some other administrator or teacher) to use corporal punishment*

*Misbehavior*

Students harassing beginning teacher**

Having suspicion that a student may be involved in illegal activity (e.g., selling drugs)**

Students stealing**

Students fighting**

Students abusing alcohol**

Teacher physically attacked/hit by student*

Evidence that a student committed a crime*

Teacher is victim of student vandalism*

Student committing or threatening to commit suicide*

Students dropping out of school*

Students who are gang members*

Students who extort money or other goods from other students*

Guns or other weapons in the school*

Students abuse drugs*

*Individual Differences*

Having a student who is being abused**

Having a student whose parent dies**

Having students who can't read**

Having students with eating disorders*

Having a student who dies*

Having a student who is murdered*

*Diversity Issues*

    Having a student who shows racial prejudice**

    Minority students (or their parents) who believe they are victims of discrimination by beginning teacher*

    Students (or their parents) accusing beginning teacher of racial prejudice*

*Gender/Sexual Issues*

    Having a student who engages in sexual misconduct*

OTHER ADULTS IN SCHOOL

*Relations with Parents*

    Parent threatens to ask that beginning teacher be dismissed*

*Relations with Teaching Colleagues*

    Other teachers are critical of the new teacher; tactless, rude, or insulting to the new teacher*

    Having to make a moral compromise to keep the peace with other teachers*

*Relations with Principals/Administrators*

    Being threatened with dismissal by principal or other administrator*

    Beginning teacher uncertain about whether she or he will be rehired next year*

*Gender/Sexual Issues*

    Being sexually harassed by another faculty member or subjected to sexual innuendo by another faculty member*

    Learning of a seduction attempt of a student by another teacher*

---

*occurred infrequently
**occurred moderately frequently

## APPLYING THE RESEARCH ON BEGINNING TEACHING

As THIS BOOK is being written, planning is taking place to modify the ACE curriculum to provide greater focus on the challenges of beginning teaching. Thus, next summer, introduction to teaching will include presentations that take up classroom management problems that can be real hassles for the beginning teachers, including the following:

- Balancing being in control versus being too autocratic
- Students leaving the classroom messy
- Managing individual students who are disruptive or uncontrollable

- Dealing with students who are tardy, talk too much, do not do assignments or homework, or do them late or haphazardly
- Dealing with a person who enters the room without authorization and will not leave
- Keeping peace with students without making moral compromises
- Keeping track of students so no student ever disappears from the classroom
- Controlling student harassment and fighting
- Dealing with theft or other illegal behaviors

In addition, what became obvious from our survey of challenges was that there are many types of student exceptionalities, rather than just the few that are officially classified (e.g., students with learning disorders, students with ADHD). Thus, the exceptionality course is being rethought to provide ACE teachers with tools for dealing with a wide range of behaviors that can cause challenges for the beginning teacher. These include dealing with students who are being abused, who are living in dysfunctional families, whose parent dies, and who can't read. There will be coverage of how to deal with students who are rude, disrespectful, or mean, have eating disorders, are sexually promiscuous, or are racially prejudiced.

Teacher educators have been aware for a very long time that beginning teaching is filled with challenges. The assumption was that the first several years of teaching were something of a baptism by fire, with the expectation that young teachers would learn through experience. For many, however, what is learned is that teaching is too challenging for them. In fact, when Roehrig et al. (2002) surveyed experienced teachers serving the same schools as the ACE teachers, they found that even the experienced teachers were challenged in ways similar to how the ACE beginning teachers were. Perhaps if ACE teacher education is reoriented to deal more directly with the challenges faced by teachers, progress can be made in better solving problems when they occur—either during the first year of teaching or much later in a teacher's career. Gaining a good understanding of just what challenges need to be covered in ACE teacher education was an important first step accomplished in the first three years of the ACE M.Ed. program.

## REFERENCES

Boser, U. (2000). A picture of the teacher pipeline: Baccalaureate and beyond. *Education Week, 19*(18), 16–17.

Dollase, R. H. (1992). *Voices of beginning teachers: Visions and realities.* New York: Teachers College Press.

Kane, P. R. (1991). *The first year of teaching: Real world stories from America's teachers.* New York: Walker.

Kowalski, T. J., Weaver, R. A., & Henson, K. T. (1994). *Case studies of beginning teachers.* New York: Longman.

Lortie, D. C. (1975). *Schoolteacher: A sociological study.* Chicago: University of Chicago Press.

Olson, L. (2000). Finding and keeping competent teachers. *Education Week, 19*(18), 13–18.

Roehrig, A. D., Pressley, M., & Talotta, D. A. (2002). *Stories of beginning teachers: Challenges of the first year and beyond.* Notre Dame, IN: University of Notre Dame Press.

Ryan, K. (1970). *Don't smile until Christmas: Accounts of the first year of teaching.* Chicago: University of Chicago Press.

Ryan, K., Newman, K., Mager, G., Applegate, J., Lasley, T., Flora, R., & Johnston, J. (1980). *Biting the apple: Accounts of first year teachers.* New York: Longman.

Shapiro, M. (1993). *Who will teach for America?* Washington, DC: Farragut.

Veenman, S. (1984). Perceived problems of beginning teachers. *Review of Educational Research, 54,* 143–178.

## 11

VLADIMIR T. KHMELKOV
ANN MARIE R. POWER

# ACE Teachers' Responsibility and Efficacy Beliefs

The 1996 study of the National Commission on Teaching and America's Future (NCTAF) followed a series of reports in finding existing practices in teacher training to be detrimental to novice teachers' professional development. Conventional teacher training fails to prepare new teachers who are professionally competent and personally committed to promote the academic success of all children. Traditional teacher education also fails to prepare novice teachers to address the special learning needs of low-income and minority students and to place talented, competent, and responsible teachers in underserved urban and rural schools (Darling-Hammond & Sclan, 1996). Finally, the NCTAF report identified the period of induction, or beginning teaching, as the most problematic time in novice teachers' development, typically characterized by high stress and lack of professional or social support. In fact, over 30% of new teachers leave the profession in the first three years of their careers due to burnout (NCTAF, 1996).

Responding to these challenges for teacher preparation, ACE had an immediate goal of attracting competent and committed individuals to work as teachers in understaffed Catholic schools, and an ultimate goal of inspiring their lifelong commitment to the education of the disadvantaged children in the United States. In following its mission, ACE seeks to avoid the failures of existing traditional models of teacher education and induction. Consistent with NCTAF's recommendations, the primary element of ACE's model is a two-year, full-time teaching internship, with most of the participants serving minority and underprivileged children. The extended internship in this environment allows ACE teachers to be fully exposed to a range of real-life classroom conditions, experience the resulting "reality shock," and attempt to overcome its detrimental impact (for a description of the phenomenon of "reality shock" in the professions, see Becker & Geer, 1958; Corwin, 1961; Hughes, 1956; Lortie, 1959).

To help its participants survive the reality shock of classroom teaching, the ACE program starts by recruiting academically successful college graduates. Academic competence is further enhanced through summer coursework designed to develop participants' understanding of contemporary educational theory and research. The field experiences during the summer session give special attention to how such knowledge can be translated into effective and responsible classroom practices. When ACE participants begin full-time teaching in the fall, the program provides additional instruction via distance-learning technologies and close on-site supervision to ensure continuous growth of professional competence.

The ACE program further distinguishes itself from other teacher development models through its emphasis on community. ACE participants live in supportive community with one another on Notre Dame's campus, taking a weekly class on community and spiritual growth during the summer sessions. During the regular school year, ACE participants live with each other in communities of four to seven preservice teachers at the service-learning sites, with teachers from several schools living in one house. These professional communities are designed to support teacher candidates through the stresses and strains of their teaching internship and to enhance their professional competence and commitment. Communities facilitate participants' constant learning from each other's experiences in the classroom and reflecting on the role that community-based pedagogy plays in enhancing the learning and socialization experiences of children.

ACE is distinctive as well because of its focus on the moral aspects of teaching. Whereas some service-oriented programs rely solely on the sense of dedication of their participants, the Notre Dame program explicitly prepares its teacher candidates to nurture ethical values, racial understanding, and social responsibility among children in a socially stratified and diverse society. This is accomplished through the program's coursework (e.g., the ACE M.Ed. program is the only teacher education program that requires a course on moral development of students) and its communities, as well as through the program's emphasis on the spiritual and ethical development of each of the ACE participants.

This chapter presents findings from a longitudinal research project that assesses the impact of the preservice teaching environment and of the organizational aspects of the ACE model on ACE teachers' sense of commitment and self-efficacy in teaching.

## BACKGROUND

TEACHERS' COMMITMENT is essential for effective teaching. Many attempted structural reforms in the last two decades, such as cooperative learning, on-the-job staff development, site-based management, and teaming, failed to demonstrate consistently positive results in the field when educators were not personally committed to improving student learning (Newmann, 1993). The importance of teachers' commitment motivated our focus on novice teachers' responsibility beliefs as the central concept of interest in the study summarized in this chapter. Following suggestions that teacher responsibility should go beyond the general formulation of a professional ethic (Oser, Dick, & Patry, 1992), our research explored two particular aspects of novice teachers' sense of responsibility: responsibility for student academic achievement and responsibility for the socio-moral development of all students.

### RESPONSIBILITY FOR STUDENT LEARNING

In contemporary schools, teachers face an increasing array of problems posed by social stratification among students and compounded by their cultural diversity. The number of students in schools who do not fit the traditional model of white, middle-class education is on the rise. Faced with poverty, limited proficiency in English, different cultural norms—and in many cases, an environment of drugs, crime, and violence—students from low socioeconomic status, nonwhite backgrounds disengage from learning. Teachers, who remain predominantly white and middle class, are likely to see this environment as problematic, perhaps a cause of student underachievement that cannot be overcome (Valli, Cooper, & Frankes, 1997). In contrast, ACE attempts to develop teachers who believe they can make a difference in such environments, who have a sense of responsibility for promoting student achievement. In this study, this sense of responsibility was conceptualized as the degree to which teachers believe they are responsible for promoting student learning, compared to the degree of responsibility they attribute to the student and the family.

## RESPONSIBILITY FOR STUDENT SOCIO-MORAL DEVELOPMENT

Although academic achievement constitutes the core of the work that schools do, another major challenge for schools is the social and moral development of students (Bellah, Madsen, Sullivan, Swidler, & Tipton, 1991). Human betterment is, in fact, a major goal of teaching (e.g., Ball & Wilson, 1996; Jackson, Boostrom, & Hansen, 1993; Sockett, 1993). Hence, in this study, we investigated teachers' sense of responsibility for promoting socio-moral development of students as an indispensable dimension of professional commitment. We conceptualized it as the degree to which teachers believe they are personally responsible for promoting students' socio-moral development, compared to the degree of responsibility they attribute to the student's family.

## TEACHER RESPONSIBILITY AND PERSONAL EFFICACY

Teachers' sense of responsibility needs to be examined together with their competence. Competence includes knowledge of the subject matter being taught, knowledge of the principles of classroom management, knowledge of learners and their characteristics, and knowledge of educational purposes and values (Shulman, 1987). Professional competence also refers to teaching skills that include an ability to analyze the situation and adapt instructional practices to groups and individual learners, without losing sight of the general educational goals.

Since direct measurement of teacher competence is difficult due to wide variation in the knowledge and skills required for effective teaching across developmental levels of students and subject matters (cf. Sternberg & Horvath, 1995; Stodolsky & Grossman, 1995), we studied teachers' sense of *personal efficacy* as a proxy measure of professional competence. Personal teaching efficacy is teachers' "confidence that they have adequate training or experience to develop strategies for overcoming obstacles to student learning" (Tschannen-Moran, Woolfolk Hoy, & Hoy, 1998, p. 205). Personal efficacy is, of course, self-perception of competence rather than an objective measure of competence, but it is a strong predictor of effective professional behavior (Bandura, 1997). In particular, personal teaching efficacy is associated with teachers' competence and effective practices (see a review in Tschannen-Moran et al., 1998). For example, Raudenbush, Rowan, and Cheong (1992) found that the level of preparation for teaching was significantly related to high school teachers' self-efficacy. In another study, both greater experience and higher levels of education were determinants of higher levels of personal teaching efficacy (Hoy & Woolfolk, 1993). Teachers with high personal efficacy are persistent when facing obstacles (Gibson & Dembo, 1984), likely to implement progressive and innovative methods (Fuchs, Fuchs, & Bishop, 1992), and experiment with instructional materials and activities (Allinder, 1994).

## DEVELOPMENT OF NOVICE TEACHERS' PROFESSIONAL BELIEFS

Schools can reinforce teachers' commitment and self-efficacy by establishing a professional working environment (Bidwell & Yasumoto, 1999; Khmelkov, 2000; Rowan, 1990). A fundamental component of such an environment is *task autonomy and discretion* in teaching that serve as a basis for a sense of ownership of one's work and, therefore, personal responsibility for the results of one's practices (see, for example, Ashton & Webb, 1986; Rosenholtz, 1989). Task autonomy and discretion allow teachers the flexibility they need to adapt their practices to the needs of diverse learners in their classrooms. Autonomy may be especially important for novice teachers who come to schools eager to apply their new knowledge and skills but may be discouraged if the older teachers, especially mentors and supervisors, do not share their pedagogical views or approve of experimentation.

The quality of *collegial relationships* is another major aspect of a professional environment for teaching (see, for example, Bidwell, Frank, & Quiroz, 1997; McLaughlin & Talbert, 1993; Talbert & McLaughlin, 1994). When teachers' shared beliefs are centered around high academic standards, the collaborative community creates an outcome-oriented environment, or *academic press* (cf. Shouse, 1996), which can be expected to promote a strong sense of personal responsibility among individual teachers. On the other hand, a strong community without an academic orientation can have negative effects on teacher commitment and student achievement (Shouse, 1996). For example, when the school faculty do not share academic norms regarding teaching for understanding, individual teachers may be more prone to pressures from parents or administrators, as well as from colleagues, to emphasize basic skills or nonacademic objectives. Furthermore, in some schools a feeling of solidarity may be built entirely around the norm of weak teacher responsibility and low academic standards (cf. Bidwell et al., 1997; Metz, 1978).

Principals or department chairs may have a positive effect on novice teachers' sense of responsibility and sense of efficacy by *buffering* them from factors outside the classroom that might interfere with instruction. Such buffering includes assistance with paperwork, managing problem students, resisting parents' demands for preferential treatment or changing instruction, and protecting teachers from excessive noninstructional tasks (Firestone, 1990; Newmann, Rutter, & Smith, 1989).

Apart from affecting teachers' sense of responsibility, collegial relationships and *peer involvement in teaching and socio-moral development of students* have important effects on teachers' sense of efficacy (Raudenbush et al., 1992; Rosenholtz, 1989; Rosenholtz & Simpson, 1990). First of all, when teachers become involved together with other teachers in defining or reevaluating school goals, in coordinating curriculum, and in sharing technical information, they develop a better understanding of long-term and immediate classroom objectives and appropriate approaches to reaching them. Most importantly, experienced teachers can offer novice teachers concrete instructional help and advice that will assist in the daily management of the classroom uncertainty and increase their sense of efficacy in teaching.

The ACE program sends its participants to work as full-time teachers in primarily underserved schools that present ACE participants with a range of educational challenges typically associated with a decline in responsibility and efficacy beliefs during the initial period of teaching. However, the negative influence of such an environment is expected to be attenuated by the ongoing professional development and social support from the university-based program. Whether that is so was evaluated explicitly in this study, along with the other issues considered up until this point in the chapter.

## METHODS

### THE SAMPLE

The study uses a sample drawn from two teacher education programs: the Alliance for Catholic Education (ACE) and Ball State University (BSU), the latter serving as a comparison group. Teachers College at BSU is a traditionally organized baccalaureate-level teacher preparation program. After completing general studies requirements, students apply to one of the programs in the teaching curriculum (such as Early Child Education, Elementary Education, Secondary, All-Grade, or Junior High/Middle School Education). Elementary and Early Child students major in education. Secondary and Junior High/Middle School students major in one or more of the subject areas. All students complete a professional education sequence that includes studies in human growth and development, educational psychology, foundations of education, cultural and ethnic awareness, content reading, and methods of teaching.

In the final year of their studies, BSU students complete a 13- or 16-week student teaching period. Student teachers are typically placed in or near their hometowns by the Field Experience Office. They are supervised by the regular classroom teacher and a member of the BSU faculty. Student teachers start teaching together with the cooperating teacher, with the idea that they gradually assume most of the responsibility for planning and teaching their classes after eight weeks of student teaching. Upon completion of all course requirements, Teachers College graduates earn a bachelor of arts or a bachelor of science degree and become eligible for Indiana licensure in their specific area.

### DATA COLLECTION

Data were collected from two cohorts in ACE: ACE IV, the last group in the University of Portland version of the program, and ACE V, the first group in the Notre Dame version of the program. Altogether, 99 ACE participants had complete longitudinal information. Three cohorts of BSU preservice teachers served as a comparison group (144 participants with complete longitudinal information). To the extent that novice teachers' beliefs and practices are influenced by their personal characteristics and experiences before teaching, it was necessary to obtain measures of teachers' beliefs prior to the beginning of the teaching experience (pre-test), as well as after the initial period of teaching experience (post-test). Baseline questionnaires, therefore, were administered before novice teachers began their student teaching or teaching internships and tapped information on participants' incoming sense of responsibility, sense of efficacy, and personal background characteristics. Follow-up questionnaires were administered at the end of the initial teaching experience and sought information on teacher outcomes and those contextual and organizational factors that were hypothesized to affect novice teachers' beliefs during teaching.

Demographic characteristics of the participants in the sample were as follows. Among the ACE participants, 49% were male and 51% female; among the BSU participants, 22% were male and 78% female. The sample was quite homogeneous with regard to the other demographic characteristics of the participants. Only 3.7% of the sample were Hispanic Americans and about 2% were African Americans. Over 93% of the participants were between 21 and 25 years old, with the remaining individuals spread evenly across the rest of the age groups (ranging from 20 or younger to 40 or older). Fewer than 9% of the sample participants were married. There were no significant associations between indicators of race, age, or marital status and teacher outcomes in these samples. Therefore, for parsimony, only the indicator of gender was included in the final analyses.

## THE VARIABLES

The dependent variables include indicators of novice *Teachers' Sense of Responsibility* and *Personal Efficacy* in two domains of teaching: promoting students' achievement and socio-moral development.

The primary predictor variable is a categorical variable ACE versus BSU. Contextual factors included three aspects of the social environment of schools that might be expected to contribute to the uncertainty of teaching and deflate novice teachers' responsibility and efficacy beliefs: (a) *high school level of teaching* (as opposed to K–8 teaching), (b) *percent minority students in the classrooms,* and (c) *school discipline and social problems.* Organizational characteristics included indicators of autonomy and quality of collegial relationships that can reinforce novice teachers' sense of responsibility and efficacy in teaching: (a) *autonomy in instruction and in socio-moral development of students,* (b) *school faculty's focus on promoting students' learning and socio-moral development,* (c) *buffering from external pressures provided by administration,* (d) *peer assistance with teaching and socio-moral development of students,* and (e) *university faculty assistance with teaching and socio-moral development of students.*

The analyses included control variables that index individual characteristics among participants, such as gender and pre-teaching measures of the dependent variables, permitting control for the participants' prior beliefs and experiences. An additional control variable was *Ratings of Training* that takes into account novice teachers' perceptions of the adequacy of the teaching skills they have acquired prior to teaching.

Detailed information on the construction of all variables can be found in Appendix A to this chapter.


## RESULTS

TABLE 11.1 PRESENTS comparisons of means by program of the background, contextual, and organizational factors that were assessed in this study. ACE teachers were more likely to teach in junior and senior high schools. As expected, ACE teachers tended to have more minority students in their classrooms and face greater social and discipline problems in their schools than their counterparts from BSU. ACE teachers also perceived weaker focus among other teachers in their schools on student learning and socio-moral development, and ACE teachers felt less protected from noninstructional pressures in their schools.

Compared to BSU student teachers, ACE teachers were less satisfied with their training, particularly in subject matter instruction. On the other hand, ACE teachers enjoyed significantly greater autonomy in teaching, especially in questions of socio-moral development of their students. ACE participants were also more likely than their counterparts to receive support from their peers, although both groups gave similar average ratings to the help and assistance provided by their university supervisors. In sum, novice teachers in the two programs taught in significantly different environments.

Table 11.2 contains comparisons of means by program of novice teachers' pre-teaching and post-teaching professional beliefs. Novice teachers in the two programs did not differ significantly in their average responsibility beliefs regarding academic achievement prior to teaching, whereas after teaching, ACE teachers reported slightly lower beliefs in this domain. While similarly not different in their percep-

**TABLE 11.1**

*Means (Percentages) and Standard Deviations of Background, Contextual, and Organizational Characteristics of Teaching by University Program*

| | ACE (n = 99) | | BSU (n = 144) | |
|---|---|---|---|---|
| | Mean | (SD) | Mean | (SD) |
| Male | 49%*** | (.50) | 22% | (.42) |
| Training in Instruction | 2.88*** | (.55) | 3.63 | (.62) |
| Training in Socio-Moral Development | 3.14*** | (.67) | 3.52 | (.79) |
| Percent in Junior/Senior High School | 55%* | (.50) | 41% | (.49) |
| Percent Minority Students in the Classroom | 38%*** | (.39) | 12% | (.18) |
| School Discipline & Social Climate | 2.34*** | (.71) | 1.99 | (.86) |
| Organizational Characteristics | | | | |
| Autonomy in Instruction | 4.25* | (.57) | 4.03 | (.90) |
| Autonomy in Promoting Socio-Moral Development | 4.37*** | (.71) | 3.87 | (1.25) |
| School Faculty's Focus on Promoting Achievement | 3.62*** | (.84) | 4.10 | (.68) |
| School Faculty's Focus on Promoting Socio-Moral Development | 3.62* | (.84) | 3.87 | (.73) |
| Buffering from External Pressures | 3.38*** | (1.21) | 3.97 | (.77) |
| Peer Network Support with Instruction | 3.77*** | (.84) | 3.05 | (1.04) |
| Peer Network Support with Socio-Moral Development | 3.64*** | (.89) | 2.85 | (1.02) |
| University Faculty Support with Instruction | 3.37 | (1.05) | 3.47 | (1.45) |
| University Faculty Support with Socio-Moral Development | 3.16 | (1.13) | 2.91 | (1.67) |

Note: $*p < .05, **p < .01, ***p < .001$.

tions of efficacy in promoting student learning prior to teaching, ACE teachers declined in their self-efficacy in this domain after the first year of teaching. As for responsibility for promoting students' socio-moral development, these beliefs were quite stable in both programs. However, ACE teachers reported considerably higher levels of these beliefs both prior to and after their teaching experience compared to BSU teachers. Finally, personal efficacy beliefs for promoting students' socio-moral development were not significantly different either in the pre-test or in the post-test.

Additional statistical analyses were carried out to determine whether there were associations between contextual and organizational characteristics of teaching and novice teachers' outcomes. The highlights of these analyses included the following outcomes. (a) Novice teachers who taught in high schools were more likely than novice teachers in elementary schools to have their sense of responsibility for achievement weakened. (b) As expected, greater autonomy in instruction, buffering from noninstructional pressures, and peer network support were positively associated with novice teachers' sense of responsibility for achievement. (c) Novice teachers who had greater autonomy and buffering from noninstructional pressures seemed to be better protected against a decline in efficacy beliefs. (d) There was some indication that better training and greater support from the collegial relationships with peers helped protect instructional efficacy beliefs against the reality shock. (e) With respect to sense of responsibility for students' socio-moral development, there was greater decline among high school teachers. (f) Sense of responsibility for socio-moral development was maintained when teachers were given a good deal of autonomy in their decisions while shielded from outside pressures. (g) There was a positive association between the degree of social and discipline problems in a school and teachers' sense of responsibility for students' socio-moral development, which may seem surprising. Perhaps it indicates greater awareness of the need to get involved in students' social and ethical development among those teachers who were sensitized by greater exposure to problems of social and moral development in their school setting. (h) The degree of school faculty's focus on socio-moral issues and support from peers for focus on socio-moral issues tended to foster the novice teachers' efficacy in socio-moral development of their students. (i) Novice teachers had greater focus on socio-moral development of students when they had greater contact with minority students.

## DISCUSSION AND CONCLUSIONS

THE FULL-TIME TEACHING internship that ACE participants experience immerses them in real-life classroom environments. Moreover, the settings in which ACE student teachers are placed are more diverse and challenging than those encountered in the conventional student-teaching program at BSU. ACE teachers have more minority students in their classrooms. They work in schools with more chal-

**TABLE 11.2**

*Means and Standard Deviations of Pre-Teaching and Post-Teaching Professional Beliefs by University Program*

| | Pre-Teaching | | | Post-Teaching | | |
|---|---|---|---|---|---|---|
| | ACE | BSU | p | ACE | BSU | p |
| Sense of Responsibility for Promoting Academic Achievement | 3.633 (.492) | 3.744 (.452) | .720 | 3.509 (.451) | 3.690 (.459) | .030 |
| Personal Efficacy in Promoting Academic Achievement | 4.006 (.475) | 4.062 (.473) | .367 | 3.843 (.569) | 4.122 (.508) | .000 |
| Sense of Responsibility for Promoting Socio-Moral Development | 4.125 (.583) | 3.827 (.622) | .000 | 4.195 (.605) | 3.818 (.642) | .000 |
| Personal Efficacy in Promoting Socio-Moral Development | 3.963 (.534) | 3.874 (.603) | .239 | 3.849 (.660) | 3.925 (.637) | .373 |

*Note:* Paired samples *t*-test, 2-tailed

lenging social and disciplinary climates and with faculty who have only average concern for promoting students' learning or socio-moral development. ACE teachers also have to deal with more issues not directly related to classroom teaching.

Given the challenging environments and the real-world experience that ACE interns encounter, one might expect that their beliefs about responsibility and efficacy in promoting students' academic achievement and socio-moral development might be much more affected than in traditional student teachers. For the most part, however, this was not the case. ACE teachers emerged from their first-year teaching experience only slightly lower than their BSU counterparts in their sense of responsibility for fostering the academic achievement of their students. This difference disappeared when contextual and organizational factors were controlled. Similarly, once some of the major characteristics of challenging classrooms were taken into account, the challenge of serving needy schools did not appear to have a negative impact on ACE teachers' feelings of efficacy in this area of teaching. Regarding socio-moral development, ACE teachers continued to feel more strongly about their responsibility in promoting this aspect of their students' growth, even when factors characteristic of their challenging environments were taken into consideration. In terms of their impressions of their own efficacy in successfully fostering their students' socio-moral growth, the ACE teachers experienced a slight negative influence, which may not be too surprising given the real-world context in which these students are operating. Indeed, one might wonder why there was not a more pronounced decline associated with the ACE experience.

What might account for the lack of any dramatic dip in the ACE teachers' beliefs about their responsibility and efficacy for promoting their students' academic and socio-moral growth? A look at the organizational factors included in the analyses, along with the factors indicative of programmatic support, may provide some answers. First, as independent, full-time teachers, ACE participants make their own decisions and, consequently, enjoy much greater autonomy and flexibility in their teaching. This organizational factor had the most consistent positive influence on novice teachers' responsibility and efficacy beliefs across the school contexts in this study. Second, ACE's focus on community building and continuous professional interactions among its participants results in a strong sense of peer support among ACE teachers. Continuous professional and social interactions within peer networks appear to foster novice teachers' professional beliefs, even though they did so to a smaller degree in the analyses summarized here than did professional autonomy and flexibility. Also, even though ACE teachers on average were less buffered from noninstructional pressures by school administration, those who were buffered certainly benefited from it.

The fact that neither supervision by the university faculty nor support from the school-designated mentor (estimated in the preliminary analyses) were significantly associated with novice teachers' sense of responsibility and self-efficacy suggests that these agents were not as successful in their mission of supporting professional development of novice teachers as hoped. This result, unfortunately, is consistent with extant research showing that cooperating teachers and university supervisors often play only a minor role in novice teachers' socialization (see review in Staton & Hunt, 1992). Nevertheless, the ACE program has considerably strengthened the supervision it provides since these data were collected. Continued research will be necessary to assess whether ACE is successful in its efforts in this respect.

In summary, ACE teachers find themselves in real-world classrooms during their teaching internships. The negative impact of reality shock, however, is reduced to a minimum for those teachers who work in professionally organized environments—who are given a great deal of autonomy in teaching and protection from noninstructional pressures by school administration and who engage in continuous professional interactions with their peers.

## APPENDIX A: DESCRIPTION OF VARIABLES

### SENSE OF RESPONSIBILITY

People differ in their views on education. Please indicate to what extent you agree or disagree with each of the following statements (1 = completely disagree, 2 = somewhat disagree, 3 = neither agree nor disagree, 4 = somewhat agree, 5 = completely agree).

*Teachers' Sense of Responsibility for Promoting Achievement*
*($\alpha = 0.6503$)*

- It is the responsibility of teachers to ensure that even difficult or unmotivated students achieve at a high level
- It is teachers who are usually responsible when their students fail to achieve to the best of their potential

- It is the responsibility of teachers to ensure that all students grow in their learning according to their individual abilities
- Since it is a personal choice of individual students at what level to achieve, teachers are usually not responsible for students' poor academic knowledge (reversed)
- Teachers should organize their instruction in such a way that all students exceed a satisfactory level of achievement
- Teachers should tailor instruction to the individual abilities of their students to ensure that all students learn to the best of their potential
- Making sure that children exceed a satisfactory level of achievement is to a larger extent the responsibility of the family than of teachers (reversed)
- Making sure that children grow in learning according to their individual abilities is to a larger extent the responsibility of the family than of teachers (reversed)

*Teachers' Sense of Responsibility for Promoting Socio-Moral Development of Students ($\alpha$ = 0.8549)*

- Teachers are just as responsible for the character and ethical development of their students as they are for academic instruction
- Character and ethical development of students shouldn't take time away from the academic curriculum (reversed)
- Students' character and ethical development is the job of their family, and schools shouldn't interfere with it (reversed)
- Teachers are just as responsible for fostering social responsibility (e.g., concern for helping others in the community, correcting social and economic inequalities, protecting the environment) among their students as they are for instruction
- Fostering social responsibility among students shouldn't take time away from the academic curriculum (reversed)
- Fostering students' social responsibility is the job of their family, and schools shouldn't interfere with it (reversed)
- Teachers are just as responsible for promoting multicultural awareness and understanding among their students as they are for academic instruction
- Promoting multicultural awareness among students shouldn't take time away from the academic curriculum (reversed)
- Promoting students' multicultural awareness is the job of their family, and schools shouldn't interfere with it (reversed)

PERSONAL EFFICACY BELIEFS

Teachers differ in views on the efficacy of their own teaching. Please indicate to what extent you agree or disagree with each of the following statements regarding your teaching (1 = completely disagree, 2 = somewhat disagree, 3 = neither agree nor disagree, 4 = somewhat agree, 5 = completely agree).

*Self-Efficacy in Promoting Achievement (α = 0.7126)*

- I expect all my students to succeed
- If I try really hard, I can get through even to the most difficult or unmotivated students
- By trying a different teaching method, I can significantly affect a student's achievement
- There is really very little that I can do to ensure that most of my students achieve at a high level (reversed)
- Without support from parents, there is little that I can do to improve my students' achievement (reversed)
- If a student's peers discourage classroom participation and/or doing homework, there is little that I can do about it (reversed)
- When it comes right down to it, I really cannot do much because most of a student's motivation & performance depends on his/her home environment (reversed)

*Self-Efficacy in Promoting Socio-Moral Development (α = 0.7823)*

- By adjusting my practices, I can meet the special social needs of at-risk students and students from diverse cultural backgrounds
- Using different methods, I am usually able to overcome the cultural (racial, ethnic) prejudices of students in my classes
- I feel inadequate relating to the social issues presented by students who come from cultural backgrounds different from my own (reversed)
- I don't feel prepared to deal with many of the social and behavior problems that at-risk students bring into the classroom (reversed)
- I have little influence on my students' character and ethical development compared to the influence of their home environment and/or their peers (reversed)
- Given the constraints of the curriculum, I have little if any opportunity to address concerns related to character and ethics (reversed)

- Given the constraints of the curriculum, I have little if any opportunity to address issues related to social responsibility (reversed)
- Given the constraints of the curriculum, I have little if any opportunity to address concerns related to racial/ethnic relationships (reversed)

### CONTEXTUAL AND ORGANIZATIONAL CHARACTERISTICS OF TEACHING

Please rate the degree of control you had in your classroom over each of the following areas of planning and teaching (1 = very poor, 2 = poor, 3 = fair, 4 = good, 5 = very good).

*Autonomy in Instruction ($\alpha$ = 0.7827)*

- selecting content, topics, and skills to be taught
- selecting teaching techniques
- selecting instructional materials
- evaluating and grading students
- determining the amount of homework to be assigned

*Autonomy in Socio-Moral Development Matters*

- fostering students' socio-moral development

Think about the school where you have been student teaching. Please indicate to what extent you agree or disagree with each of the following statements (1 = completely disagree, 2 = somewhat disagree, 3 = neither agree nor disagree, 4 = somewhat agree, 5 = completely agree).

*School Faculty's Focus on Promoting Students' Learning ($\alpha$ = 0.7601)*

- The school places a high priority on helping all students to learn
- The grading practices are consistent and fair in this school
- The rules against cheating are actively enforced in this school
- Most teachers in the school don't really care whether their students fail or succeed in learning (reversed)

- The academic standards in this school are too low (reversed)

*School Faculty's Focus on Promoting Students' Socio-Moral Development* (α = 0.8392)

- The school places a high priority on fostering character and ethical development among students
- The school places a high priority on promoting multicultural awareness and understanding among students
- The school places a high priority on developing social responsibility among students
- Most teachers in the school don't really care about their students' moral or ethical development (reversed)
- Most teachers in the school don't really care about fostering social responsibility among their students (reversed
- Most teachers in the school don't really care about developing multicultural understanding among their students (reversed)

*Buffering from External Pressures Provided by Administration* (α = 0.8359)

- This school's administration knows the problems faced by the staff
- The principal takes an interest in the professional development of teachers
- The administration deals effectively with pressures from outside the school (parents, school board, budget) that might otherwise have affected my teaching
- My principal enforces school rules for student conduct and backed me up when I needed it

Please rate the help you received from your peers/university faculty in the following (1 = very poor, 2 = poor, 3 = fair, 4 = good, 5 = very good).

*Peer Assistance with Teaching* (α = 0.8993)

- academic instruction
- managing students' behavior
- evaluating the effects of your teaching decisions on students

*Peer Assistance with Socio-Moral Development of Students*
$(\alpha = 0.9391)$

- fostering students' character and ethical development
- promoting multicultural awareness and understanding among students
- fostering students' social responsibility

*University Faculty Assistance with Teaching* $(\alpha = 0.8660)$

- academic instruction
- managing students' behavior
- evaluating the effects of your teaching decisions on students

*University Faculty Assistance with Socio-Moral Development of Students* $(\alpha = 0.9253)$

- fostering students' character and ethical development
- promoting multicultural awareness and understanding among students
- fostering students' social responsibility

CONTROLS

*Male*—separate item

*Percent Minority Students in the Classroom*—*a separate item*

Please rate the preparation you received during your training for each of the following aspects of teaching (1 = very poor, 2 = poor, 3 = fair, 4 = good, 5 = very good).

*Rating of the Training in Instruction* $(\alpha = 0.7535)$

- selecting content to be taught, appropriate teaching techniques, and instructional materials
- developing individual interests and abilities of all students
- helping disadvantaged children achieve better academically
- fostering critical thinking and problem solving skills

- evaluating and grading students
- determining the amount of homework to be assigned

*Rating of the Training in Promoting Socio-Moral Development (α = 0.6856)*

- fostering students' character and ethical development
- promoting multicultural awareness and understanding among students
- fostering students' social responsibility

Indicate to what degree each of the following matters presents a problem (i.e., exists) in this school (1 = very low, 2 = low, 3 = mid-level, 4 = high, 5 = very high).

*School Discipline and Social Problems (α = 0.8898)*

- students' tardiness and/or absenteeism
- students' cheating
- physical conflicts among students
- robbery or theft, vandalism of school property
- gang activity among students
- students' use of alcohol and/or drugs
- racial/ethnic tension among students
- students' disrespect for teachers
- lack of parental involvement with their kids' learning

### REFERENCES

Allinder, R. M. (1994). The relationship between efficacy and the instructional practices of special education teachers and consultants. *Teacher Education and Special Education, 17*, 86–95.

Ashton, P. T., & Webb, R. B. (1986). *Making a difference: Teachers' sense of efficacy and student achievement.* New York: Longman.

Ball, D. L., & Wilson, S. M. (1996). Integrity in teaching: Recognizing the fusion of the moral and intellectual. *American Educational Research Journal, 33*, 155–192.

Bandura, A. (1997). *Self-efficacy: The exercise of control.* New York: W. H. Freeman.

Becker, H. S., & Geer, B. (1958). The fate of idealism in medical school. *American Sociological Review, 23*, 50–56.

Bellah, R. N., Madsen, R., Sullivan, W. M., Swidler, A., & Tipton, S. M. (1991). *The good society.* New York: Knopf.

Bidwell, C. E., Frank, K. A., & Quiroz, P. A. (1997). Teacher types, workplace controls, and the organization of schools. *Sociology of Education, 70*, 285–307.

Bidwell, C. E., & Yasumoto, J. Y. (1999). The collegial focus: Teaching fields, collegial relationships, and instructional practice in American high schools. *Sociology of Education, 72*, 234–256.

Corwin, R. (1961). The professional employee: A study of conflict in nursing roles. *American Journal of Sociology, 66*, 604–615.

Darling-Hammond, L., & Sclan, E. M. (1996). Who teaches and why: Dilemmas of building a profession for twenty-first century schools. In J. Sikula (Ed.), *Handbook of research on teacher education* (pp. 67–101). New York: Macmillan.

Firestone, W. A. (1990). The commitments of teachers: Implications for policy, administration, and research. *Advances in Research and Theories of School Management and Educational Policy, 1*, 151–183.

Fuchs, L. S., Fuchs, D., & Bishop, N. (1992). Instructional adaptation for students at risk. *Journal of Educational Research, 86*, 70–84.

Gibson, S., & Dembo, M. H. (1984). Teacher efficacy: A construct validation. *Journal of Educational Psychology, 76*, 569–582.

Hoy, W. K., & Woolfolk, A. E. (1993). Teachers' sense of efficacy and the organizational health of schools. *Elementary School Journal, 93*, 356–372.

Hughes, E. C. (1956, Winter). The making of a physician: A general statement of ideas and problems. *Human Organizations*, 21–25.

Jackson, P. W., Boostrom, R. E., & Hansen, D. T. (1993). *The moral life of schools.* San Francisco, CA: Jossey-Bass.

Khmelkov, V. T. (2000). *Developing professionalism: Effects of school workplace organization on novice teachers' sense of responsibility and efficacy.* Unpublished doctoral dissertation, University of Notre Dame, Notre Dame.

Lortie, D. C. (1959). Laymen to lawmen: Law schools, careers and professional socialization. *Harvard Educational Review, 20*, 352–369.

McLaughlin, M. W., & Talbert, J. E. (1993). *Contexts that matter for teaching and learning.* Stanford, CA: Stanford University.

Metz, M. (1978). *Classrooms and corridors.* Berkeley: University of California Press.

National Commission on Teaching and America's Future. (1996). *What matters most: Teaching for America's future.* New York: Author.

Newmann, F. M. (1993). Beyond common sense in educational restructuring: The issues of content and linkage. *Educational Researcher*, 4–13, 22.

Newmann, F. M., Rutter, R. A., & Smith, M. S. (1989). Organizational factors that affect school sense of efficacy, community, and expectations. *Sociology of Education, 62,* 221–238.

Oser, F. K., Dick, A., & Patry, J.-L. (Eds.). (1992). *Effective and responsible teaching: The new synthesis.* San Francisco, CA: Jossey-Bass.

Raudenbush, S. W., Rowan, B., & Cheong, Y. F. (1992). Contextual effects on the self-perceived efficacy of high school teachers. *Sociology of Education, 65,* 150–167.

Rosenholtz, S. J. (1989). *Teachers' workplace: The social organization of schools.* New York: Longman.

Rosenholtz, S. J., & Simpson, C. (1990). Workplace conditions and the rise and fall of teachers' commitment. *Sociology of Education, 63,* 241–257.

Rowan, B. (1990). Commitment and control: Alternative strategies for the organizational design of schools. *Review of Research in Education, 16,* 353–389.

Shouse, R. C. (1996). Academic press and sense of community: Conflict, congruence, and implications for student achievement. *Social Psychology of Education, 1,* 47–68.

Shulman, L. S. (1987). Knowledge and teaching. *Harvard Educational Review, 57,* 1–22.

Sockett, H. (1993). *The moral base for teacher professionalism.* New York: Teachers College Press.

Staton, A. Q., & Hunt, S. L. (1992). Teacher socialization: Review and conceptualization. *Communication Education, 41,* 109–137.

Sternberg, R. J., & Horvath, J. A. (1995). A prototype view of expert teaching. *Educational Researcher, 24,* 9–17.

Stodolsky, S. S., & Grossman, P. L. (1995). The impact of subject matter on curricular activity: An analysis of five academic subjects. *American Educational Research Journal, 32,* 227–249.

Talbert, J. E., & McLaughlin, M. W. (1994). Teacher professionalism in local school contexts. *American Journal of Education, 102,* 123–153.

Tschannen-Moran, M., Woolfolk Hoy, A., & Hoy, W. K. (1998). Teacher efficacy: Its meaning and measure. *Review of Educational Research, 68,* 202–248.

Valli, L., Cooper, D., & Frankes, L. (1997). Professional development schools and equity: A critical analysis of rhetoric and research. *Review of Research in Education, 22,* 251–304.

## PART IV

## ADMINISTRATION: FROM RECRUITMENT UNTIL CAREER

T*he current ACE program is an enormous effort, involving faculty, administration, and staff at Notre Dame as well as dioceses and schools across the southern and southwestern United States. The many components all require resources, which must first be raised and then managed properly to accomplish the many tasks comprised within ACE. Managing the money is no small task. ACE is also ambitious in scope concerning the development of participants, interacting with ACErs first as college seniors, then as program participants and graduate students, and ultimately as alumni and working professionals. The administration of ACE is not stagnant, but rather, always changing to respond to new opportunities and new needs. An important message in the three chapters that follow is that the administration is never far from the ACErs themselves, always thinking about their needs and how those needs can be best met, wisely using the resources available to the program. The admissions, management, and alumni programs that serve ACE are detailed in the three chapters that follow. Another important message in these chapters is* *that administration never loses contact with the foundational pillars of the ACE program: the academic development of teachers, their growth in community, and the development of individual teacher spirits within the ACE spiritual whole.*

# 12

# RECRUITING AND RETAINING TEACHERS

"Saying no to nuns!" That's my answer when people ask about the hardest part of my job as administrative director of ACE. Every April, we have a retreat at Notre Dame that convenes for the first time the new cohort of ACE teachers and their superintendents and principals. It is always profoundly moving. Good things happen when you bring together leaders who have dedicated their lives to Catholic education, often at great personal sacrifice, and enthusiastic young people who are about to embark on two years of service through teaching in Catholic schools. The sight of 80 new talented and faith-filled ACE teachers often reduces veteran superintendents and principals to tears. "They give me hope for the future of Catholic schools," is a consistent refrain. At the same time, the ACE teachers are inspired by those who have committed their energies to Catholic schools for years, all the while underpaid and under-appreciated.

The April retreat begins on a Friday night. By Saturday morning, the questions begin. "John, I love my ACE teachers! Any chance I can have one more?" The nuns make it hardest on me. They know, or at least suspect, my upbringing. After 16 years of Catholic school, how do you say no to nuns? "John, the chair of the religion department just told me last Thursday that she's retiring. How will I find a religion teacher in a state where only 3% of the population is Catholic? Can you help me?"

Sometimes we can. Sometimes a candidate on our wait-list proves to be a perfect match and happily accepts over the phone. Other times we cannot help, and I am vividly reminded of the challenges facing Catholic schools across the nation. By the end of the weekend, I'm exhausted, in part because the April retreat represents the culmination of an intense three-month process of selecting and placing the new cohort, in part because I have had to deny requests for more ACE teachers from some dear and quite persistent friends.

Though tired, the ACE staff is also exhilarated at the end of the retreat. We feel blessed to play a role in the annual infusion of 80 new teachers into under-resourced Catholic schools. We see the continued high demand as the ultimate sign of the program's health. These requests are affirmation of the men and women drawn to ACE, especially since ACE teachers mean more work for their superintendents and principals. There are houses to locate and furnish, mentor teachers and chaplains to appoint, hospitality to extend to newcomers who know no one in the city, and individual attention to give to teachers who begin with all of six weeks of classroom experience. Yet the extra work is never an issue, even when problems occasionally arise.

These administrators repeatedly tell us that they don't mind the work because of the quality of the ACE teachers. They cite their intelligence and content-area expertise—in recent years, participants have an average G.P.A. of more than 3.4 in a variety of academic disciplines ranging from engineering to history. They appreciate the increasing diversity of ACE—with over 15% of recent cohorts composed of under-represented groups, it is already the most ethnically diverse teacher education program in Indiana. They welcome their enthusiasm and desire to serve in schools with the most need—faculty often praise ACE teachers for bringing new life into their schools. Most of all, they value their faith and warm embrace of the mission of Catholic education—to teach as Jesus did.

Recruiting is the lifeblood of ACE. This is not to diminish the importance of programmatic structures and procedures; in the long run, they are essential to perpetuate large and diverse applicant pools. Still, nothing is more important than attracting first-rate people. Every year, ACE must renew itself with a new cohort to replace its graduates and, typically, to expand to new sites. Getting the right people means everything. In the end, recruiting is the only issue that keeps me up at night—not because I'm a worrier by nature but because I've come to appreciate and never take for granted the generosity of more than 250 people who apply each year for the opportunity to work harder than they ever have for less money than they could make doing something else.

Of course, money is rarely an incentive for most applicants. At its best, ACE is counter-cultural in the sense that living the Christian life challenges much that is taken for granted in the modern world. In the words of Nichol Hill of ACE VI: "Success has come to bear new meaning. Success formerly meant having money, living comfortably, driving a nice car, and those kinds of things. My vision of success has turned around since I began to view teaching as a vocation rather than an occupation." A different vision of success is something that unites ACErs, no matter what their background or discipline. ACE continues to be blessed with participants who have many options professionally. Among our current participants and alumni are a Notre Dame valedictorian, an NSF fellowship winner in physics, and winners of Fulbright awards. Teaching is not their second choice.

Most come to ACE fresh from completing their undergraduate experience. Increasingly, however, we see applicants with experience in corporate America who seek to pursue teaching in their search for more fulfilling work. That many of ACE's recent graduates choose to remain in education would suggest that they are finding it in service to children.

## THE APPEAL OF ACE

WHY HAS ACE ATTRACTED increasing numbers of talented applicants? Why do over 90% of the accepted candidates—people who typically have a number of prospects—accept our invitation to join ACE? Through entrance interviews and focus groups of undergraduates and those in the program, we constantly strive to understand how ACE is perceived and how to attract the best candidates. What follows is our best sense of the elements central to ACE's popularity and recruiting success.

In *Field of Dreams,* a voice badgers Ray Kinsella, "If you build it, they will come." The history of ACE is exactly the opposite; they came and it was built. Who could have predicted at the outset that within a few years, almost 10% of the senior class would apply? Three seemingly unrelated features of university life converge to create a climate hospitable to ACE's recruiting efforts at Notre Dame: a strong tradition of service, the absence of an education department, and a close-knit campus community.

The culture of service that pervades ACE flows from Notre Dame's tradition of undergraduate and post-graduate service and, more broadly, the Church's traditional emphasis on social justice. Nearly 90% of Notre Dame's undergraduates participate in volunteer service at some point during their four years. Historically, 10–12% of its students perform at least one year of service after graduation. Most ACE teachers cite as their primary motivation the desire to serve the less fortunate out of Christian love and duty. Most actively pursued service opportunities as undergrads through Notre Dame's Center for Social Concerns; many completed Summer Service Projects sponsored by the center. They see teaching, particularly in Catholic schools where they can openly connect values with faith, as an effective and fulfilling way to serve. "People enter the ACE program because they want to make the world a better place," according to Katie Sutliff, who taught high school religion for two years in Baton Rouge. "Teaching allows them to do this, and the educational component of ACE allows them to learn how to teach. ACE teachers enter with the passion and desire, learn skills along the way, and leave with experience and a charge to continue the mission." Sutliff speaks for many drawn to ACE.

At first glance, such widespread interest in service through teaching seems even more astonishing at a university without an education department. Though Notre Dame has an agreement with neighboring Saint Mary's College in which Notre Dame undergraduates can pursue education courses and become eligible for a teaching license, few students matriculate to Notre Dame with the intent to become teachers. ACE offers great appeal for those who come late to the idea of teaching or, even more commonly, for those who wish to give it a try without abandoning their major and adding a year or more to their undergraduate experience (and expense) to pursue licensure in a conventional manner.

Consider the case of Christian Dallavis, now an associate director of ACE, after teaching English in Biloxi, Mississippi: "I looked into doing the Saint Mary's program during my junior year, but I wouldn't have been able to continue my double major and still graduate in four years if I did it. I had a professor for an English class that inspired me to consider teaching, and ACE offered the perfect opportunity to give it a test run without burdening my undergrad courseload. I figured I could try it for two years, and if I didn't like it, I could always try something else. Like most people in ACE, I loved it and ultimately plan to go back to it."

Now that ACE has established itself as a reputable and permanent campus fixture, having satisfied participants is especially useful at a place like Notre Dame, where news travels fast and fully among under-graduates. This efficient grapevine is largely a function of Notre Dame's emphasis on residential life, where students live in the same dormitory for four years or until they decide to move off campus. As a result, students come to forge many friendships outside their graduating class. Recent alums provide plenty of informal vocational and career counseling to their younger friends, who place implicit trust in their experience. Among the Notre Dame applicants to ACE, more than 70% report first hearing about it via friends in the program. We continue to work hard to make sure that everyone on campus hears about ACE, ideally in multiple contexts (mailings, volunteer and career fairs, our website, and personal contact with staff, faculty, and friends of the program) and as early as possible. However, we recognize that the enthusiasm of those in the program serves as our most effective marketing strategy for Notre Dame undergraduates.

The success of our recruiting efforts at other institutions augments our sense of what it is about ACE that holds broad appeal. ACE benefits greatly from its focused and unambiguous mission. The need is manifest; the work is clear. From the beginning, ACE has been construed and perceived as a service program, unique in that it adds value to its participants through graduate work that culminates in a master's degree. ACE envisions teaching as a form of service and the study to become a better teacher as a crucial part of that service. In fact, we approach the application process as a process of discernment in which a number of candidates come to realize that, although they want to join a service program, teaching is not the type of service they envision for themselves.

Related to the focused mission is the communally shared sense of purpose that ACE teachers experience. More than group solidarity, this sense of community springs from common motivation (service informed by faith), values, and desire to be part of something larger than oneself. At the December retreat, for example, weary teachers who have tasted challenge of one sort or another frequently speak of how consoling it is to be with each other and share their stories. Trish Sevilla, who had a particularly difficult assignment in a tough urban school, expressed heartfelt gratitude for the larger ACE community: "How inspiring it is to be united with so many great people doing so many great things! It motivates me to return each day to do my best." We observe among the ACE teachers a hunger for meaning in life, for a transformative experience in which participants enjoy being surrounded by like-minded young people who are not seduced by the siren song of economic gain.

The program enjoys a reputation among Notre Dame students as an excellent transition from undergraduate life. The move to a new geographic region holds appeal to those with a spirit of adventure, as the sense of community provides comfort to those who have heard tales of how isolating life can be following college. I recall overhearing Tara Mahnesmith, at the time our office intern, tell a fellow undergraduate who had come in to inquire about ACE: "The main reason I want to do ACE is the people I'll be surrounded by for the first two years after college. I have spent the past two summers here in the office, and I am totally impressed by the quality of people that do ACE. How can you beat the chance to be with great people, give service to children, and get a master's degree at the same time?"

Living and working with such people also serves as an aid to discerning one's professional calling. Many are drawn to ACE as a chance to give of themselves in a context that helps them decide how to direct their gifts and energy. "Anyone who has the idea that they might want to be a teacher ought to give it a try," says Laura Eideitis, who taught biology in ACE before moving on to doctoral studies at the University of Michigan. "The worst that happens is that you give a huge effort, learn a lot about yourself, human nature, and parenting, and find out that teaching is not for you. The best that will happen is that you find a vocation that ensures that you will never have a boring day at work, positively impact uncountable lives, pour out love and receive it in abundance, and have the satisfaction of serving your country, world, and Church."

ACE teachers tend to be risk-takers with a spirit of adventure. For example, the majority of ACE teachers have spent at least one semester abroad. Many have done service in distant places and challenging environments during summers or breaks. The program's regional focus on the South and Southwest attracts those looking for new and different living experiences. ACE teachers are the kind of people who get excited about spending two years in a different part of the country and immersing themselves in the local culture.

At the same time, ACE presents few real risks for its participants, other than occasional fatigue and the challenge to grow from the trials of first-year teaching. The program's multi-tiered support system is accompanied by the personal attention and genuine care of staff, faculty, and fellow participants. Participants receive an attractive series of benefits, a package that prompted one applicant from Boston College to say in his interview: "And you call this a service program?" We do. The work is grueling and the pay below minimum wage. But there are a number of compensations.

First, the Master of Education (M.Ed.) degree from Notre Dame is obviously attractive, especially as it comes free of tuition. We construe ACE, with its rigorous professional development, as a value-added service program. Service remains the primary motive of most applicants (and must, if the program is to continue to attract the number and caliber of applicants it does). Still, ACE teachers recognize the value of the degree for what it means to their teaching during the program and for the professional doors it can open upon their graduation. Good teaching demands far more than good intentions. ACE teachers thus value their graduate education as a way to enhance their ability to serve. Study, preparation, and practice become key elements of their service to the children who most need well-prepared teachers. That ACE is simultaneously a service program and graduate school has obvious appeal to its participants and their parents.

In addition to their tuition-free degree, ACE teachers receive a stipend of roughly $900–$1,000 per month, indexed according to the cost of living in their community. As Americorps members, they also qualify for an educational award of $4,725, which can be applied to federally subsidized student loans or to future graduate schooling. The stipend and the educational award, combined with automatic loan deferrals, travel stipends, summer room and board, and excellent health care benefits, enable ACE teachers to maintain financial independence. To be sure, no one will prosper financially by doing ACE, but the level of support they receive allows ACE to recruit students from any socioeconomic group, regardless of a potential participant's debt load. ACE is not just a service program for those who can afford it.

That said, ACE represents a tremendous professional opportunity. While increasing percentages of our graduates remain in education—most of them in Catholic education—participants also recognize that this two-year experience prepares them for professional success in a diverse range of fields. In the field of education, ACE graduates are already principals and administrators. Take Clara Finneran of ACE III, who serves as the principal of St. Anne's School in Ridgecrest, California: "ACE certainly inspired me as to the importance of Catholic education and its needs. . . . When I graduated from ACE in 1998, I felt prepared to undertake the role of principal." Others have matriculated to topnotch graduate programs in education, public policy, law school, and medical school. Still others have entered the business world. Regardless, ACE graduates find themselves highly sought after, given the skills acquired and responsibilities assumed in a program that combines two years of employment with an intense degree program.

## RECRUITING STRATEGIES

How do we recruit? We explicitly invite all Notre Dame and St. Mary's graduating seniors to consider ACE. Our invitations are consistent and personal, from the location, design, and friendly spirit of the ACE office to the many campus events at which ACE establishes a visible presence. Every October at Notre Dame, for example, students experience an advertising blitz aimed at stoking interest in ACE. One cannot travel very far on campus without encountering the ACE logo, either on the hundreds of brightly colored posters or in full-page ads in the daily campus newspaper, *The Observer*. Massive mailing campaigns target every senior with a glossy brochure and an invitation to apply. Students recommended by current ACE teachers also receive a personal invitation. All faculty receive a letter briefing them on the program and asking them to encourage their students to consider ACE. We make a special effort to establish strong relationships with dormitory rectors and hall staff, sending them information early in the fall, along with the coveted ACE T-shirt, which comes out in a different color each year. All of this publicity points to one key date—the ACE informational night. In fact, program applications, invariably changed slightly from the prior year, are withheld from distribution until that evening, helping to generate a large audience.

Ritual matters in ACE—whether it's a Mass on a retreat or our informational session—and enthusiasm is the hallmark of ACE rituals. The large, energetic crowd at the November informational meeting may cause potential applicants some anxiety about the odds of getting accepted, but it also reassures them that they are not alone in responding to the call to teach. We have experimented with different campus venues and have settled on the student union ballroom, a large social gathering place, as the ideal environment. With lively background music, food and drink, and lots of conversation before and after the formal presentations, we ensure a festive atmosphere. Many, if not most, of the 250–300 people gathered in the room know about ACE through friends. We want them to experience the culture they've heard about. As they enter, ACE staff and alumni greet them personally and welcome them. The presentations are a healthy mix of information and inspiration. We always want to model good teaching! This well-choreographed information night whets student interest, although we do not sugarcoat the experience. We are up front with potential applicants that the next two years will likely be the most difficult in their lives to this point.

In ACE, faith is not something that sneaks through the back door. The evening opens with prayer, and Fr. Tim Scully, the founder of ACE and the university's executive vice president, leads off the event. The ongoing energetic involvement of such a prominent university administrator gives ACE enormous credibility. Scully also happens to be a great teacher—the restless, passionate sort that inspires students to "trust their hearts and take risks for the Gospel." After Scully comes a recent ACE graduate whose short talk is designed to give an endorsement of the experience that is at once realistic and compelling. The room then darkens, and the evening moves from the motivational to the informational through the 15-minute ACE video. Keeping the video fresh requires considerable staff time and budgetary resources; we are convinced of its value, however, and believe that a professionally produced video is essential to give any audience, especially potential applicants, a succinct and powerful sense of ACE through images and words of participants. Finally, we distribute applications and detail the process and timeline.

The entire program lasts about an hour, though the staff remains long afterward to mingle and answer any individual questions. Potential applicants certainly want to know what the program can do for them; however, most are motivated even further by the desire to give of themselves and are seeking avenues that allow them to do so. Hence, as we answer questions, we underscore teaching as a profound act of love and highlight the potential life-changing nature of participation in ACE. Over the years, we have learned the value of explicitly describing the balance between service and graduate study that makes ACE so unique. We present the master's degree not simply as a benefit but as a way to empower them to be better servants in the short-term as well as the long-term, either as Catholic educators or as lifelong advocates for Catholic education no matter what professions they ultimately pursue.

As ACE has grown, our recruiting strategies have evolved to reflect the developing identity of the program. To ward off any potential decline in interest as the program moves from youth to maturity, we have sought strategies to project the dynamic nature of ACE. Our informational brochure receives an annual revision, and we supplement it with an academic brochure as well as a colorful photo- and quote-filled pamphlet called *Faces of ACE,* which, like the video, is another effort to give prospective applicants a window into the ACE experience. These have their electronic equivalent (and more) in the ACE website, which has become, not surprisingly, an increasingly powerful recruiting tool, especially to reach a large audience off campus. Small giveaways (pencils for example) bearing the ACE logo provide a nice touch without seeming gimmicky. This is important, for it could be perilous for a program like ACE, which draws candidates with strong motivations to serve, to appear too slick.

Still, as ACE has grown larger, we make every effort to personalize recruiting. As a staff, we know that ACE teachers and potential applicants are more important than any paperwork. Our office culture emphasizes hospitality and warm attentiveness to visitors. Interruptions to meet with interested candidates are routine and, ultimately, at the heart of our work. Why schedule a later time to meet with a drop-in who has questions about ACE when the present moment holds such promise? At the same time, we look to extend that hospitality beyond the walls of the office. The generosity of the ACE staff and, increasingly, the ACE alumni who work at Notre Dame or in the South Bend area is invaluable in promoting awareness. Someone connected with ACE attends every relevant campus event to spread the word about ACE, whether at the campus ministry cookout to open the academic year, the volunteer fair sponsored by the Center for Social Concerns, the Arts and Letters career fair, or Activities Night, which is a perfect example of our desire to reach everyone early. A few seniors attend this event, but most in the crowd are freshman and sophomores. At all events, we get names and contact information of those who express interest, and we follow up with regular correspondence. The trick, of course, is to continue to invite people to consider ACE without annoying them with too much information too often.

The visible presence of ACE staff and alumni on student retreats, campus choirs, and a variety of organizations also helps. We reach out to under-represented groups on campus in a variety of ways, most notably through special dinners where, in a fairly intimate setting, we can field their questions about ACE and encourage them to consider strongly the value of serving as role models in the under-resourced schools where ACE places its teachers. Finally, we ask current ACE teachers to provide us with names of excellent candidates. Over 70% of those who apply to ACE hear about it first through someone in the program. To augment this trend, we send personal letters to those recommended by current ACE teachers, inviting them to apply upon the advisement of their friends.

We regularly conduct focus groups with a variety of people across the campus to discern trends and maintain vigilance about the program's image and reputation among undergrads. Recently, for example, we realized that undergrads were making concrete post-graduate decisions earlier than ever before. Probably because of the economic boom, juniors were getting summer internships that often led to full-time offers before the start of senior year. We needed to make them aware of ACE long before the invitation to all seniors in early October.

On the Notre Dame campus, ACE maintains strong personal relationships with a variety of people and organizations: campus ministry, the dormitory rectors and staffs, the leaders of multicultural student affairs, the career center, the athletic department, the Center for Social Concerns. We send letters to every faculty member inviting them to talk about ACE with their students. Representatives from all of these areas and groups sit on our selection committee, which usually numbers at least 30, so that we can marshall 10 three-member teams to cover the 160–180 on-campus interviews. The collective wisdom of the selection committee gives us great confidence in the process. Those who serve on it exemplify the tremendous institutional support ACE enjoys at Notre Dame. These busy people commit to doing between 15–20 one-hour interviews in a 10-day span.

Once the first round of interviews is complete, teams rank their candidates and summarize their judgments for each individual. With 30 or more people in the room, it is typical for one or more to know the candidate in question. Because of its emphasis on residential life, the Notre Dame community has an intimacy that belies its 8,000 undergraduates. Generally, there is convergence of opinion on the initial ranking, but not always. When there is disagreement, the real value of a large and diverse selection committee emerges. I have seen candidates rise and fall in this process, none more infamous in ACE lore than the candidate who was ranked by an experienced team as the highest rated ever but who turned out to have run afoul of the law on several occasions, which wasn't mentioned on the application. Fortunately, the applicant's former rector sat on the committee and enlightened us all.

In situations where disagreement exists either among the interviewing team or among the larger committee, the ACE staff conducts second interviews that focus on areas of concern. More commonly, second interviews are granted where areas of uncertainty remain among the interviewing team. In the end, the selection committee at Notre Dame allows for a level of thoroughness and personal attention that not only ensures a successful admission process but also represents ACE well to the campus. One cannot ignore the recruiting power of having more than 30 well-known and trusted campus figures serve as advocates of ACE to the students they encounter.

Though Notre Dame undergraduates form the nucleus of our applicant pool, we increasingly strive to recruit at other institutions. We actively recruit at a number of Catholic colleges, among them the University of Portland, Boston College, Holy Cross, Villanova, and the University of St. Thomas. In addition, we welcome applications from those who hear about ACE via our website, by word of mouth, or through information distributed at graduate school or volunteer fairs. These applicants add a richness and diversity to ACE; without them, we could not mount cohorts of the quality and size we do. Of late, 25–30 undergraduate institutions are represented in the roster of current ACE teachers. Indeed, we typically season our ranks with an international flavor, having enrolled students from Ireland, Australia, and Chile.

Our recruiting strategy at other campuses parallels that at Notre Dame, though on a smaller scale. First, we try to identify key allies on each campus. The ideal figures are popular faculty members and energetic service coordinators or staff members from campus ministry who regularly interact with a number of students interested in post-graduate service. We then advertise the ACE informational session with colorful posters and in campus newspapers. Usually, an ACE graduate from the local area conducts the informational session—showing the video, distributing applications, and answering questions. Potential applicants value the chance to meet people who have done the program, who speak with the authority of experience. Establishing continuity and networks at other colleges is vital to ensure a large and outstanding applicant pool.

In light of our focus on recruiting at colleges and universities, one misperception we consistently confront is that ACE limits itself to those just finishing undergraduate studies. On the contrary, we welcome applications from those who have experience in the working world. What began as a drop a few years ago has become a stream of late—candidates who experience a lack of fulfillment in corporate America and are looking to make a difference in the lives of children by becoming teachers. If present trends continue, we expect this to become a considerable and valuable part of our applicant pool. To this end, we consistently remind seniors who express interest in teaching but feel pulled in other directions to consider ACE in the coming years. We also invite current ACE teachers and alumni to convey this to friends who may be searching for vocational direction.

Ultimately, we see a strong connection between the selection process and recruiting. Perhaps because of the changing nature of intercollegiate athletics, the very word "recruiting" carries with it a certain set of negative connotations and, given ACE's philosophy, is more than a slight misnomer. We take great care to ensure that all applicants to ACE are treated with respect. Doing the right thing has practical benefits. I often joke with the selection committee that we at ACE pride ourselves on our inefficient admissions process, but, as with most jokes, there is a core truth at the heart. We prefer to sacrifice expedience for thoroughness for several reasons. First, admitting the best people is obviously vital to the ongoing success of any program, but it also has an important and easily overlooked benefit. Getting the right people on the front end allows for a leanly staffed office that uses resources prudently. As much of our energy is directed at the formation of stellar teachers who understand and live Christian community and grow in their faith, we do well to admit those who have the openness and potential to flourish. Second, ACE seeks to maintain, indeed improve, its reputation as an organization that cares deeply about all who apply. Everyone is taken seriously; everyone gets a full hearing. To inform a generous and gifted applicant that there is no suitable placement is difficult for all involved. Therefore, we offer to help those we do not accept to find other opportunities to serve in Catholic education, education in general, or other areas—in short, to help all applicants discover and live out their vocations.

Because we believe that teaching is rightly seen as a vocation, we share with potential candidates our conviction that the application process is best understood as discernment of one's calling. Everyone who applies from Notre Dame and Saint Mary's College is granted a one-hour interview. We also commit to interview every candidate from the institutions where we actively recruit, sending an ACE staff member, who is typically joined by our liaison at that campus or an ACE alum in the local area. We review the files of all at-large applicants and invite for an interview those who can reasonably travel to either Notre Dame or a regional interviewing site (such as Boston, Philadelphia, Minneapolis, or Portland). That leaves a small percentage of files, which we carefully review before conducting phone interviews with those who seem to have promise. In the end, no one is admitted to ACE without an interview, and we typically interview about 90% of our applicants.

While undergraduate transcripts are an important determinant (ACE teachers must thrive as graduate students at Notre Dame), we remain convinced that grades are not the sole determinant of one's potential to be an excellent teacher. We review transcripts carefully, looking for improvement if the overall G.P.A. is low. Common examples are the students who begin in science or engineering before finding their niche in the liberal arts. Often, these candidates make excellent science and math teachers at the middle school level, as they relate well to students who struggle a bit in these subjects. ACE casts a wide net, and we consistently spread this message in individual conferences and group presentations. We place great weight on the two essays and the interview, which are designed to measure interest and the likelihood of successful contributions in teaching, community, and spirituality. A strong record of participation in service activities certainly adds strength to an application, as does demonstrated interest in working with children or youth. Likewise, evidence of leadership in student organizations or athletics, signs of commitment to community life (working as a resident assistant, for example), and involvement in campus ministry often serve as excellent predictors of success in ACE. Notwithstanding the occasional grumble (or presumption), there is no checklist, no ACE poster child. A few years ago an anonymous, disgruntled candidate phoned the office to complain: "I guess ACE doesn't take anyone who lived off-campus." Ever vigilant about campus perception, we reviewed our acceptance statistics controlling for this variable. It turned out that a slightly higher percentage of off-campus applicants had been accepted! What matters is that the applicants' passion is genuine and that they are open to growth.

## THE PLACEMENT PROCESS

APPLICATIONS ARE DUE in late January, and the selection and placement process begins almost immediately. In February, at the same time that the ACE staff are evaluating the applicants, dioceses submit their specific requests for teachers. Principals forward their needs through the local superintendent's office to keep information organized and all stakeholders involved. Once all candidates have been interviewed and ranked, the placement process begins. This challenge is akin to piecing together a complex jigsaw puzzle. Subject-area competencies and grade-level preferences are the most important determinants, and we strive to ensure gender balance in individual households for the good of community. As ACE has expanded to serve inner-city schools, many with predominantly Hispanic students, we have begun to try to take into account geographic and demographic preferences as well. We make every effort to place those with backgrounds in Spanish, for example, in schools and communities where this knowledge will benefit both the ACE teacher and the students. However, we cannot guarantee a particular type of school or region; our degrees of freedom are simply too restricted to please everyone. Here the openness and generosity of the applicants come into play, for only in rare instances do people turn down ACE because of their specific placement.

As applicants are notified of their status in mid-March, we send individual files of those we have placed to their schools and dioceses, which have right of refusal. Sometimes, principals and superintendents wish to conduct phone interviews to get a fuller sense of the teacher we have assigned to their school. Acceptance letters are thus provisional until the school and diocese sign off. Such is the quality of the applicants and the generous trust of the local leadership that we have never had to rescind our provisional acceptance. Over the years, less than 10% of those accepted to ACE have declined our invitation. Still, we generate a substantial waiting list, since we cannot anticipate the background and grade level of those who may decide to pursue other options.

Schools and dioceses are given one week to approve or reject the placement. Once approvals are finalized, we hold an informational meeting for all accepted candidates at Notre Dame. Here they learn of their placement and meet the other members of their community (or at least see their pictures if they are from other institutions). We video this presentation and send copies the next day to all off-campus acceptances. This evening session has a ceremonial feel not unlike the ACE information night in November, and for much the same reason—we want people to make an informed decision, to listen to the questions of their peers, to feel comfortable airing their doubts, hopes, and most frequently, their enthusiasm. Accepted candidates now have a week to decide whether they wish to join ACE. At the end of this meeting, each person signs up for a 15-minute interview with the ACE staff.

Over the next two days, we hold these entrance interviews to assist ACErs in the discernment process. Some sign the contract immediately. Most have specific questions about their school, the placement, and the city in which they'll spend the bulk of the next two years. A few express the desire for more time with a staff member, and this gives us a personal mechanism to set up that appointment. During this week, we also telephone every out-of-town acceptance to conduct a similar series of conversations. At all times, our goal is to listen carefully and offer counsel when it is sought. Obviously, we project great enthusiasm about ACE. At the same time, we want potential ACE teachers to be confident in their decisions, for the road ahead is often difficult, though invariably worth traveling. Being gracious and understanding when people decide not to do ACE is an important part of the recruitment and selection process.

When openings occur, we immediately contact individuals on the waiting list in an effort to fulfill the school's specific request. Then there occurs an accelerated version of the acceptance process—files are faxed to principals and superintendents and we meet with those called from the waiting list. This is a frenetic week, as we look to put the finishing touches on the newest cohort. Flexibility on all sides is essential at this point. Ultimately, we only place those in whom we have great confidence—to do otherwise would be to compromise the program's quality and, more importantly, the education of those students in greatest need of first-rate teachers. Fortunately, ACE has been blessed with an abundance of talented applicants. So I do not have to begin saying no to nuns until the April retreat, several weeks after the full cohort is established.

Notwithstanding the enthusiasm of April retreat, the overall success of ACE's recruiting is best measured at graduation. The program's graduation rate consistently exceeds 90%, and virtually all ACE teachers complete their first year of service—giving ACE the highest retention rate of any Americorps program over the past several years. Why do they stay in ACE? They do so mostly for the reasons that drew them in the first place, though those reasons become more deeply understood over the two years: motivation grounded in religious belief and a commitment to service, multilevel support systems that ultimately reduce to an intense care for the individual, and a strong sense of community and identity that nourishes and affirms their intrinsic motivation. That ACE is an intense two-year program also matters. For one, many students choose not to apply because they are reluctant to commit to such an intense and long service experience.

More importantly, from the outset, the new teachers realize how difficult the first year in the classroom is likely to be, but they also regularly encounter veteran ACE teachers who have experienced similar challenges and are now thriving. Their example lends credence to our advice to those who come to doubt themselves: "Trust the process." Most do. I recall a conversation with a young man facing great struggles in his first semester, particularly in the area of classroom management. Based on his initial teaching experience during the summer, he expected to be every student's favorite teacher—entertaining, enthusiastic, and inspiring. By October, when I asked him whether he was happy with his decision to do ACE, he responded with refreshing candor and simple faith: "Right now, it's very tough . . . but I know I will be when I finish ACE."

# 13

AL STASHIS

# FINANCING THE ACE PROGRAM

The aim of this chapter is to outline the financial resources that allow the mounting and administration of the ACE program. We start with a brief explanation of the program's beginnings and its early financial needs, and then move on to focus on ACE's current needs and development strategy. In particular, we explore the major sources of current support for ACE and further examine Notre Dame's efforts to build an endowment for generating additional revenue to support ACE's operating expenses.

Operational costs during the early years of the program were minimal in contrast to the program's current needs. Nonetheless, substantial start-up funding is of course essential to a program's long-term viability. Thanks to generous in-kind gifts from the University of Notre Dame and the University of Portland and the benefaction of Joseph Gallo, the W. K. Kellogg Foundation, the Humanitas Trust, and the Corporation for National Service (CNS), which each provided programmatic support, ACE was able to begin its efforts on sound financial footing. Each school hosting an ACE teacher also paid to Notre Dame an administrative fee of $4,300 per year. Notre Dame provided office and classroom space, along with free summer rooming for participants. Portland provided faculty from its School of Education quite affordably and generously. Neither school charged tuition or sought any income-generating revenue from the program. The administrative fees from the schools, along with the support of Joseph Gallo, Kellogg, Humanitas, and CNS allowed ACE to cover its other operational expenses: staff salaries and other associated costs, including summer meal plans, retreats and special events, development and public relations efforts, staff travel and participant travel vouchers, duplication and postage, telephone, supplies, and so on.

Let us turn to the current operational model for today's much expanded program. As one considers the program's benefaction, it is helpful to reflect that the Alliance for Catholic Education is appropriately named. The partners within this alliance are drawn from diverse constituencies—K–12 Catholic schools across the South and Southwest; K–12 public schools in and around South Bend; the University of Notre Dame, and formerly the University of Portland; their alumni and development bases; private and corporate foundations; the federal government; and individual benefactors. The diversity of the alliance provides diverse types of resources.

## ADMINISTRATIVE FEES PAID BY SCHOOLS

We should begin with a discussion of the hard money or guaranteed support that ACE receives each year. Principally, this support comes in the form of administrative fees paid to Notre Dame by the one hundred or so schools served by ACE teachers. At present, these fees provide support sufficient to cover roughly one-third to one-half of ACE's annual operating expenses.

Over the program's first five years, each diocese calculated an average starting salary for its new teachers. From that figure was deducted the cost of health care for that teacher and a $4,300 fee sent to ACE for programmatic and educational expenses. What remained was the annual stipend for the ACE teacher.

As we considered this arrangement, we became aware of two principal inequities in such a model. First, the savings resulting from the ACE teachers tended to favor schools with less financial need. Schools with the lowest starting salaries (typically the parish elementary schools with the fewest resources) saved less than schools with starting salaries above the diocesan average. The fixed school fee, therefore, helped the neediest schools least of all. Second, there was great variability in stipends received by ACE teachers from diocese to diocese, far exceeding the cost of living differences for the sites, especially considering that rents were kept relatively similar (usually $150–$200 per month per teacher) and expenses like utilities, groceries, and telephone rates did not vary widely across the regions ACE serves. In 1997–1998, the stipend scale stretched from $702 per month on the lower end to $1,100 per month on the upper extreme.

Recognizing the need for a change, we considered it important to preserve two important features of the original system. First, though the principal mission of ACE had never focused on the financial benefits to schools, ACE had historically served as a financial boost for two reasons: health care premiums were deductions rather than additions, and schools paid FICA only on the stipend received by the ACE teachers. We sought to continue to offer such substantial financial relief to schools; however, we hoped to do so in such a way that made the benefit more equal across all schools. Second, all ACE teachers within a diocese must earn the same stipend regardless of their school's salary scale, and stipends across dioceses needed to be more equal than they were in the early years of ACE. To accomplish these goals, we enacted changes to the fees system.

To achieve the first financial goal, the cost of an ACE teacher to a school is now indexed according to the school's starting salary for a new teacher (bachelor's degree, zero years experience). This plan established the cost of an ACE teacher to each school at $1,000 less than the starting salary for each school, plus the FICA on the stipend. The difference between this figure and the teacher stipend—which ranges from $10,000 to $13,000 annually, depending on the diocese—represents the school fee, the amount that comes to ACE. School fees, then, are no longer fixed at $4,300. ACE still provides a substantial savings for each school relative to the cost of hiring a new teacher, however. For beyond the initial $1,000 savings, each school pays FICA only on the stipend (a savings that ranges from $600–$1,000). Also, schools and dioceses no longer provide health care coverage to ACE teachers. Instead, ACE now pays the premiums for its teachers under a group policy for Notre Dame graduate students. (This plan is entirely portable, allowing ACE teachers to choose any physician they prefer. Each teacher is also entitled to one free routine medical examination per year, including diagnostic testing. The plan also features prescription and mental health benefits. Participants are responsible only for meeting a $250 annual deductible.) We estimate the savings to schools having an ACE teacher versus a new teacher to total roughly $3,000–$5,000, depending upon the benefits package extended to regular employees.

To achieve the second financial goal of more equal stipends for ACE teachers, stipends for ACE teachers in any given diocese are established according to an index based on the average starting salary within that diocese (i.e., all teachers are paid the same stipend within the diocese). In addition, maximum and minimum stipends are established for the ACE program as a whole. In academic year 2000–2001, we capped stipends in the highest-paying dioceses at $1,100 per month and raised stipends at the lowest-paying dioceses to $850 per month. ACE recalculates this stipend each year and informs dioceses and schools in a timely manner.

## SOFT-MONEY SUPPORT

IN ADDITION TO THE HARD-MONEY support offered by the school fees agreement, ACE must fund the remaining 50–65% of its annual operations through the soft-money support of various benefactors. To this point, ACE has succeeded in gaining generous in-kind support from Notre Dame and the University of Portland, from private and corporate foundations, from the federal government, and from individual benefactors.

Interestingly, the bulk of this support has not come from Catholic foundations. Indeed, we have aimed to involve a variety of stakeholders interested in education in general and Catholic education in particular. We contend that the mission of ACE is so universally appealing as to make the program uniformly attractive to a variety of benefaction constituencies. All of them are interested in producing the next generation of energetic, talented, intelligent, and creative teachers. All hope that these teachers might serve under-resourced and often under-represented student populations. All recognize the need for developing successful alternative models for teacher preparation. All identify with ACE's call to service.

Both the University of Notre Dame and the University of Portland brought tremendous credibility to the ACE effort. Nonetheless, both also gained much from sponsoring ACE, a meaningful enterprise linking the universities with K–12 school systems locally and nationally. Done well, this program provides an ideal blending of the academic (teaching and research) and service missions of a university. For Catholic universities like Notre Dame and Portland, ACE represents a splendid opportunity to give back to the impressive K–12 Catholic school system that has historically contributed to the health of Catholic higher education.

Foundations, both corporate and private, have also offered substantial targeted support to assist ACE's efforts. Typically, a foundation's board identifies particular funding priorities that are to receive support. In seeking foundation support, we take great effort to identify discrete aspects of ACE operations that qualify appropriately for foundation funding. In the case of the Koch Foundation, we sought support to fund expansion to underserved Hispanic communities in the Southwest. Humanitas lent its assistance in supporting the costs of the summer program, particularly the very expensive costs of faculty salaries and travel. The Annenberg Trust has funded our efforts to develop permanent lines for tenured faculty through Notre Dame's Institute for Educational Initiatives, and the UPS Foundation offered an unrestricted gift toward general operations while we built the endowment. Meanwhile, the Helen Brach Foundation has supported our efforts to provide stipends to program graduates who return to serve as summer mentors to beginning ACE teachers. Finally, the W. K. Kellogg Foundation has generously supported ACE's novel teacher preparation program, especially its focus on service learning and emphasis on mentoring underserved student populations.

In 1994, the Corporation for National Service selected ACE as one of 11 National Demonstration programs and has generously continued to serve as a benefactor to ACE for the past seven years. Through CNS's Learn and Serve America, Higher Education, and Americorps departments, the corporation has provided program funding—especially the funding of ACE's summer teacher-training and service-learning program—as well as a $4,725 per year education award to each of the ACE participants, who are also considered full-time Americorps members. This year, 147 of ACE's participants were eligible to earn an Americorps education award, which may be used to reduce student loans or to pursue future graduate education.

There is little doubt that the availability of the education award, in particular, allows ACE to attract a more diverse applicant pool and membership in terms of racial/ethnic and socioeconomic composition. Given the typically high debt load of economically disadvantaged graduates from private universities like Notre Dame, participation in postgraduate service simply would not be an option without relief as provided through the education award. Attracting diverse teachers is important, since Notre Dame's outreach to underserved communities across the South and Southwest intentionally targets high proportions of poor, frequently African American and Hispanic students. The Americorps awards go far in permitting minority youth to be served by minority teachers, who are models of what is possible for Americans of all backgrounds.

## GROWING PAINS

IN THE PAST THREE YEARS, ACE has incurred substantial increases in operating costs. Particularly, these increases are associated with the development of the Master of Education program. In order to help offset these increases, we have sought additional funding from a number of foundations that support education efforts.

We also sought increased financial support from the Corporation for National Service. Unfortunately, budget constraints made further federal funding impossible. Instead, however, CNS suggested that we consider recovering some of the education awards that Americorps provides to ACE participants. After all, CNS contended, ACE teachers receive graduate degrees at essentially no cost. Hence, ACE now requests that one of the two Americorps education awards earned by each ACE teacher be paid to Notre Dame. That is, each participant uses one of his or her awards (amounting to $4,725) to defray the cost of continuing education in Notre Dame's M.Ed. program. Considering that the educational benefit ACE teachers receive amounts to $50,000 to 60,000, most ACErs recognize the arrangement to be quite a bargain. More importantly, the award revenue helps to cover in part the costs of operating a first-rate academic program.

## ENDOWMENT

SIMULTANEOUS WITH OUR EFFORTS to generate sufficient operating revenue have been our efforts to build an endowment to insure the program's long-term sustainability. Principally, these gifts to endowment have come from individual benefactors, with particular thanks due to the fund-raising acumen of ACE's founder, Fr. Tim Scully. Individuals making large gifts are accorded their own endowment accounts. Often these funds are specified for a particular purpose, as an endowed professorship. In other circumstances, the endowment produces revenue on a quarterly basis that may be reinvested or used to offset program operational expenses. One particular endowment account has also been established as a general fund housing smaller contributions to ACE—from alumni, friends of ACE, etc.—with the revenue used to support program operations or special projects. It is our hope to build the endowment over the coming years to a level that we might minimize ACE's reliance on soft-money contributions, and thereby solidify the program's long-term future.

Our principal development tools include the ACE video (now in its third edition), which describes in detail ACE's mission, and profiles and summarizes well the day-to-day life and impact of ACE teachers. We have also developed an annual report and a number of brochures, and we continue to upgrade our program website (http://www.nd.edu/~ace). Each year we unveil the now famous ACE T-shirts to aid us in the development process. Of course, the program's main fund raiser remains its founder, Fr. Scully, with his many contacts, his creative ideas and tremendous vision, and his relentless drive. Scully is responsible more than any other for building the endowment from the ground up.

Thanks to the dramatic success of the ACE teachers, along with prudent planning, careful spending, and a great deal of hard work, ACE has been financially self-sustaining throughout its history. Indeed the program has even generated new revenue for Notre Dame, all of which has allowed ACE to expand its numbers while simultaneously improving the quality of the program and its participants. In short, the financial solvency of ACE has been fundamental to our capacity to enact ACE's mission of training, developing, and providing the next generation of teachers and leaders for our children.

# 14

CHRISTIAN DALLAVIS

## AFTER ACE . . .

When John Cardinal O'Connor came to Notre Dame to preside over the ACE program's fifth annual Missioning Mass at the end of the summer of 1998, he was struck by the enthusiasm of the participants in the program. Noting their zeal and dedication, he told Fr. Scully, "Pretty soon, you'll have a movement on your hands." Indeed, ACE attracts high-quality, faith-filled, intelligent people who often become life-long advocates for Catholic education, and the enthusiasm and energy these young people bring to ACE follows them throughout the country as they move on to life after ACE.

By the end of 2000, ACE had more than 250 graduates; with 75 graduating each year, the program's alumni will number more than 1,000 in another 10 years. In the first five years of ACE, almost three-fourths of the graduates have stayed in education after their service in ACE (see Table 14.1). This is a particularly remarkable statistic considering almost none of these people would have entered education had they not joined the ACE program. They would be engineers, consultants, doctors, and lawyers. After completing ACE, most are teachers. Clearly there is something special about the ACE program that inspires people who otherwise would not have considered education to become career teachers. During their time in ACE, members recognize the importance and appeal of education as a profession.

**TABLE 14.1**

*Fall 2000 Status of ACE Graduates*

|                              | ACE I    | ACE II   | ACE III  | ACE IV   | ACE V    |
|------------------------------|----------|----------|----------|----------|----------|
| Teaching                     | 14 (44%) | 24 (58%) | 30 (51%) | 33 (58%) | 53 (81%) |
| Education *(Total in Education)* | 8 (69%)  | 5 (71%)  | 6 (61%)  | 6 (68%)  | 1 (83%)  |
| Nonprofit                    | 3        | 4        | 3        | 3        | 2        |
| Religious                    | 0        | 0        | 1        | 2        | 2        |
| Graduate School              | 5        | 5        | 12       | 6        | 3        |
| Business                     | 1        | 3        | 3        | 7        | 4        |
| Totals                       | 32       | 41       | 59       | 57       | 65       |

Total ACE graduates = 254; total ACE graduates teaching = 154 (61%); total ACE graduates in education = 180 (71%)

What happens to someone in ACE that elicits such strong dedication and commitment to schools, often the schools they served during their time in the program? It is tempting to attribute this success to the quality of the people in the program, and certainly, ACE attracts dynamic, intelligent, dedicated, and driven leaders who are committed to making a significant impact with their service. However, credit also the communities in which these people work and serve. The experience of serving a great need and seeing concretely the impact one can have on a child, class, and school creates loyalty and advocacy among ACE graduates.

One job for the ACE program is to harness the energy generated by this dedication and assist our graduates as they embark on a lifetime of advocacy for Catholic education. One thousand teachers across the nation, tied by the common experience of serving America's neediest schools, sharing a vision of the future of Catholic education in terms of teaching, community, and spirituality—this is the movement Cardinal O'Connor anticipated.

## ACE'S SUPPORT FOR ITS GRADUATES

ACE IS DETERMINED to tap the enormous resource of leadership, creativity, and commitment of its alumni to facilitate their permanent involvement in education. ACE supports those who choose to remain in Catholic education, identifies and develops further service opportunities, and most importantly, provides the spiritual support that was so crucial to the success of these graduates during their two years in ACE.

## PROFESSIONAL SUPPORT

ACE has taken a number of steps and provides numerous services, all with an eye toward professionally supporting our graduates and facilitating their desire to stay in education. Professionally, ACE serves its alumni as a clearinghouse for education and service-related jobs and by facilitating post-ACE service opportunities domestically and internationally. ACE compiles, organizes, and distributes lists of education and service-related job openings biweekly by e-mail. Usually, the job postings come from other ACE graduates whose schools are searching for teachers or administrators. Often the job postings come from schools who have no affiliation with ACE or ACE graduates but who have heard that ACE is the place to go to find excellent, committed Catholic teachers.

Recently, ACE added to its resources the ACE Alumni Online Network, which comprises a database of lesson plans, chat forums to facilitate professional resource sharing, a job-posting database, and an alumni directory. The lesson plan database, available to teachers everywhere, will provide lessons arranged by grade level and subject area, all submitted by ACE participants and graduates. By collecting, organizing, and distributing lesson plans geared toward Catholic schoolteachers, who rarely enjoy the material resources of their public school counterparts, ACE hopes to provide its graduates with the opportunity to engage in professional resource sharing, enabling them to use the ideas of their colleagues in Catholic education.

The online alumni chat forums enable graduates to meet one on one to discuss strategies and issues pertinent to Catholic education and teaching. The chat rooms serve an important function as a forum for current ACE teachers to interact with alumni. These discussions are valuable for current ACE members who are contemplating teaching different subjects or grades, or in different geographical locations. ACE alumni provide an outstanding network of professional support for recent graduates who hope to teach in Catholic schools in particular cities. For example, Portland, Oregon, is home to more than a dozen ACE graduates, nearly all of whom are teaching in Catholic schools. Current ACE members interested in moving to Portland can interact with these alumni online, learn about job opportunities in the area, and begin making professional contacts through the alumni.

Those who choose to teach in Catholic schools make sacrifices, not the least of which is financial. Often ACE teachers pass over lucrative job offers from corporate America, originally intending to return to those job offers after finishing their two years in the program. Inevitably, however, the majority choose to remain in one of the lowest-paying professional jobs available—teacher, particularly in a Catholic school. Many graduates want to stay in Catholic education but would not be able to do so because they must begin repaying their student loans six months after graduating from the ACE program. ACE helps them stay in Catholic education by reimbursing a portion of their recaptured Americorps educational award, which can be used to offset their loans.

ACE also hopes to serve its alumni with academic expansion, at the same time expanding its capacity to serve the Catholic schools of America. The ACE administrative licensure program to be inaugurated in the summer of 2002 will allow ACE graduates the opportunity to earn certification to become principals at ACE schools. The courseload will consist of two summers of academic work at Notre Dame, co-hosted by the Institute for Educational Initiatives and the Mendoza College of Business. During the academic year, participants will serve an internship as an assistant principal, working with a veteran principal in a diocesan school. Upon completion of the second summer of coursework, participants will be eligible for licensure as a principal.


### Spiritual Support

Participants in the ACE program are treated to spirited, vibrant liturgies during the ACE summer and retreats. These experiences are a highlight of the week during the summer session, and the first Mass to begin each event—the summer program and the December retreat, for example—is always a joyful, enthusiastic celebration. In their communities, ACE teachers often engage in active communal prayer, and the atmosphere in most ACE houses fosters spiritual growth. Most ACE graduates cite the spirituality pillar of the program as a strength of ACE.

Unfortunately, ACE graduates have not always found such vibrant faith communities or opportunities for spiritual growth after they leave the program. We have often heard complaints about lackluster spiritual environments within their new parishes, and apathy can set in. When ACE graduates get together, they often fondly recall the Sunday night Masses from their ACE summers, and nearly every recollection ends with the observation that Mass at one's new parish is nothing like an ACE Mass.

In response to the needs of our graduates, in 1999, ACE inaugurated the Post-ACE Spirituality Initiative, which proactively seeks to provide opportunities for communal spiritual experiences and continued growth in one's faith. In addition to providing chances for graduates to share in the community of ACE in a spiritual context, the initiative hopes to help ACE graduates become productive members of their home parishes, and it challenges them to be the change they wish to see in their parishes.

The primary vehicle for spiritual growth and explicit reflection in the two-year ACE experience is the retreat. ACE's retreats follow a 12-step progression, and every graduate of ACE has been to at least five ACE retreats, possibly seven or more. Therefore it is logical that we use the ACE retreat experience as a primary means of continuing to serve our alumni.

The focus of alumni retreats is reunion and renewal, and the sessions emphasize refocusing one's life on God and putting one's faith into action. The retreat is a great chance for old friends and community members to meet and share their post-ACE experiences. Members of different ACE classes who had never met before mingle effortlessly. The retreat provides personal spiritual reflection and growth. Participants often write that these retreats are exactly what they need. Several alumni seriously have reconsidered their vocations during this experience, and one graduate even began a job search to return to Catholic education after a few years in corporate America. She wrote, "I guess you could say the reunion retreat inspired me more than even I thought it would."

ACE II member Andrew Alfers, who received a master's degree from the Kennedy School of Public Policy at Harvard after completing ACE, is now working for a start-up educational consulting firm. He describes the qualities of the ACE retreats and community that make the post-ACE retreats unique and vital for so many alumni: "What I liked most about ACE was the phenomenal collection of people driven to serve others, grow their spiritual lives, and learn from each other both within their local community and the ACE community as a whole. What I miss most . . . I will never be a part of another community where I'm challenged by all members in my community to deepen myself in these ways like I was in ACE."

Smaller regional retreats are being inaugurated in cities where ACE graduates have settled in large numbers. Staff members will travel to Portland, Boston, and Atlanta to conduct retreats for local ACE graduates, making it easier for alumni to take part in the Spirituality Initiative by bringing the ACE retreat experience to them. In addition, manuals will be available that will enable local ACE graduate communities to conduct their own regional retreats on a regular basis, allowing these regional ACE graduate communities the opportunity to build an identity based on their shared experience in the ACE program. One goal of these retreats is to create a regional network, similar to Notre Dame's regional Alumni Clubs. These groups will comprise post-ACE graduates and spouses who continue to seek the fellowship of community provided by ACE, enabling graduates to meet socially, strengthen the bonds of community and spirituality, and continue the faith journey many participants enjoyed as members of the ACE program.

These regional retreats will complement the annual retreat held at Notre Dame, and ACE will continue to subsidize travel for those in need. Top retreat leaders from across the country will be invited to serve as retreat masters.


## DEDICATION TO EDUCATION

Annemarie Welch, a member of the ACE class of 2000, had planned to be an actuary throughout college and received a mathematics degree with a concentration in business. She did an internship with a large insurance company and loved it. However, she soon became frustrated with her work and wanted to make an impact beyond the reports and investments she dealt with every day. Annemarie decided to try ACE to determine if she would like teaching. During ACE, Annemarie taught in Atlanta and loved her school. In fact, she decided early to remain at the school beyond her commitment to ACE, in part because she enjoyed the strong connection between her students, their families, and the local parish.

It is tempting to attribute Annemarie's situation to luck and say that she stayed at her school for reasons very specific to that particular place. However, more than 30 of Annemarie's classmates remained at their ACE schools beyond their two-year commitment. Why are these talented leaders with newly minted M.Ed. degrees staying in poor schools and making low wages? Annemarie explained: "When I was growing up, I went to private, public, and Catholic schools, and the Catholic schools were by far the most influential in my life. I want to remain teaching in Catholic schools because I get to have that kind of influence on students. I get to educate the whole student, and most importantly, I get to share the things that are most important to me. We—my students, their families, the community, me—share a common faith that is so much more important than their math problems. Catholic schools provide an opportunity to share that faith, and so are the perfect backdrop for kids to develop, grow, and learn."

ACE VI member Clare Deckelman, who teaches at St. Jude School in Montgomery, Alabama, is in the midst of her final semester as an ACE teacher. Over the past year and a half, she has realized what most ACE participants also conclude, echoing a popular sentiment of many ACE teachers in their second year of teaching, as well as many alumni: "This is absolutely my life's vocation!"

ACE V graduate Scott Bishop's experience teaching at St. Jude in Montgomery made him realize what an enormous impact he could have in such a needy place. Like many other ACE members, Scott also realized that he needed what St. Jude's had to offer him as much as St. Jude's required his service. Scott found that he thrived on this combination of needs—that he could serve and simultaneously receive gifts in abundance from his school community. The support, love, and faith of his students, fellow faculty, and administration instilled in Scott a strong desire to continue teaching in Catholic schools.

Tom Kessler, an ACE IV graduate, has a similar story. Tom was a computer science engineering major in college, and he saw many of his classmates head to Silicon Valley and New York for high-paid consulting jobs. Tom taught for two years in Pascagoula, Mississippi, and managed to raise enough money to buy new computer hardware for the school. He decided to stay for a third year to finish the networking project he began his first year, and he and his students networked the entire school with new equipment. Three years out of college, many of Tom's computer engineering classmates are now clearing well over $100,000 a year, but Tom is still in Pascagoula at Resurrection Catholic School, one of the lowest-paying schools in the nation. He explains that his ACE experience has shown him that he can directly impact the lives of others positively—something a computer engineering job cannot provide. He says, "What I value most about teaching in a Catholic school is the opportunity to be involved in the development of my students. As an engineer, I would be involved in the development and testing of new technologies, but as a teacher, I am privileged to play a role in the development of another person— on a number of different levels: academic, emotional, physical, spiritual. Of course, working with students is often more difficult than working with computer chips—chips don't have bad days, they don't talk back, and they are never mischievous. But working with students is also more rewarding; I look to Emerson for my definition of success: 'To know that even one life has breathed easier because you have lived: this is to have succeeded.'"

Tom teaches math and computers, drives the bus, coaches the track team, and loves everything about his job. He has started doing some consulting work on the side for families of his school and parish and some local businesses, which supplements his income. He comes back to Notre Dame during the summers to help the ACE staff with its technology projects, and he is planning to spend a fifth year at Resurrection in the 2001–2002 school year.

Susan Fischesser, ACE IV, explained how her experience in ACE led her to continue in Catholic education as a second grade teacher in Cincinnati: "For me, staying in Catholic education isn't a choice; it's a calling. By participating in the ACE program, I knew that I am called to be in a Catholic school. I have thought about what teaching in a public school would give me: money, more time, more benefits. But teaching in a Catholic school provides me with so much more. The parents and students have a desire not only to learn, but to walk the path God has set for each of us. As we talk about Jesus and God, not only are the students learning, but so am I. ACE gave me the opportunity to become more aware of how I can serve God every day. I once thought I would teach in a Catholic school for a few years and then move to the public school system. ACE gave me the knowledge that I am more than just a teacher who is Catholic; I am a Catholic school-teacher." Susan, Annemarie, Scott, and Tom have all identified the common links that continue to compel ACE teachers to remain in Catholic education: faith and community.

The faith-based communities within which ACE teachers live and work provide the motivation to stay in Catholic schools. The strong communal and professional support of the ACE program, combined with these supportive faith-based communities, results in an ACE experience that instills in its participants a dedication to teaching, education, service, and their communities in a way that has the potential to revitalize Catholic education across the country as the ranks of alumni grow.

ACE has succeeded far beyond its founders' imaginings. The program was intended to provide teachers for two years to a few dozen schools, but it has grown to serve hundreds of schools. More importantly, the vast majority of those graduates who have remained in education have stayed in Catholic education. Something about the ACE experience instilled in these graduates a sense of the importance of Catholic education while revealing the dire needs of the system.

### Advocates for Catholic Education

While the number of ACE graduates who remain in teaching and in the field of education is impressive, perhaps even more striking is the advocacy for Catholic education evidenced by the graduates who move out of the field and into the worlds of business, law, medicine, or government. The experience and fulfillment of meeting a need in a Catholic school often instills strong dedication to Catholic education in ACE graduates. After graduation from ACE, those who do not serve Catholic education directly through teaching often serve it indirectly in their parishes and dioceses by contributing their free time and personal resources, as well as their voices, to the cause of Catholic schools.

ACE IV graduate Ted Lefere liked his placement in Biloxi so much that he decided to stay in Mississippi upon graduation from the program. However, Ted was ready to move out of teaching and was interested in getting some experience in the business world. Through a contact he made in his parish in Biloxi, Ted found a job and has been learning sales, marketing, and finance for two years after ACE.

His dedication to his students and to the local Catholic school in which he taught remained strong, and Ted wanted to continue working with his students and help out his school and diocese. He conceived of and organized annual retreats to the University of Notre Dame, taking about 20 students from southern Mississippi to South Bend each January, spending a great deal of his own time and money to arrange and facilitate the retreats. The theme of the retreats, "Faith in Action," summarizes Ted's approach to his life as a business professional in Mississippi, and it is a chance for him to share his faith and dedication to education with his former students. In 2001, Ted expanded the retreat program and opened it up to students from the entire diocese of Biloxi, bringing 20 students from four high schools across the Gulf Coast up to Notre Dame for a long weekend of reflection and prayer.

Ted Caron, another ACE IV graduate, was also drawn to Catholic education by his ACE experience. Instead of remaining in teaching, Ted moved to Iowa to pursue graduate studies in education. He says his experience in ACE heavily influenced his decision to remain in education, however, and writes, "I felt that ACE provided me a solid practical experience, teaching in parochial schools that grounded me in the nuts and bolts of teaching in a way that inspired me to stay in education." He plans to be an advocate for Catholic education after finishing his studies, and he says, "I hope to support Catholic schools, though in some ways I feel as though there are professional, policy, and moral concerns that also call me to public education. However, I wish to continue to impact Catholic schools in any capacity I can." Ted identifies ACE's professional and community pillars as two of the program's strengths: "I enjoyed both the development of friendships as well as the summer classroom experiences, both of which helped me to think more deeply about education."

## DEDICATION TO SERVICE

PARTICIPANTS IN ACE frequently cite the desire to do service as the overriding factor in their decision to join the program after college. They wanted to help the neediest, most under-resourced Catholic schools and reach out to the underprivileged children in the Catholic schools of the nation. Most of them had extensive experience serving the poor during their undergraduate careers, and so ACE was the next step in deepening their commitment to a life of service.

Many of these service-oriented people continue to serve the poor beyond ACE, and the ACE staff actively seek opportunities for graduating ACE members to continue doing service, both in America and abroad. Recent ACE graduates have served in Thailand, Australia, Chile, East Africa, Northern Ireland, Ecuador, and Nicaragua. One graduate has organized an ACE-like service program that provides teachers from the University of Notre Dame–Australia for Catholic schools in East Timor.

In 1999, ACE established a community of four graduates in Dhaka, Bangladesh, where they taught English. ACE IV member Sean Byrne, who had taught middle school science in St. Petersburg, Florida, was one of these teachers. In Bangladesh, he taught seminarians, religious sisters, and Catholic school teachers from village mission schools. Sean lived with his ACE community at Notre Dame College in downtown Dhaka, a city of 10 million, among the most crowded cities in the world. When he first arrived in Dhaka, it was difficult to find enough work to do, but within a few months, all of Sean's classes were full. Sean and his three post-ACE colleagues were teaching 50 teachers at a time, eight hours a day, six days a week. Ultimately they taught more than 100 teachers directly, indirectly serving more than 8,000 students across the country through these intensive ESL teacher-training workshops. The noise, crowds, smells, and poverty of Dhaka were overwhelming and unfamiliar. It also was difficult to be away from friends and family for so long. However, Sean found strength in his ACE community and fulfillment in his service.

Upon returning from Bangladesh, Sean joined two other ACE graduates on the faculty of his alma mater, St. Ignatius College Prep in Chicago. He teaches high school chemistry and biology and even has some of his younger siblings in class. When asked about his decision to teach, Sean related, "I never thought I would be a teacher. I hadn't even given teaching a thought, until I started looking into the ACE program in order to do service. The bottom line is that I would not be in the profession I am now without the ACE program. ACE helped me to learn to love teaching by allowing me to teach right away. By jumping in with both feet, and learning by doing, I have learned more about teaching than I ever thought possible. Even as an alum, the ACE community continues to give me the support that I need to stay in Catholic education."

Sean also took part in the second Alumni Retreat, and he looks back on his time in ACE with pride. "I loved the feeling of being part of a program that was making a significant change in the world. I knew that my own contribution to that change was incredibly small, but the overall effects of a program like ACE are really awe-inspiring. Every once in a while I would take a step back and realize how many other teachers around the South were going through the same challenges. The St. Petersburg ACE community kept me going when the days were hard and celebrated with me when they got better. I miss being directly involved in the ACE community but am proud to be an alum."

ACE is currently working to continue post-ACE international service opportunities in Dhaka. New post-ACE communities also are in the planning stages for Santiago, Chile, and San Juan, and Dublin, Ireland.

## DEDICATION TO COMMUNITY

WHEN THE FIRST CLASS of ACE graduated, many members wanted to remain in teaching, but they also wanted to continue enjoying the support of their communities. In 1996, one group of post-ACErs decided to move together to Washington, D.C., as the first post-ACE community of teachers. Since then, this has been a popular option for many ACE members who enjoy the community of ACE and want to continue teaching. Currently, post-ACE communities can be found in Charlotte, North Carolina, Atlanta, Georgia, and Chicago, Illinois, with a large contingent of ACE VI now making plans to be together in the Washington, D.C., area.

Scott Bishop, Melissa Harraka, Brian Fulmer, and Annemarie Welch are the Atlanta community. They all decided to continue teaching in Catholic schools after completing their commitment to ACE in 2000. Annemarie and Brian both decided to remain at their ACE school. Scott and Melissa wanted to remain in Catholic schools but desired the challenge a larger city could offer. Hence, they moved from their ACE site in Montgomery, Alabama, to Atlanta, joining Brian and Annemarie. The opportunity to continue living in an ACE community was the deciding factor for Scott in his choice to move to Atlanta. More than anything, he wanted the spiritual support offered by his friends in ACE. As a post-ACE community, Melissa, Scott, Brian, and Annemarie eat together, pray together, share chores, and pool resources—all of the practical and logistical concerns that are the backbone of the ACE community experience.

### "I NEVER WOULD HAVE THOUGHT I'D BE DOING THIS"

Among graduates of ACE, this common refrain—"I never would have thought I'd be doing this"—reflects the dynamic, truly life-changing experience that is the hallmark of the program. Annemarie Welch never thought she'd be a teacher for life. Sean Byrne never guessed he'd go to Bangladesh. Ted Lefere never expected to be sharing his faith with high school kids while working as a sales representative. Tom Kessler never imagined he'd be using his computer science engineering degree to teach typing, drive a bus, and coach track. During their experience in ACE, each of these teachers developed a professional dedication fostered by the support of community and inspired by their faith. This dedication and spirit have changed their outlook on life, altering career plans across the board. Few of those who graduate from ACE ever imagined they would be teachers for life. In some capacity, all of them are. As more ACE alumni stay in Catholic education every year, the movement of which Cardinal O'Connor spoke is quietly taking shape.

This chapter is necessarily incomplete—the "After ACE" life has just begun, and the true impact of the program will not be fully realized for quite some time. Already, however, it is clear that life is different after ACE—for the alumni who stay in Catholic schools or bring their energy and advocacy to their parishes, for the schools directly served by the program, and for Catholic education and the American Catholic Church.

# Epilogue

The final touches are being made to this book in July 2001, and much has been happening in the ACE program. In March 2001, the ACE staff completed interviews for the ACE VIII class, with the selection process occupying almost 100% of the energies of John Staud and the ACE associate directors. As in recent years, the new ACE M.Ed. class includes outstanding graduates from Notre Dame and St. Mary's as well as from a number of other universities. A new twist is that three members of ACE VIII are from South Bend, each an adult who has been out of college for a number of years and who now seeks to teach in Catholic schools. These individuals will live and work in South Bend during the school year. Since all are married, they will have community experiences as a group but will not live together. As the admissions process unfurls, the staff believes they may be admitting the strongest class ever. This would be consistent with the trend in the program for every class to be a little bit bigger and stronger than the previous class.

The summer program expanded its technological instruction to students and faculty. For example, program faculty were instructed about all the technology available in the main classroom building serving the program. This session was a huge success. ACE gets stronger with respect to technology every year.

All members of the program are enrolled in a course in moral development and education. There are eight sections of the course, each devoted to a particular topic in moral development and education. Professor Clark Power is coordinating this effort, which includes some lectures in the summer. These will be followed by Internet experiences during the year. Many of our faculty, students, and staff believe that moral development and education should be central foci of teaching. With the mounting of this course, Notre Dame became the first teacher education program to require moral and ethical development in its curriculum. This represents an expansion from having the course as an elective in previous years.

In addition, the moral development and education course signals a permanent change with respect to the use of the Internet in instruction. Beginning with summer 2001, no courses are Internet-only courses (i.e., taught over the Internet during the school year with little or no professorial contact in advance of the course during the summer session). From now on, courses on the Internet during the year meet at least six times during the summer session. The goal of the summer session meetings is to cement the personal relationship between students and faculty as well as to jumpstart student thinking with respect to the topic of the Internet course. Because some of the course coverage will be completed in the summer, Internet seminars will be less demanding during the school year than they have been in the past. An important goal of the ACE M.Ed. program is to continue to improve its courses.

A committee to reflect on the capstone portfolio experience met in May 2001. There were concerns about the size of the portfolio, the scheduling of feedback to participants, what the role of the portfolio should be relative to the role of field supervisor observations in evaluating overall effectiveness, the costs, and the academic rigor of the approach. The result was a new capstone, which involved the second-year students making a public poster presentation about their teaching. The students also will be filing a series of reflections and artifacts over their entire two years in the program, which will sum to a portfolio. Continued thinking about and revision of the program is consistent with the reflectivity in this program in general.

With respect to spirituality, the ACE office has formalized relationships with a priest and a female chaplain in order to increase the pastoral counseling available in the program. In the spring, Tim Scully renewed his call to Holy Cross priests to develop homilies that mesh well with the interests and needs of ACE participants, and there were many stimulating moments at this summer's 10 P.M. Masses. The folk choir is better than ever on Sunday nights. Steve Warner is providing an additional 1 credit of the liturgical music and education course for ACE participants who want to be part of the folk choir for a second summer. The ACE participants do much more of the planning of the Sunday Masses, making it an even more complete educational experience for ACErs. An additional 125 chairs have been added to the chapel where Sunday ACE Masses occur, reflecting their great appeal to the campus. The folk choir recently released another CD, providing yet another set of contemporary hymns that will travel to ACE classrooms next school year.

A few more faculty will be involved in the Biloxi retreat next December in order to strengthen connections between the academic M.Ed. and the spirituality and community pillars of the program. Spirituality, community, and professional education more completely intermingle as the ACE program continues to develop.

Expansions of the program are much on our minds. There is another community of four teachers in Los Angeles in 2001–2002, a new community in Tucson, and the new community of career changers in South Bend. These expansions are consistent with the continuing westward movement. Expansion of another type is on the horizon as well.

The principal's licensure program is getting on firmer footing; the first participants in it will begin in summer 2002. High-quality administrative training will be provided at low cost to the aspiring principals. The expectation is that these principals will serve many of the same dioceses now in the Alliance for Catholic Education. Although some ACE graduates have been promoted to the role of principal, this is the first time that Notre Dame will offer a principal's program specifically tailored to those overseeing Catholic schools. With every passing year, ACE is serving a wider range of Catholic education.

As the faculty and staff gain years of experience with the program, our understandings of the challenges facing ACE teachers increase. We are also growing in our understanding as to how to solve at least some of the problems confronted by the ACErs, especially serious ones that land on our desks. Our success in mediating problems is best reflected in the completion rate for the program. Although 83% of those starting ACE V completed, the corresponding figure for ACE VI is 92%, and 95% of those who began ACE VII are with us during the summer 2001 session. We have gotten better at understanding when ACE teachers have legitimate reasons for changes in their school positions or community, and we've gotten better at figuring out how to execute effective changes. The ACE faculty and staff have matured in their comprehension of this complex program as a function of designing and carrying it out. That said, as the final touches are put on this manuscript, we are working hard with one ACE community that had difficulty living harmoniously with one another last year. We have asked a psychologist with expertise in small-group interpersonal relationships to work with this group of ACE participants to increase the odds that their second year will be better than their first.

As should be obvious, as we carry out the program every year, it continues to be reinvented and refreshed in light of experiences and opportunities. We are convinced more completely than when we started that a teacher education and teacher service experience blending academic, community, and spiritual dimensions is rich with possibilities. We are heartened that with every passing year, new ideas for improvement continue to emerge, ones that get carried out. We are grateful that this is not a program steeped in tradition to the point of stagnation. A great bonus for those of us privileged to teach and administer ACE is that every passing year leads each of us to new academic, community, and spiritual understandings about teaching and learning and living. We are better educational researchers, teacher educators, and ministers to teachers because of ACE. We feel that we have met Jesus at this well called ACE, just as Jesus once visited the Samaritan woman at a well. We are captured, just as the Samaritan woman was captured two millennia ago:

THE SAMARITAN WOMAN

It joined us together, the well;
the well led me into you.
No one between us but light
deep in the well, the pupil of the eye
set in an orbit of stones.
Within your eye, I,
drawn by the well,
am enclosed.

—*Karol Wojtyla (Pope John Paul II)*

# INDEX

Page numbers followed by letter *t* refer to material presented in tables.